CW01498076

WORTHY

The Scouting Adventures and Football Life of

DAVE WORTHINGTON

with Philip Dawkes

First published by Pitch Publishing, 2025

1

Pitch Publishing
9 Donnington Park,
85 Birdham Road,
Chichester, West Sussex,
PO20 7AJ
www.pitchpublishing.co.uk
info@pitchpublishing.co.uk

© 2025, Dave Worthington with Philip Dawkes

Every effort has been made to trace the copyright.
Any oversight will be rectified in future editions at the
earliest opportunity by the publisher.

All rights reserved. No part of this book may be reproduced,
sold or utilised in any form or transmitted in any form or by
any means, electronic or mechanical, including photocopying,
recording or by any information storage and retrieval system,
without prior permission in writing from the publisher.

A CIP catalogue record is available for this book
from the British Library.

ISBN 978 1 83680 166 5

Typesetting and origination by Pitch Publishing

Printed and bound on FSC® certified paper in line with
our continuing commitment to ethical business practices,
sustainability and the environment.

Printed and bound in India by Replika Press Pvt. Ltd.

Contents

Acknowledgements

FIRST AND foremost, I would like to say a massive thank you to Chris Dawkes for introducing me to his 'brilliant' brother Phil. Phil has worked tirelessly to understand my strange mind and my often erratic memory to write this book, so well done for all your time and effort, Phil.

I must thank Maggie, my wife, for her patience and understanding throughout and ALL my family for reminding me of names of people, places and pets or for correcting some of my distant memories from such a full and often frenzied life at times.

My thanks must also go to 'Big Sam' Allardyce for his foreword and for his wisdom in taking me to Bolton Wanderers, firstly as just one of his scouting team and eventually to be his chief scout. To this day, he is a good friend.

Thank you also to the club historians from the clubs for which I have played for their knowledge and input.

It would be remiss of me to not say a thank you to all of the team-mates who I have played alongside throughout my sporting life, be it in amateur or professional football, rugby, cricket or golf. They all brought a mix of fun and frustration, which always brought out that competitive nature in my character.

I am certain that I will have missed out someone's name within the chapters. I am 80 years old now, so if I have done so, I do apologise. Rest assured, you do still pop up in my memories at times and I hope that you all enjoy my story because somewhere you are still in there and also in my heart.

Finally, thank you again Mum and Dad for giving me the strong upbringing that you did during those very tough and troubled times immediately after the Second World War in which you both served your country proudly, bravely and so well.

Worthy

P.s. I really do feel that I must apologise to my two neighbours and drinking partners, Mick and Steve, who have been seriously deprived of their usual alcohol intake whilst I have been working on this book. Normal service will be resumed ASAP.

Foreword

WORTHY IS a rare breed today – a dedicated, loyal scout who has played the game, knows it inside out and has the track record to prove it.

We first worked together at Bolton from 2002 – although I knew of him, having shared a dressing room and a few adventures with his younger brother, Frank, during my playing days. At Wanderers, he proved himself an invaluable colleague, moving to France, where he helped us expand our scouting network and recruit some of the players that served us so well in the Premier League. During this time, he would drive hundreds of miles to watch games, sometimes sleeping in his little Fiat Punto. Thankfully, he eventually listened to my advice and got himself a proper car to get around!

That we subsequently worked together at three others clubs – Blackburn, West Ham and Everton – shows just what I think of him professionally. As well as having a good eye for a player, Worthy is also honest in his assessments. His reports were always detailed on every aspect of the players he watched.

Over our years working together and since, he has become a good friend. His sense of humour makes him great company and always worth catching up with, which we do regularly, wherever we are in the world. He works hard and plays hard – a man after my own heart!

Sam Allardyce

One

Shelf Life

(1945–1954)

Tucked away on a small street in the tiny, evocatively named village of Shelf near Halifax is a humble one-up, one-down stone terrace house. One of many like it. In the one downstairs window stands a woman. She's ironing but not concentrating on the task. Instead, she's watching what is going on just over the street, in the car park of the pub opposite. In the tight, triangular space in front of her, three young boys are playing football. Her boys.

The smallest and youngest of the three is on the right wing, dribbling the ball between his feet, in a world of his own, where all that matters is the next flick to beat his man.

The middle brother stands to near military attention in front of the metal garage door – the makeshift goal – patiently waiting for a cross and the end of an attack that could signal his chance to be back playing outfield.

Finally, there's the lad in the middle, the eldest, a look of determination on his face. He is waiting for the ball, for the chance to score.

WHEN I think back to those games, fiercely contested between my brothers and me on our very first pitch in front of the Duke of York, I remember my mum at the window, her dark hair piled high with rollers, a look of contentment on her face. She watched on partly to make sure we were safe, not because she was fearful of the small community – these were the early 1950s and the horrific, wrenching experiences of war had given people a renewed sense of care for each other – but because she knew her boys. We were competitive siblings, winners at all cost, cut from a cloth she helped sew. Happy play could descend into argument and confrontation in a heartbeat if one of us felt another had crossed the line. Fights were frequent and often in need of an impartial referee.

She also watched because she loved football. In her childhood, she would accompany four of her brothers – Arnold, Arthur, Ernest and Jack, all fanatical – to watch Halifax Town. Later, as her three sons grew and moved to different parts of the country to play, she would travel to Holker Street, Blundell Park, Meadow Lane, Leeds Road, Filbert Street and more but her true supporter's heart always lay at The Shay.

She had been a player herself during the war. A small joy to savour when she wasn't fulfilling her duties driving troops to and from RAF Woolsington, near Durham. All of us kids – Bob, Frank, our younger sister, Julie, and I – would regularly hear the story of the time she scored nine goals in a single game for her women's RAF side. We never had cause to doubt the claim. She backed it up on family summer holidays to sunny Bolton or Manchester, playing up front in overgrown fields, hammering the ball home past one of us with the crest of her bare right foot, where the laces of a boot would be. The technique of an old pro.

She would enhance her credentials in a mind-blowing way on the one real family holiday I remember – a four-day trip to Blackpool.

Throughout the 1950s, Joe Smith's Seasiders had been one of the best teams in the country, containing the magical Stanley Matthews, rock-solid defender Harry Johnston and South African-born outside-left Bill Perry. They also had Stan Mortensen, one of the finest centre-forwards in the game, with a gravity-defying leap and a shot of unnerving power and accuracy. Despite being a football superstar, he owned and worked in a sports shop in Blackpool – a real sign of the times – and it happened to be 200 yards away from the guest house in which we were staying. One day, my mum took us there.

With his beer-barrel chest and defender-repelling cornflake box shoulders, Stan was immediately recognisable behind the counter. For a moment, I was in awe, dumbstruck. 'I'm just going to say hello,' declared my mum, breaking the spell. I was indignant: 'You don't know him? He's a famous footballer!' But off she went, to not only say hello to one of the greatest goalscorers the English game had ever seen but to have a long, warm chat like long-lost friends. To this day, I'm none the wiser as to whether she actually knew him or not. It forever cemented in my mind, though, that my mum knew her football.

I like to think she was also savvy enough, as she watched on from that downstairs window, to recognise the burgeoning talent on display in that tiny, gravel-decked space over the road. She might even have foreseen all three of us forging a future in the game, so long as we applied ourselves properly, listened and learned. And we did. Mostly. In many ways she was the very first scout in my life, before the concept of the job that would come to consume the latter part of my career had even entered my mind.

If Mum was the talent spotter, Dad was the man who nurtured it. He was our first coach. There was no doubting his credentials. Born in Manchester, he had played for United's A team as a youth with the likes of Johnny Carey and Stan Pearson, future giants of the club and who both would go on to make more than 300 first-team appearances. He also impressed in local league football for Manchester North End and Denton United. Pride of place in one of my scrapbooks are the beautifully embroidered badges awarded to him to mark his appearances for the Manchester County Football Association between 1937 and 1939. A now faded and battered newspaper cutting below attests to his quality as a youngster in the Cheshire County League. 'Better wingers than Worthington and Hazeltine, of North End and Salford, will be hard to find,' it states.

Just prior to the war, he moved to Halifax Town, where he would finally make a mark in the professional game, in the Third Division North. While there, over four largely wartime seasons, he would play with the likes of Tom Barkas, an inside-right and Town legend famed for his craft and vision, and full-back Bill Allsop, who has still played more games for the club than any other player – more than 500 of them. Again, the prized snippets of reports, wafer thin and frayed, clinging desperately to the coloured pages of my scrapbook, speak of my dad as a 'forceful raider' down the right wing and a 'robust and energetic leader'. He was a 'player of promise'.

His career, like so many others, could have been much more fruitful had the war not interrupted and taken him away to help with a much greater cause. He began as a Royal Engineer but opted to become a paratrooper when he discovered such roles paid better. I'm not sure he fully grasped that this would mean having to jump out of an airplane with a parachute on his back and Germans shooting at him.

He was one of more than 10,000 soldiers to drop on Arnhem as part of Operation Market Garden in September 1944. He was one of only 2,000 to return. He never spoke of it. I don't think anyone who survived the horrors did. The only time he ever expressed to me any feelings regarding the war was during a cinema trip to Halifax Odeon. I can only have been six or seven. It was to see a film called *Theirs Is the Glory*, which was about Arnhem and mixed original footage from the battle with re-enactments shot on location. More than 200 veterans appeared as actors. I recall sitting in the back row, enraptured by the aircraft setting off en route to the Netherlands on the big screen. Next to me, my dad was animated. He kept leaning forward and pointing, excitedly exclaiming: 'I'm sure that's my mate Dinky Durkin from Keighley.' He was picking out soldiers he thought he recognised from the footage, men preparing for battle or later in hospital beds, their ultimate fate uncertain.

His sacrifice, in comparison to so many, was relatively minor but it deprived him of the opportunity to fully realise his dream. In the latter years of his playing career, the ones I was old enough to witness for myself, he would appear for the local team down the road, Shelf United. The thing I remember most from watching him is the ferocity of his shot, blasted from a cannon of a right foot and almost spiteful in its disregard for opposition goalkeepers. Fury mixed with frustration.

The coaching sessions by the pub, which comprise some of my earliest memories, saw my dad teach me how to crack a ball like him, along with something far more delicate. He would stress the importance of close control – a quality I would strive to perfect as a player and later, as a scout, spend 20 years seeking out in others. He demonstrated how to trap the ball with the sole of the foot and then watched as I repeated the skill. It was thrilling for me and convenient for him, as he could balance out imparting advice with a trip inside the Duke of York for a well-earned pint or two.

I had a head start on my younger brothers but we all received the same tutelage from the stocky man with slicked back hair, deep-set, focussed eyes and a near constant cigarette in his mouth. Once we were old enough to play together in the car park, we were well drilled in the requirements of a cushion-like first touch. And nothing hones the need like a floaty plastic ball and a tight, angular pitch down one side of which flew regular passing cars and buses. One errant touch and our next onrushing opponent would be the No.47, rumbling up the road from Brighouse. Not even our Frank had a trick to get around that.

We didn't live in luxury. We weren't showered with gifts. The house was barely big enough to fit us all, with one bedroom in which we all slept and an outside toilet you'd need to creep across freezing cold cobbles to reach. I would have cardboard strips put in my shoes to plug holes and eke out a few extra precious months of wear from the soles. My parents were not wealthy people nor were they truly poor. They were like so many folk after the war, striving to pick up the pieces, make ends meet and move on by reclaiming lives that had been so unjustly halted.

We three boys didn't receive an abundance of affection either – no cuddles or regular displays of tenderness – but we were never left in any doubt that we were loved. Care and support were always there, as was a clip round the ear when you'd earned it. Along with her comforting presence at the downstairs window, the other thing I remember most about my mum from my youth is her narrow-eyed, exasperated look when she caught one of us being naughty. Her mantra would soon follow: 'If you boys don't stop it, I'll tell your dad when he gets home.' Often she didn't but the threat itself was enough. Having seen the ferocity of his shot, I certainly didn't fancy being on the receiving end of his palm to the back of my calves or backside. On the rare occasions she did tell him … oof! Mum provided the assist and dad finished it.

The most significant gift they bestowed on us, though, was one of the finest things any parent can hand down to their child. Something that has tailored our lives, provided us with careers, connections, lifelong friends and immeasurable joy. They gave us a passion for the game of football.

I was born on 28 March 1945 in Halifax General Infirmary, the first child of Eric and Alice Worthington. Bob and Frank would follow at two-year intervals. My parents waited until 1957 to have another child, my sister, Julie, arriving to finally provide them with the girl they longed for to complete the family. I imagine it must have been a relief after 12 years of us boys running amok. Little did they know that Julie would prove to be just as boisterous as her three big brothers. A Worthington through and through.

During the week, dad worked as a labourer, principally for a machine tool parts company, although his eye for an opportunity and a bit more money saw him change jobs fairly regularly. In fact, such was his ethic, he would even find casual work on our holidays to Bolton to stay with my mum's sister, May, and her husband, Harry, getting up early to head down to a nearby farm to muck out the stables from eight in the morning until two in the afternoon. The need placed on him to support a growing family meant he wasn't as solid a presence in the house as my mum. He would be up early to catch the bus into Halifax for a shift and return late, even later if money was tight at the end of the week and he had to walk the journey.

After giving birth to her three sons, my mum worked on a till at Woolworths and Brow Lane Stores in the village. She also cleaned for the Whitaker family of Halifax brewery fame and did shifts at Mackintosh's sweet factory. She would often return laden with misshapen, leftover toffee for us kids to fight over, the one consistent luxury we were afforded.

For the first year of my life, Dad would leave us on winter Saturdays to turn out for Town, the result and standard of his performance dictating the evening mood. With luck, he would return energised, with tales of derring-do on the field – a dominant display in a 5-2 victory over Carlisle, a lobbed finish over a helpless

Bradford City goalkeeper, two-goal heroics against Sheffield Wednesday. If things didn't go to plan, a sombre silence could descend on the house. I was way too young to understand why but I imagine that even then I sensed the difference that winning or losing brought to my own little world.

It wasn't long before I cottoned on as to why the village, and our house in particular, was such a hubbub of emotion on a Saturday. There were other places to be and other things to do, of course. Every Sunday, the popular Shelf Working Men's Club would host bingo, a particular love of my mum's, and the Duke of York, another hub of the community, was literally over the road and seemingly never shut. My parents loved music, too. Dad had played in a jazz band in Manchester and was a keen piano player.

There was never a shortage of pastimes for a young lad. In the summer, we would go swimming at Wibsey Baths, funded in part by the rewards provided for sliding down the coal shoot of our neighbours to help them get back into their house if they had locked themselves out. During the winter, when snow fell, we'd sledge down the sloping streets that fell away from the house. All year round, we raced each other over ever-increasing distances on an improvised track along the roads. Football, though, was the thing that truly energised us all.

I still have an old picture, taken close to our house, of my brothers and me and three of our friends – Davey Lewis, John Cutts and Kenny Reilly – ahead of a game on the street. Little Frank stands near the centre, a cheeky look on his face. Bob is on the end, stood to attention, with me looking casual next to him, each of us sporting a big, expectant grin. All of us are wearing full kit, including boots with leather studs. Ready for action.

After a cartilage injury did for my dad's slim remaining hopes of making it as a professional player, he turned to local football for his fix. I would delight at being taken to watch him play for Shelf United, standing on the touchline of a mudbath of a pitch, enraptured alongside my mum as she held young Bob. As the years passed, he would join me by her side to be replaced by the infant Frank in her arms. I was blown away by the energy and ferocity on display. It might only have been local amateur football but it was keenly contested, with plenty of ability on show from players who had previously represented Football League clubs, some as high as the First Division. It was an early education in the levels required if you were going to make it in the game.

Dad would also turn out for the pub team on a Wednesday. Mr Gregson, the landlord, played too, as a defender. He would also ferry the team to away games in his big American limousine-style car. There would be two players in the long front seat next to him, two on backward-facing seats behind and at least three in the back. Our Bob and me would sit in the footwell. We were like the Ant Hill Mob, chugging up hills to the likes of Wainstalls, Midgley and Heptonstall.

By the time I was able to kick a ball, I was quickly put to good, albeit nefarious use in the operation. Just before a game, my dad would call me over for our own secret team talk. 'David, I want you to head off down the bottom there with your friends,' he'd say, pointing to the goal housing the opposition goalkeeper. 'You go kick the ball about behind that goal.' Off we would go, to play away merrily and, to the unsuspicious eye at least, innocently. If we did our job properly, we would create enough of a distraction that the keeper might allow one of my dad's trademark 30-yard thunderbolts to fly past him. Eventually, the goalkeeper would cotton on and we'd receive a stern demand to 'sod off, you nippers!' Unwittingly, I was making my first strides into competitive football, as Shelf United's unofficial 12th man.

The game made local celebrities of us. Even the shortest walk out with Dad would last an age as he stopped to chat to everyone we came across, me listening in at his side. They would ask about last week's game, about this week's, about a goal someone had seen him score or even just discuss whether he thought Halifax might go up that year.

With my dad's influence, his origins over the other side of the Pennines and youthful experiences with Manchester United, it was, perhaps, inevitable that I would look for the results of the Reds as I began to discover football fandom. This was the Matt Busby era, before the Munich air disaster stripped them of so much when Duncan Edwards, Dennis Viollet and David Pegg were breaking through and league titles followed. As I grew a bit older, Halifax inevitably came to the fore – a passion I could share with both my parents and wider family. There was also an early indication of my rebellious side when I decided to lend my support to Bradford City. They and Bradford Park Avenue were the other significant local sides in the area – both in the Third Division North at the time – and a lot of the lads in the village supported the latter. Not wanting to follow the crowd, I declared myself for City. On one occasion, I caught a train on my own to go and watch the Bantams play away at Scunthorpe. It was a stubborn early foray to a part of the world I would later get to know very well.

The only other significant club in my pre-adolescent life were Newcastle United. Not the real Newcastle side mind but a one-inch-high version made of plastic that I kept in a tray and controlled by flicking around a felt pitch. Subbuteo, the famous football game in which you direct a team of small players by tapping them about with your index finger, was our indoor vice and Newcastle were my prized side. Every year, we would have a cup knockout competition at one of the lads' houses, in which I would strive to tap my way to victory, led by a miniature, blank-faced but nonetheless prolific Jackie Milburn. Most of us could only afford to have a team of players but Kenny Riley, who was a few years older and had a bit more money by dint of his parents owning the local greengrocers, had a proper pitch and even the little floodlights to put in each corner. There was never a debate over whose house held major finals.

In stark contrast to later in my life, I had little concept of football or the players that played it beyond England's shores. There would be newspaper reports of World Cups and descriptions of exotic-sounding Brazilian forwards like Ademir but little else. There would be very few foreign players or managers in England – a country still firmly holding on to the belief that, having invented the game, they did it better. That would all begin to change on 25 November 1953.

It was a Wednesday and England were playing Hungary at Wembley. The game was being televised but, back then, few people had a TV set. We certainly didn't. However, a lad who lived near us, Martin Lister, had the luxury of a set. For two days ahead of the game, he became my best friend. When gameday came around and school finished, I was straight around to his house. 'Hi, Mrs Lister, is Martin home? Oh, he's watching the game? Mind if I join him?' She barely had time to respond before I was through the door, my coat off, heading for the living room.

The next 90 minutes, sat glued to that black-and-white, hazy screen, were a football education. Hungary tore England to shreds. The way they passed the ball, their movement and skill was light years ahead of anything I'd seen before. They had Nándor Hidegkuti, who scored a hat-trick playing as a deep-lying centre-forward, a position we didn't know was even possible, and, as a second striker, a stocky lad by the name of Ferenc Puskás. He was some player – strong and quick but also crafty and gentle, with little feints and touches to take him past opponents and into empty space. He ran poor England defender Harry Johnston ragged.

I didn't appreciate the Hungarians' brilliance at the time. I'd gone round to Martin's house to watch England win, to see Stanley Matthews and my mum's mate, Stan Mortensen, put on a show, playing the English way. It was the naivety of a young football fan that knows no different. I didn't particularly enjoy watching our lads get embarrassed by these fancy foreigners, flicking it around so brilliantly with the outside of their foot or over their head. It clearly struck a chord, though, with all of us. It wasn't long before we were all out on the street or in the park, trying to emulate Puskás.

I was often the youngest in my group of mates. The creep towards adolescence brought with it a desire to establish myself in a bigger, braver world, prompting me to hang out with the older lads. It occasionally got me into bother. The savvy ones of our gang would make the youngest like myself do the naughty stuff, so if we were caught they could deny involvement and lay the blame on us. There would be fights, too, with other gangs from Buttershaw or Queensbury. I would often be the littlest one, keeping to the back, but I quickly learned how to look after myself and not to back down – a trait that has never left me.

Thankfully, my parents had planted a smart enough head on my shoulders to recognise the far more positive and pointed inspirations to be drawn from my peers, chief amongst them Dennis Wilkinson. Dennis was the older brother of my mate Neville and served in the forces, although he was too young to have gone to war. Nev wasn't a great footballer but Dennis had real talent. He was a giant of a lad, 6ft 5in, strong and quick. On occasions when he was back home on leave, he would join us for kickabouts and we would bounce off him as we tried to get the ball. What made him truly special, though, was his trial with Aston Villa. He didn't end up signing for them but it still meant something to me that a big First Division club had scouted a lad from Shelf and that I'd shared a pitch with him. It laid a pathway for me to follow, provided the inspiration I needed to achieve my dream of becoming a professional footballer.

Inevitably, Shelf has changed much over the years. But many of the landmarks of my youth remain. My childhood home is still there, as is the Duke of York, although the car park has changed. Instead of an open gravel space, perfect for football, it is now decked in part and strewn with picnic benches and planters. In the wall is a modern glass-filled archway that would be threatened by even the lightest of impacts from a misdirected plastic ball.

In my mind, it will always be that empty, triangular patch of gravel, the spot where three young lads learnt how to play and a woman with rollers in her hair and a contented smile watched on from a nearby window. Even a scene so humble owes itself to the hard work and sacrifices of my parents. It was they who provided the platform, allowing me to go off and pursue my dreams. In my most reflective moments, I'm left with questions. Did I give it my all, achieve all I could and become the man my parents hoped? Was I decent, dependable, deserving? Worthy?

Two

Worthington Drive
(1954–1961)

If you were to head out of the Duke of York and set off up the road towards Queensbury, you would soon arrive at a street on the right. It has not been there long, since 2016 in fact.

It is a nice spot. The gardens are all manicured, the 13 limestone, new-build houses on its winding, brick-paved road in stark contrast to the weathered, stone buildings that have stood in Shelf since the Industrial Revolution.

However, the homes on this street are of no concern to this story. Nor are the people that live in them. In fact, the actual street itself is largely irrelevant.

What matters to us is its name. Worthington Drive.

I HAVE tried to find out why this street, so close to the house where my parents lived and we three boys grew up, was given the same name as my family. Could it have been handed the moniker by a knowledgeable fan in the council, aware of the footballing family from just round the corner? Maybe it was just to mark the achievements and fame of Frank, the only one of us who graduated from the Duke of York car park to the dizzy heights of Wembley? There is also the possibility that it may just be a huge coincidence. I visited the town hall and library in Halifax in search of answers but left with none. As a last resort, I knocked on the front door of one of the houses on the street to enquire about the company that had built them. A girl at their offices took my call and told me she would get back to me but never did.

Even if the street has nothing to do with my family, I've often thought it a fitting tribute regardless. From the youngest of ages, I had a drive instilled in me. My parents set the tone, providing an example with a determined and stoic attitude to work that I have carried with me throughout my life.

It first began to show itself in my youthful sporting endeavours. I could never stand to be beaten in the running races we staged on the streets around our house, no matter the opponent, regardless of the distance. A mate of mine, Tommy Coulson, suffered from a chest problem, so only did the shorter sprints, but I still revelled in my victories over him. I was ruthless. I quickly began to realise that I had honed the ability to take on long distances and, so, would continually increase the length of the races to further emphasise my superiority. Four laps of the village would become five, six, more – the rest of the lads trailing in my glorious wake.

I brought the same will to win to cricket, playing for Shelf Juniors CC, along with Bob and then Frank. I opened the batting with Tony Flesher, whose own brother, Peter, captained the side. One glorious summer, we won the Bradford Central League, with me chipping in runs at the top of the order. Tennis was another sport I enjoyed, although I wasn't often able to afford the four pence required for an hour on the park courts. Instead, a couple of scallywags and I would wait until the park keeper had left for the evening and then scale the fence. We'd play for free until it got dark. No matter how, I wanted to be out playing sport and, of course, winning.

My competitiveness occasionally got me into scrapes, some more dangerous than others. As a young boy, I was a big fan of the appropriately named Dan Dare, the comic book space hero who appeared in *Eagle*. I had an outfit – a space suit, complete with a grey felt helmet – given to me one Christmas so that I could play as my hero. I wore it often around the village, on dangerous missions to the hostile planets of West Street and Score Hill. I was in my element in the winter of 1953 when heavy snow fell, turning Shelf into an alien landscape. In the real world, my dad had to dig himself out of the house to get to work but, for my friends and me, it was constant adventure. And Dan Dare never loses.

The snow had created a prime sledging track near to our house on Score Hill, which ran down a slope towards a wall with a gate in its centre. Inevitably, a competition was born. The gate was fastened back and the first one down the slope and through the now empty gap would be the winner. I positioned myself at the start line, felt helmet on, plotting my route to victory. I remember the thrill of hurtling down the hill, a blast of cold wind in my face, only for it to be interrupted by the sight of one of my friends slowly overtaking me to my right. I wouldn't have it. I had to win. I fought back, went sledge edge to sledge edge with my rival, clawing the snow with my hands to increase my speed. He flew through the gate. I went straight into the wall.

I have a hazy recollection of being dragged up the hill on my sledge by my panicked friends, of a commotion being made in the house and the sensation of wetness all around my head. By the time I regained some sense, I was on the bus with my mum, my head wrapped in towels to stem the blood. I can only imagine what a sight it must have been for the other passengers. After a short walk from the bus station to Halifax infirmary, I was quickly assessed and ten stitches put in my head before we headed off for a slightly less gruesome journey home. It should have taught me a lesson about curbing my instincts for my own good, risk versus reward. But the only thing I lost that day was a felt helmet.

Thankfully, I had a smart and knowledgeable teacher in my dad, who was able to help me channel my determination into something more productive on the football pitch. He imparted wisdom from his own experiences as a centre-forward of 5ft 9in, who regularly had to tolerate the physical attentions of monstrous centre-backs and beat them with grit and guile. He would tell me to use my speed, smaller size and stamina to my advantage. 'Don't let them know they're hurting you,' he would insist. 'If they're kicking you, whacking you, just get up and have a little smile … then go and stick one in the net!' So that's what I did. I'd take a kick but bounce straight back up and grin. It doesn't matter if you're an 11-year-old school kid or a 27-year-old hardened pro, when an opponent you've just booted up in the air dusts himself off and smiles at you, it gets under your skin, especially if they then get the better of you to score.

I began playing formal competitive games at junior school, alongside and against 11-year-olds at the age of just seven. I was at least a foot smaller than many of them but I was armed and ready for it. One of my first games was against Fox Hill School in Queensbury and I scored four, nipping in regularly past two big defenders to slot the ball home. With the hours spent outside the Duke of York and the teachings of my dad, I found it came easy. I was sharper, my touch was superior and I had an instinct for where to be and when. I remember scoring against Lightcliffe. We went to Hove Edge, Northowram and the church school in Shelf. The goals kept coming. I was on my way.

One of my team-mates in that junior school side was Stuart Harrison – or 'Nipper' as we all knew him because of his size. He was the only lad younger and smaller than me in that team but, like me, he could play; a very tidy midfielder. Away from school, the pair of us were also regulars for Shelf Juniors, playing on the same sloping mudbath of a pitch on which I'd witnessed my dad rocket in 30-yarders with such alarming regularity. Such was our ability, 'Nipper' and I would play well above our age group, turning out for the under-18s at just 11 and 12 respectively. Not only that but, in recognition of my talent and temperament, I was made captain of the side. In 1957, I led them to victory in the Halifax & District Red Triangle League, beating Wibsey to lift the first proper cup of my career. In the team photo that appeared in the local paper, taken at Savile Park in Halifax, the contrast between 'Nipper' and me – mere boys on the front row – and the young men that comprise the rest of the team is stark. At the back, arms crossed, forearms as wide as my neck, is Kenny Todd. He soon went to play for Bradford City's youth and second team – another inspiration. And I was his captain!

'Nipper' was good enough to have played professionally. He certainly had scouts from a couple of clubs watching on with interest but his size must have counted against him. Nowadays, there is a more sophisticated view of physical characteristics and an understanding that protecting the ball can be developed, likely helped by the huge success of diminutive but dynamite players like Lionel Messi. But back then, being small meant immediate dismissal. It is one of life's cruel twists that by the time he hit 18, little Stuart had shot up to about 6ft 1in. A nipper no more but his window had closed. He became a top player in the local leagues, though, playing for Luddenenfoot and Queensbury.

He lives in Wibsey now and I still meet up with him to go for a walk or a pint in the Duke of York and reminisce about football. Even now, we can still remember it all. We talk of Shelf games and about the equally competitive matches on the street of my second childhood home on Burnside Avenue. We moved there when I was 12, helped into a larger home by the council after Julie's birth had made it unmanageable to stay where we were. It provided me with my own room for the first time, a proper garden and a long street on which to stage games. At the end was a wall, into which we drew a chalk goal. When the rain washed that off, I picked up a rock and carved and carved until there was a permanent goalpost alongside the street lamp for 'Nipper', myself and others to try and score between. After I had left to pursue my career, Julie would take part in games there with her friends. 'You know, Dave, I used to hate the lads running at me and getting past me,' she would later confide in me. 'It drove me mad. If I couldn't tackle them, I'd trip them up to make sure I didn't get beaten.' Competitiveness is a family trait.

My switch to secondary school brought fresh challenges. I wasn't a stellar student but I was smart and motivated enough to hold my own academically. Not every subject appealed to me but I threw myself into those that did. I enjoyed geography and, in particular, studying maps with Mr Day. I especially thrived in languages, studying both French and German under the tutorship of the hard and sometimes cruel Mr Oates and then the gentle and attentive Mr Wood. I was good enough across the board to get the marks I needed to gain entry to the most prominent school in the area. Hipperholme Grammar was a posh institution, with history dating back to the 17th century, which prided itself on standards – ones that occasionally clashed with my, shall we say, less refined characteristics. I would often be corrected in class for how I spoke. 'Hipperholme has two Hs in it, Worthington,' I would be told by my teachers. 'It is not on you to drop the middle one as you see fit.' It was a concession I was willing to make. In other areas, I was unyielding.

Hipperholme was a rugby school, proudly pushed by a Welsh headmaster with the sport in his veins. He insisted on the correct kit, including a red and navy hooped shirt. My parents didn't have the money for a new one and, so, I acquired a hand-me-down from an older lad up the road, Alan Rhodes. He became a regular and trusted source of sporting kit over the years. I fondly remember a pair of old running spikes he gave me that proved invaluable in adding extra speed to my runs. The shirt, though, had been through the mill over the years, with a multitude of washes to remove repeated grass and mud stains. By the time I had use of it, the navy had become grey and what was once red was now a light pink – no worse colour for a boy engaged in the rough and tumble sport of rugby. I was mocked for it by my peers. Never one to take a backwards step, I made a mental note of each tormentor. When the opportune moment came in games, I would go in hard on them in the tackle, occasionally adding a late elbow or knee for good measure. My pronunciation they could alter but my temperament was set in stone.

The real conflict was off the field. A rugby school meant no football, formally or for fun – a rule I begrudgingly accepted on their time but not my own. I had moved on from Shelf to make early strides in senior football for Lightcliffe and it was going well. On Saturday mornings, I would play rugby for the school and then get changed and head off to play football in the afternoon. One Monday morning, though, I was called into the headmaster's office. He had found out about my double sporting endeavours through my maths teacher, Mr Flynn, who was a Lightcliffe fan and had seen me play for them two days earlier. 'I'm not happy, Worthington,' he began. 'As a member of the school rugby team, I expect you to give it your full focus. We cannot have players who split themselves between rugby and football. If you wish to continue representing the school at the former, you must give up playing the latter.' I was stunned. I loved playing rugby and was proud to do so for Hipperholme. I wasn't the best player but I threw myself into it with gusto. But his stance made no sense. What difference would it make for me to play football afterwards, provided I gave my all on the morning? One thing I knew for certain was that I was not giving up football, so I stood my ground and told the headmaster as much. His response was to ban me from playing any kind of rugby at the school, be it double games sessions on a Monday, house or representative matches.

I felt I'd been hard done by and told my parents. The upshot was a visit from the headmaster, during which my dad pleaded my case to continue playing both sports but to no avail. From then on, for two hours every Monday afternoon while my friends were out playing rugby, I would have to sit alone in the art room, frustrated and aggrieved, writing out the same line hundreds of times: 'Disobedience and insubordination are two undesirable qualities in the character of a schoolboy.' That may be so but, as time would tell, a fierce determination, coupled with an urge to prove someone wrong, are desirable qualities in the character of a budding young footballer.

Lightcliffe represented a significant step up. I was a slight 14-year-old forward coming up against grizzled defenders a decade and more my senior. It was literally men against boy. Maybe it was my youthful enthusiasm, the wise teachings of my dad or that I was just simply good enough but it felt like a natural progression to which I was quickly able to adapt. We would train twice a week, on Tuesday and Thursday evenings, often on a small pitch illuminated by two huge lamps on the big Nissen huts they used for dressing rooms. The games would be on Hove Edge on Saturday afternoons, requiring me to travel down on the bus with my dad, who had quit playing by then and had transformed himself into a vociferous fan. It made for a busy week, combining all of this with both school and the paper round I was performing for the local newsagent every day.

The West Riding Amateur County League had some good clubs: Thackley, Golcar, Guiseley, Yeadon Celtic, Luddendenfoot. The sides each had a spattering of old pros, coming off the back of brief careers with significant West Yorkshire teams like Leeds, Bradford and Huddersfield. There were plenty of ex-Halifax lads. These were proud men, competitors wringing the final games, and a few extra quid under the counter, from their ability. It was amateur in name only and fiercely contested. There was certainly no leeway given to some young upstart. I took plenty of thumpings designed to put me in my place and cow me into fearful submission. If I wanted to fulfil my ambition to make it in the game, though, there could be no hiding.

Thankfully, I had support. Off the pitch, my dad could impart advice. On it, I had hardened team-mates who took me under their wing. Jackie Barrett, a big, bald full-back in his late 30s was an ally, as well as a smashing player. He had lost a yard of pace but was quick enough across the pitch if ever I took a whack from a bullying centre-back. Brian Hendy was another. He had come out of the forces, the RAF I think, but had played at Halifax as an amateur. He supplied me with copious advice on fitness.

My dad had his own theories on the subject. After games at Hove Edge, my team-mates would all head to a pub up the road called The Pond, where they would drink beer alongside supporters. I would join them with the old man. I wouldn't drink. He would. During one session he told me: 'You know, you're not really strong yet. You need something to build you up.' His solution was a trip to the bar and the purchase of a pint of Guinness. After that, it became a ritual after every game – I received one pint of the black stuff, to build up my strength. It was only later that I cottoned on to my dad's plan. The buses from Lightcliffe to Shelf ran every hour and he was conveniently delaying our departure to buy himself more time in the pub. 'Oh, we've missed the bus now,' he'd declare, heading to the bar to get himself another pint. 'Ah well, we'll get the next. Your mum won't mind.'

This was my first entry into the ritual of social drinking in the aftermath of a game. It would later become a staple part of life during my professional playing days but rarely to excess. I believe it was the discipline in largely abstaining from drink in my youth that helped me to thrive while many of my friends – some of them just as talented as me – fell away. My philosophy on life has been to work hard and play hard. Sadly, many of my peers embraced the latter, with too little of the former.

I welcomed the responsibility of making something of myself and I learned quickly. I was sharp, smart and scored goals. Soon, I was getting glowing write-ups in the local paper. My progress was recognised by the league when they invited me to be part of a West Riding County representative side for an FA County Youth Championship cup tie against Sheffield and Hallamshire at Hillsborough in December of 1960. I was listed amongst the travelling reserves. Starting at half-back for that side was Paul Madeley, then of South Leeds but soon to form a key part of the dominant Leeds side of the 1960s and 70s under manager Don Revie, as well as going on to play for England.

My efforts soon brought reward in the form of my first-ever football pay cheque, albeit one not strictly in the rules for an amateur club. One Thursday, the secretary handed me a brown envelope containing 15 shillings for expenses. This was twice as much as I received for the paper round. The majority of it went to my parents, although I kept a little bit for myself, a little symbol to show I was getting closer to the dream. I carried on delivering papers, of course. I didn't want to let down the newsagent and it's always nice to have a few extra coins in your pocket. I'm my father's son, after all.

I have played on many great and famous pitches in my career. There are few I remember as fondly as the unconventional or makeshift ones of my youth. Leading a black-and-white clad Shelf Juniors through the tree line at the bottom of Shelf Hall Park and up to our sloping pitch remains a proud memory. In my head, it was like charging out at Wembley for the cup final. Just behind me would be big Kenny Todd, Keith Ormerod, the goalkeeper, Paul Woodhead and, of course, 'Nipper' Stuart Harrison.

Years later, I would admit my pride to 'Nipper' at having captained a side of under-18s at the age of just 12, telling him just how important that had been for me going forward. A smirk came over his face. 'You know why they made you captain, don't you?' he told me. 'It was because the coaches had heard Northowram were trying to sign you and they didn't want you to leave.' You can always rely on your mates to keep you grounded.

Burnside Avenue, that other key Worthington pitch, is still there. Much of it has changed since my childhood but one key feature remains. If you were to walk to the end of the street, you would find the wall that served as our goal. Even now, 70 years on, faded but clear, is the carving of a goalpost.

Three

It's Pro Time

(1961–1964)

This is how it could have happened ...

A man stands on the touchline and watches. He is not a regular at any one club's games, more of an infrequent but very eager observer of many. He is a student of the leagues on his patch, of the game itself. He tries to keep a low profile, hiding himself inside a large overcoat and a flat cap. So long as he can see and hear, he can do his job. This is to watch footballers, to judge them, sort the wheat from the chaff. His lot is to identify the ones who could make it, do a job for his employer, maybe even go on to bigger and better things.

More often than not, he leaves frustrated. Finding a diamond in the rough is a rare occurrence. But when it does happen, it makes all the cold, wet, fruitless afternoons on muddy touchlines across West Yorkshire worth it.

Today, he is at Hove Edge, the home of Lightcliffe, to see a teenage striker who has been getting good write-ups in the paper. It takes less than ten minutes for the man's interest to be piqued. The young striker is sharp, fleet of foot and mind. He's got a touch on him, knows where the goal is and he's not overawed. He's taken a couple of kicks already but has bounced straight back up with a grin on his face.

This league is full of footballers. Only a few earn the right to precede that with the word 'professional'. Even fewer make it stick. Maybe this kid is one of them ...

I HAVE no idea how I came to the attention of Halifax Town. It is likely they had at least one scout watching the most prominent leagues in the local area to try and snare the best talent. This was the lifeblood of clubs, especially those further down the food chain and lacking financial clout. Halifax were a Third Division club and had never been higher on the league ladder. If a scout had attended Lightcliffe games to watch me in the winter of 1961, I'm certain he would have liked what he saw. I've stood on those touchlines and made those calls. Whatever the cause – a scout recommendation, word of mouth or an educated decision based on local newspaper reports of my nine goals in eight games – I was invited to attend a trial at the club in October.

I was ready for it. Two months earlier, I'd suffered the disappointment of being rejected by Bolton after having attended a trial at Burnden Park. They were a First Division club at the time, clearly a level beyond my promise. I wasn't going to let a second chance slip by me, though, especially not with my dad's club. His prime years had been taken from him but, in my own small way, I could restore some of what he had lost. With the proud old man watching on from the sidelines, in a game featuring a mix of youth and reserve players, I scored a hat-trick before half-time. As I was walking off, the coach pulled me aside. 'You won't be playing in the second half, lad,' he informed me. A sinking feeling gripped me. Had I not done enough? Was the dream over? Perhaps sensing my concern, he quickly added: 'Get over to the offices – the manager wants to see you.' As soon as my dad and I got inside, I was ushered to a seat, a form and a pen placed in front of me and I was told Town wanted to sign me. Delighted and dazzled at suddenly being presented with everything I'd ever wanted, I signed the form there and then. In my head, I had become a professional footballer. I would soon discover, though, that one must earn such a status.

For the first five months at Town, I wasn't even technically a pro. The form I had signed was an amateur contract but tied me to the club until I could sign full terms on my 17th birthday the following March. They wanted me to become an apprentice upon joining but I was less keen. I had seen what apprentices had to do around the club – setting up and clearing up after training, sweeping the dressing rooms and the steps of the stands after matches and other menial tasks. The first-team players had to look after their own boots during the week but it was the job of an apprentice to clean them all thoroughly ahead of games. I didn't fancy that much. I just wanted to play football and I told the club as much. My proud stance lasted less than a week.

I owe my acquiescence to friendship. Malcolm Russell was the only apprentice at the club at that time. He was eight months younger than me and from Southowram, about five miles from Shelf, on the opposite side of Halifax. He lived in a council house with his mum, dad and siblings, just like me. He was a good footballer – taller than I was, strong and a solid tackler. He was good enough to attend England youth trials at Lilleshall. We quickly became firm pals and you don't leave such figures in the lurch. I often found myself alongside him after training, a broom in my hands, sweeping the dressing rooms or the steps of the Skircoat Stand at The Shay. I was the apprentice's apprentice. We had some fun, too, though. When there was nobody else about, we'd race each other to the top of the two floodlight pylons at the southern terrace end of the ground, him up one, me the other. They were unnervingly high, often slippy, and the only tangible reward for scaling them was the quid we'd bet each other beforehand but my old instincts kicked in and I would frantically clamber to the top in pursuit of victory. In the afternoons, with the sweeping done, we'd go into Halifax town centre for a coffee and to chat to the girls that had suddenly started to pique our teenage interest.

Slowly, I was discovering the responsibilities and application of a professional life. As an amateur, I had taken on a paid job outside football, which I found at Halifax Town Hall, delivering mail for the town clerk's office. The role involved a lot of running around, dropping off letters to other council offices and solicitors. As a result, I became something of a delivery boy for the six or seven women who worked in the office with me. 'David, if you're going past Marks & Spencer, do you mind picking me up some tights?' they would ask and they'd write down the size and colour. 'David, if you pass the bakery, bring us some cakes for lunch.' I may not have been an official apprentice for Halifax Town but I certainly was in my second job. I enjoyed the work, being part of another team, and it kept me fit.

There was no doubting where my true focus lay, though. I would relish every training session with the Town first team, getting put through my paces alongside seasoned pros. We would do laps of the speedway track that ran around The Shay, between its pitch and the stands, and I'd pride myself on being one of the fittest. Partway round, there would be a leather ball hanging from a rope to practise heading.

Unfortunately, regular exposure to rain meant it was more like trying to nut a bag of cement. Too much enthusiasm meant a near concussion. There was no actual training ground, so much of our work with a ball was done in the narrow car park, on cinders, trying to ensure you didn't lose it down the banking on the right side.

Alternatively, we'd jog about a mile and a half, past the bus depot and hospital, up to Savile Park to play seven- or eight-a-side in front of couples out for a stroll and the odd bloke walking his dog. Regardless of location and surface, the quality and ferocity of it was on a level I'd not previously experienced.

The Town squad was full of tough, committed players. Back then, every team played a 2-3-5 formation, with a trio of uncompromising, unflappable and occasionally unhinged half-backs. I especially remember the brutal combination of Derek Leck, Terry Branston and John Kurila (or 'Gorilla' as we knew him because of his size and strength) at Northampton. These were beasts not men – snarling and snapping into tackles with relish and rage. Halifax had their own fearsome half-back crew in Eric Harrison, Alex South and Frank Large.

Eric was a local lad, from Mytholmroyd. He had a bit of quality to his game, which would show itself most obviously in his range of passing and a little drag-back of the ball he would use to beat onrushing opponents. He wasn't the quickest but he was strong and possessed the heart of a lion. Unquestionably, his biggest asset was his character. He was a born winner, at all costs. He clearly saw similar qualities in me because I was quickly tucked under his wing, in the least tender way possible. In training games, he would ensure he was on the opposing side to me so that he could give me a whack, to test and harden my resolve. I soon grew confident enough to give him one back, much to his delight. He enjoyed it even more if I whacked someone else, especially if they lacked the same work ethic and moral code as himself.

I recall one particular player in the squad that Eric thought was lacking in the right stuff. He was a big lad and would use his size to bully people smaller than him and lacked the courage to stand firm. During games, he would have plenty to say, knowing he'd only have to face his opponent twice a year. Underneath it all, though, he was a big softie, a bag of wind. In one early training session, he tried to use his size against me. I could see him coming out of the corner of my eye, ready to hit me. Instead, I readied myself and clobbered him first and hard, leaving him in a heap on the floor. It was a clear foul but I'd stood my ground. As we were walking back down to The Shay after training, Eric was the first man by my side, wrapping me up in his big wing. 'Worthy, well done pal, that's what you've got to do, sort a few out like that.' It was with Eric's help that I realised there are people who talk a good game and then there are those who get the job done.

Eric's personality had a way of expressing itself that I was a bit less eager to emulate. For one of my early games for the first team, I was sat next to him in the changing room beforehand. Near to kick-off, I watched him get to his feet, line up one of the cupboards with his hands and then begin to bang his forehead into it. 'I hate Barnsley!' he growled. Bang, bang, bang. 'I hate Barnsley!' He was winding himself up, getting in the zone to go out and give it his all. For future games, he would try and recruit me to follow him in his ritual of aggressive, amateur carpentry. 'Come on Dave,' he would yell, 'you hate Tranmere, don't you?!' Bang, bang, bang. 'Dave, we hate Bradford City, we hate them!' Bang, bang, bang.

The man in the middle of that half-back line, Southy, was a classy centre-half – tall and slim but hard as nails. He'd been a boxer in his youth in Brighton, a southpaw, which I found out to my cost on more than one occasion. When I arrived for training in a morning, he'd often greet me with a left hook. 'Morning Alec,' I'd say and then, from nowhere, this fist would catch me on the shoulder or in the chest, never full strength but enough to wind. I got used to bobbing and weaving whenever I passed him in a corridor. On the pitch, Southy didn't pull his punches. If ever I got in any bother, he'd be there to back me up. He was always a good source of information on opposing players, too. 'This centre-half is tough but he'll wobble if you hit him early on,' he'd say or

'Watch out for him raking his studs down your calf.' These are the dark arts, those snippets of knowledge and experience on the very borderline of the rules that give you an edge. Knowing when and where to use these separate the amateur from the pro.

The third member of the trio, Frank, was a different animal. He was large by name and nature. Where Eric and Southy were channelled, he was unrestrained and nasty at times. He was a Leeds boy and would invite Malcolm and me to come to the city with him to take part in gang fights. I've no idea if he was just messing with us but we came up with all manner of excuses not to go. In general, despite his size, he wasn't that intimidating off the pitch but, once he got on it, you knew he was there. He started as a midfield player with Town but ended up at centre-forward, where he scored plenty of goals for a succession of different clubs. In 1962, he moved to QPR but then quickly went on to join Leck, Branston and Kurila at Northampton. Whenever we faced them, I made sure that wherever he was on the pitch, I was not.

My early competitive games for Halifax were in the reserve side, playing alongside Malcolm and others, including Rod Green. Rod was a giant Adonis of a man, with a body shaped like an upside down triangle. He was a character, too, a proper joker who was always looking for an accomplice to help him get ahead. He would regularly recruit me to go to the lido in Bradford, not so he could swim but as an excuse to parade his physique in a pair of little white trunks … well, 'budgie smugglers', as they say. He would stand on the diving board, showing off, never getting wet, while I tear-arsed around, flinging myself into the pool, still a kid at heart.

The first away trip I went on with the reserves was to Middlesbrough – a Second Division side at the time but still a big club after a number of seasons in the top flight either side of the war. Keen to provide support, my dad travelled with the team on the coach. At the ground, he was allowed to sit in the VIP seats with the well-to-do, besuited Town directors. Midway through the first half, I was sent in on goal, drew the keeper and finished neatly. My first senior goal for the club. We would ultimately lose 2-1 but little Town had put up a valiant show and I had starred. It was only later I found out that my dad had greeted my goal by leaping to his feet and cheering boisterously, much to the disapproval of the prim and proper directors sat around him. Apparently, it was not considered 'the sporting thing to do'. Clearly, I wasn't the only one still learning how to be professional!

There would be another trip to a big club soon after, this time of a different nature. Manchester City had contacted me to offer a trial – an opportunity I could not turn down. While not quite the behemoth they are now, City were a huge club even then. They'd won trophies, including the FA Cup only a few years prior. Denis Law was there at the time. With all due respect to Halifax, it was a significant step up. I travelled over secretly, played in a game and stayed at my grandad's pub, the King's Head, on Moss Side. It must have gone well, because they enquired with Halifax about signing me. However, the form Town had asked me to sign after that trial in October had no release clause. If City wanted me, they would have to pay and they were unwilling to part with any money for a relatively untested 16-year-old. It was a small lesson in reading the small print before signing.

As I promised I would, on my 17th birthday I became a full-time professional with Town, beginning my football career with them in earnest. A photo of the moment, probably cliché even then, appeared in the local newspaper. It depicts me sitting at a table, sporting a pretty dapper duffle coat, just about to put pen to paper. The manager, Harry Hooper, is stood over me, one hand on my shoulder and the other pointing to where I needed to scribble my name. Neither of us seem all that delighted but I can promise you that I was. It may only have been the Third Division but it meant everything. The wage cap back then was £20 for every player, even those in the First Division. I think I earned £14 a week to begin with when playing in the first team – hardly a fortune but it was more money than I'd ever seen before.

Harry was a strange old man. He smoked like a trooper, walked with a limp and signalled his impending arrival in any location by singing to himself. It was always the same song. I'd be in the changing room and suddenly, echoing down the corridor, getting steadily louder, I'd hear: 'Do not forsake me oh my darlin', on this our weddin' day, do not forsake me oh my daaaaaarlin', waaaaiiiit, wait along ...' And then he'd appear, shuffling out of a billowing cloud of smoke like the world's worst *Stars In Their Eyes* contestant. He'd perch the tiny butt of his fag in his mouth to pin the teamsheet on one of the cupboards and then off he'd shuffle down the corridor, his song getting quieter and quieter: 'I do not know what fate awaits me, I only know I must be brave, and I must face a man who hates me ...' It was always high noon in Halifax when Harry was about.

He was an old school manager, the kind that wore a three-piece suit and resided almost entirely in his office. Usually back then, the gaffer was someone who had been a player, a good name, which Harry certainly was after having played a long time for Sheffield United in the First Division. Managers weren't necessarily someone with a coaching background, although Harry had been assistant trainer at West Ham prior to getting the manager's job at Town. These managers garnered respect by virtue of having played but you wouldn't often find them at practice during the week, with the trainer doing the work. We didn't receive the sort of tactical detail you get today, gleaned from sending scouts to watch an upcoming opponent to get reports on players or corner routines – the sort of tasks I'd later begin my scouting career performing. Harry's advice was limited to imparting his expectations – to do your job, stop an opponent playing, get in the face of a defender or maybe use pace if a marker was especially cumbersome.

I'll always be grateful to him for handing me my debut. He had promised to play me if and when the club were safe from relegation at the end of what had been a difficult 1961/62 season. With two games to spare, the moment came, against Coventry. Up until the morning of the game itself, I had no idea I was playing but, at around 9am, I received a phone call from Harry at the town hall. 'Dave, I want you to leave work now,' he said. 'I want you to go and get your hair cut, go home and have a sleep if you can, because you're playing tonight.' I think he purposefully held back the news to prevent me from getting nervous but my excitement could not be contained. I shot out of work and headed straight for the barbers. What little sleep I did manage that afternoon was riddled with nightmares of Coventry's fearsome centre-back, George Curtis. He was a monster of a man, an absolute clogger who had hammered every centre-forward from pillar to post that season. Once again, my dad's words echoed through my head: 'Don't let him know he's hurt you … get up, dust yourself off and smile.'

I did what I could, took the odd kick and even tried to reply with an occasional dig in the ribs when he rose for a header behind me. I didn't score and we ended up losing 2-0 to what was a decent City side but I made my presence felt. Afterwards, Harry came to me and put his arm around me. 'You've done well there, son,' he told me. It would be the only game I would play that season but it was a start. For the gaffer, though, high noon had arrived and there would be no heroic ending. Harry Hooper was no Gary Cooper. In the summer of 1962, Town sacked him.

Harry's successor would end up being one of the most important figures in my career, someone who would truly teach me what it meant to be a professional footballer. Don McEvoy was from Golcar originally and spent the majority of his playing career as a formidable defender with Huddersfield and Sheffield Wednesday. Halifax was his first managerial job but he quickly impressed us all with his coaching skills. He'd done his badges at Lilleshall while still with Lincoln near the end of his playing days. Unlike Harry, he was hands on, getting involved in training, where he proved he could still mix it. He was only a bit taller than me but solid as a rock. I would bounce off him if I attempted to go in for a tackle. He came armed with tactical ideas, too. He was a student of the game and aspired for his teams to play attacking football, on the front foot. I'd say the squad learned more about how to play the game from Don in six months than they had in five years under Harry.

He was particularly eager to work with and educate the younger lads. He recognised the need for Town to bring through its own players if they were going to thrive. This was of particular benefit to Malcolm and me. Often, after training, Don would drive the two of us to watch Sheffield Wednesday or Huddersfield Town reserves. Throughout the games, he would constantly point things out, telling us to observe specific players. 'Dave, watch the centre-forward, see what runs he makes,' he would say. 'See what positions he takes up when the full-back gets the ball and where he lays it off when it gets fed into him.' It wasn't just a players' tutorial, it was an early lesson in scouting. I still have a cutting from the *Halifax Daily Courier* from 1963, Jack Dunhill's 'Soccer Survey' column, in which Don details his youth plans for the club. I am described as 'perhaps the keenest and most dedicated trainer on the staff'.

My brother, Bob, was in the youth team at that time, too, taking his own early steps in the professional game as a tough-tackling full-back. We played together in an A team fixture that year, a West Yorkshire League Watson Cup semi-final, which we won, me playing up front and our Bob at left-back. It would be another decade before we were named in the same team again. Later in Jack Dunhill's column, under a section headed 'Quality', he describes an 'outstanding 14-year-old prospect' who 'has all the qualities required to make it in the game'. He's referring to our Frank, who was now dazzling people at The Shay rather than patrons at the Duke of York with his ball control, tricks and flicks. Sadly, Don would never get a chance to work with my younger brother, who left soon after to join Huddersfield, tempted away by their chief scout at that time, one Harry Hooper.

Don was a good man. He was honest and genuine. It didn't always help him in the job but the players respected him for it. Whilst fierce when he needed to be, he was part of the team rather than a distant authoritarian. This was helped by his eagerness to involve himself in training. In addition, during the summers he would play alongside us in our cricket team, just one of the lads in a side captained by Alex South and with me wicketkeeping. Don was fun-loving, too – good company. We built up a brilliant relationship off the pitch, so much so that I would babysit for him on a Saturday night, looking after his daughter, Kathy. He looked after me and I'd have done anything for him in return. In many ways, he was my football father figure.

Unfortunately, for all the good work Don was doing off the pitch, results on it were disastrous in his first season. We showed fight and played some decent stuff at times but it wasn't enough to stay up. On a personal level, it was a breakthrough year and a huge learning curve – one that provided plenty of memories. At the start of the season, I experienced my first trip to London, travelling with the squad as a reserve for a double-header of games at Crystal Palace and QPR. The furthest I'd been before that was a school trip to Filey. Driving into London was mind-blowing, seeing Trafalgar Square – something I'd only seen on the TV before. We drew the first game at Palace in front of a huge 17,500 crowd but got hammered 5-0 at Loftus Road. That result set the tone for the season.

I got my first run in the side in September. Goals followed. I was the width of a post away from netting in a 2-0 win over Barnsley but then scored my first for the club in a home 3-2 League Cup defeat to Mansfield, who were flying in the Fourth Division at the time. My first league goal followed two days later, in a 2-1 win over Brighton. The ball broke to me on the edge of the box and I smacked it through a crowd of players and into the bottom corner. I was flying, eager for more … perhaps a bit too much so. Two days after Brighton, we travelled to Northampton for our fourth game in seven days. At that time, the Cobblers played on the county cricket ground, which meant one touchline did not have a stand, with the roped-off wicket behind it. That was soon of little concern because we were 3-0 down inside 35 minutes and down to ten men because of an injury to Brian Redfearn (there were no substitutes back then). Northampton added a fourth and a fifth before I pulled one back, heading in a Willie Carlin cross. Pumped up by the goal and naïve youthful enthusiasm, I began running back to the halfway line shouting 'come on lads, we can do this!' I met Eric and Southy on the way, their hands on their hips, shaking their heads. 'Calm down, Worthy son.' They knew the score. We ended up losing 7-1.

You quickly learn the difference between losing causes and the games when you don't give up the ghost.

At the end of September, Swindon came to The Shay. They were unbeaten in eight games and ultimately destined for promotion, along with Northampton. With 55 minutes gone, they led 3-0 and we all feared another drubbing. Many of the fans gave up – I remember looking up in the second half to see many walking up the banking of the stand, heading for home. More fool them, because they missed an absolute treat. In the 70th minute, Barry Tait pulled one back and Swindon began to wobble. He got his second ten minutes later and then, in the 88th minute, completed his hat-trick to draw us level. With seconds to go, Brian Redfearn charged clear and drove in from an angle to win it. The team and the remaining fans in the crowd went bananas. We were unbeaten against Swindon that year, drawing 1-1 at their place. Mike Summerbee, who would go on to play for England and become a Manchester City legend, played for them in both games. I occasionally see him during visits to City's Etihad Stadium and I delight in reminding him of those games. 'Hey Mike, do you remember when you were 3-0 up with 20 minutes left and little crappy Halifax came back and beat you!'

I learned another lesson that day, courtesy of our hat-trick hero Barry Tait. In my mind, he was a lazy player. He wouldn't put a shift in and often didn't track back when he lost the ball. It was the opposite of what I'd been taught but he scored goals and every team needs a player like that. So long as he kept doing his main job, popping them in, earning the team a win and the players a nice little bonus (we got £4 extra for a victory, £2 for a draw) then we could see past his lack of effort at times. It's a realisation I carried into scouting. Someone might not be your kind of player or lacks qualities you personally cherish but you have to identify what he does bring to a team and how this might complement your own.

That was a long, hard and cold season. We didn't have a home game for three months at the start of 1963 because of snow and freezing temperatures. At one stage, concerned about the lack of money coming in, the club opened the ground as an ice rink, allowing people to pay to skate on the pitch. It was an apt move. We were on a slippery slope in all regards. We would finish bottom, with just 30 points. While it was obviously disappointing, after scoring five times in 16 games, I was hopeful that a campaign in the Fourth Division would mean more involvement for me in the first team and a chance to continue learning under Don. There would at least be some positives before the season ended. In late May, I was part of the team that beat Leeds United 5-0 in a West Riding Senior Cup semi-final. It was a largely second-string Whites team but did include my former team-mate from the West Riding County days, Paul Madeley. We would lose to Bradford in the final but the win over Leeds ensured a few drinks from fans in the months that followed.

I'd also started courting. Larraine lived in Shelf, just down the road from our house. We got to know each other initially on bus journeys into Halifax, with me heading into training and her to her job. We hit it off immediately and quickly gravitated from sharing a seat on the double decker into town to the bowling alley and newly opened jazz club. It was fun and excitement at a time when, sadly, Town weren't providing a whole lot of either.

The 1963/64 season would be my last at Halifax. It was an important one for my development and establishment as a professional. I discovered versatility to my game, born from my willingness to do whatever job was required for the team. I was still a young man – just 18 – and, so, would move between the first team and games for the reserves in the North Regional League. Often, I would play in my usual role of centre-forward, or wide right, but occasionally I would drop back to operate as an attacking midfield player. I got stuck in, regardless. In one first-team match, away in the FA Cup first round at Workington, I started in midfield but ended up playing nearly the entirety of the second half in goal when our goalkeeper Mick Granger broke his finger diving at an attacker's feet. We were 2-0 down at the time. I would concede two more. Mick, now playing up front, grabbed a late consolation goal. We would joke about it with each other for years after. 'I conceded the same number of goals as you Mick and I'm not a goalkeeper,' I'd say. 'Ah, but I scored, though, didn't I, Worthy?' he'd respond. I was no keeper but Mick, like every lad I've ever met who played between the sticks, secretly thought he was a centre-forward.

Perhaps the most obvious example of my growth as a player, certainly in the eyes of Eric Harrison and Alex South, was one I knew very little about. It occurred in a League Cup tie against Rochdale at The Shay. Dale's keeper at the time was Ted Burgin, who had played for a long time at Sheffield United and been a member of England's squad for the 1954 World Cup. Before the game, Eric pulled me aside and told me: 'First chance you get, go in and hammer Burgin, show him you mean business.' In the first minute, we won a corner, so I readied myself. As Frank Twist's delivery came in, Burgin set off to catch the ball and I set off to catch Burgin. The next thing I knew, I was being hauled up from the turf by my jubilant team-mates. 'What? What's happened?' I asked groggily. 'We've scored, Worthy, Willie's scored,' they replied. As the ball had come in, I had charged in on the keeper, leaving me in a dazed heap on the floor. I had done just enough, though, to throw him off and give Willie Carlin the space he needed behind me to nod in the opener. It was a real feather in my cap; I, a green 17-year-old, had put myself on the line against a serious opponent for the good of the team. It set us up for a 4-2 win and felt to me like the moment I'd truly arrived as a pro.

We would finish tenth in the Fourth Division that season, something of a consolation after the previous year's relegation. It was not enough for the club, though. Don departed his role as manager to take over at Barrow, where he had ended his playing career. Halifax were struggling financially and came to me in the summer with an offer of a part-time contract. It was not something I was willing to entertain. I had worked so hard to become a full-time footballer, living the right life, playing the game the right way. I wasn't taking a step backwards now. I wasn't prepared to lose my hard-won status. I rejected it and backed myself to successfully navigate the uncertainty of what came next as a professional.

Four

Barrow Boy to Man
(1964–1966)

In the tiny village of Shelf, on a street with a wall into which is carved a single goalpost, is a house alive with activity.

In the kitchen, the woman of the house is cooking tea for her family, an apron wrapped tightly around her waist. Sat at the table nearby is her husband, the paper in front of him and a cigarette in his hand. In the living room, their daughter plays with her Sindy doll while, outside in the garden, two of their boys practise juggling a ball. In almost every part of this happy home, contentment can be found.

The one exception is the bedroom at the front, in which lies the eldest son, staring up at his ceiling and deep in thought. He's contemplating the future or, to be more precise, the uncertainty of his chosen one.

He is a professional footballer, living the dream of so many. For two years, he has been learning, growing and getting better. Until now, his destination and the directions on how to get there have been clear – listen, work hard and never give in. It has taken him far. But now there is only one option in front of him and that involves putting everything into reverse.

As he contemplates his fate, he hears the phone ring in the downstairs hall and listens in as his dad answers and talks in muffled but warm tones to the person on the other end. After a minute or two, he appears at the bedroom door, a knowing smile on his face. 'Dave, it's Don on the phone,' he says. 'He wants to talk to you about joining Barrow.'

A LOT went through my head when I received that call. There was relief and happiness that my career as a full-time professional footballer could continue. I was humbled, too. Don had left Halifax but thought enough of me as a player to want me alongside him in his next job. I also couldn't help but be excited by the money on offer. The £20 wage cap had been abolished in 1961 and what Don was proposing to me was considerably more than I was on at Halifax, plus it also included a small signing-on fee.

There was caution and concern, though. Halifax was all I had known so far, both personally and professionally. In a career sense, while the club's offer of part-time terms was a complete non-starter, this didn't mean I would find it easy to wave goodbye to the place. The humble Shay, with its creaking stands and peeling paint, was the setting for some treasured memories. I'd swept its terraces, climbed its floodlights and covered every blade of grass on its pitch. I would also be leaving a fine group of team-mates, some of whom had been pivotal in my development as a player and a person.

In addition, there was the Worthington connection. Halifax had been my dad's club and was also currently that of my two brothers. Me leaving would end any hope of the three of us all turning out in the same Town team – a moment that would have truly swelled my parents' hearts with pride. Most significantly, I would be departing from family and friends for the first real time, saying goodbye to the warm, familiar security of home. How would I feel without the comforting regular presence of my parents and siblings? Would I find friends up there? And what of the budding relationship with Larraine – could we continue it over a distance?

Perhaps sensing my reticence, my parents gave me a push, handing me the scissors so I could cut the apron strings. It was the same advice they would soon offer to Frank when Huddersfield came with an offer to take him from Halifax and to Bob a couple of years later, with Middlesbrough offering him a new home. True to the man I knew him to be and the relationship we had built, Don was equally supportive. He took me on a recce of the area, giving me the highlights reel of the Lake District and the coastal road with a lovely view of Morecambe Bay. He later helped me get a car of my own, driving me up to an old mechanic friend of his in Bowness-on-Windermere. The signing-on fee he secured for me was not huge – around £120 – but it was enough to put down a deposit on a little 875cc Mini. It would provide me with the means to get about and also get myself home to Halifax if required. All I had to do was learn how to drive it.

The gaffer's biggest show of empathy and respect came with the signing of my contract. After I'd completed the paperwork in his office, he took the sheets and put them in his desk. 'I'm going to keep this in here,' he explained. 'You get on with pre-season, throw yourself into the club and training and give it your all. But if you come to me in a month and say you're not enjoying it and you don't want to be here, I'll tear the contract up and that'll be that.' It was the safety net he felt I needed and a huge show of faith. I'm not sure how he would have squared it with his board of directors had I come and asked him to rip up the deal but I never had any doubt he meant what he said.

Despite Don's best efforts, the early weeks in Barrow were hard, tapping into all my initial fears. It was a quiet place and unfamiliar. I was lonely. I would enjoy a pint after games on a Saturday but wasn't much of a drinker outside of that. Away from training, I quickly became bored. My only real connection to the place was through football and, so, to occupy myself, I would go to watch the part-time and reserve players train on Tuesday and Thursday nights. They must have thought it odd to see the new young striker stood on the sidelines watching them do laps and other drills.

My living arrangements didn't help. I stayed in digs when I first moved up, with a retired couple in their big house on Ainslie Street, near to the club's Holker Street ground. They were good enough to take in two of the club's new signings in the summer of 1964, myself being one and Ray Brennan the other. Ray was a forward and had joined from First Division club Blackburn Rovers. He was a nice player, although maybe a bit too nice for the division into which he was dropping, where opposing players gave him little of the time he wanted on the ball. We got on okay, initially, but he wasn't my sort of pal. We certainly didn't hit it off as quickly nor develop the kind of friendship Malcolm Russell and I had forged at Halifax.

Any chance there might have been of us becoming friends was ended during one particular training session. We were playing an eight-a-side game on the cinders of the car park next to the ground. As I made my way down the right, I could see Ray coming from the side to challenge me. In he flew with an unnecessarily aggressive tackle that took all of me and none of the ball, sending me flying to the rough ground. My knee and thigh took the brunt, scraping off a long chunk of skin. The pain was secondary to my anger. I leapt to my feet, the red mist swirling, and got a few punches in before we were pulled apart. Later that evening, we both sat silently seething at the dinner table as our hosts tried to make pleasant small talk, me with scabs forming on my leg, he with a black eye. We didn't speak to each other at all for a few days and kept it largely civil afterwards.

As my thoughts began to wander to the signed but not yet sealed contract in the top drawer of Don's desk and the escape route it offered, a chance discovery brought me back from the brink. I have never been much of a reader but, during one of my evenings alone in digs, I ended up studying one of the bookshelves. I'm not sure why, possibly because of the mindset I was in, but I reached for a self-help book and began flicking through the pages. There was a chapter on positive thinking and it drew me in. Its core message – to focus on the good opportunities around you rather than the negatives – resonated with me. I thought to myself: 'Your mum and dad and everyone else are back in Halifax, you're on your own now. It's time to stand up and do something for yourself.'

A week before the deadline Don had given me, I walked into his office once again. 'Gaffer,' I started. 'You can file that contract away, I'll be all right up here.' The safety net was gone. It was all on me now. I threw myself wholeheartedly into my new life, especially my career. I trained furiously, striving to run harder and faster, to perfect skills and learn whatever, whenever and wherever I could to help better my game. Nothing could satisfy my quest for improvement. I would get frustrated in training because there were usually only two or three balls between 20 of us, hampering my development. So, after the morning session had finished and everyone had drifted off, I would return to Holker Street in the afternoon to practise on my own. I would sometimes climb over a fence near the turnstiles and get access to the pitch through the door to the drying room, which was always left open to allow air to get to the freshly washed and hung kit. Once inside, I had free rein to practise whatever I fancied in the empty ground.

A favourite drill of mine was to stick two corner flags near the edge of the penalty area to represent the two ends of the defensive wall and then practise curling free kicks around them. I would try to steer them into the top corner from one side with the inside of my right foot and then the other with the outside, over and over and over. On a good day, I'd get a few hours of solid practice time to myself. On others, I'd have to quickly scarper, the shouts of an irate groundsman following me.

I started to develop friendships with some of the other players. Lads like Bobby Tait, a good goalscorer who had come down from Scotland and joined from Notts County after impressing as their inside-forward. Malcolm Edwards was an ex-Bolton full-back but found a home in Cumbria. Brian Arrowsmith was Barrow through and through, a smashing lad and a really tough full-back. There was Barnsley lad Roy McCarthy, Keith Eddy, George Smith and Mick Hartland. Bobby Knox, a part-time player for the club, would gain some fame on the first day of my second season when he became the first substitute to score in English football, in a 4-2 win over Wrexham.

It was a small squad that bonded during training sessions on the beach at Walney Island, over the bridge from the mainland. Don would take us down there to run on the heavy sand, the Isle of Man visible across the sea on a clear day. Near the end of the session, lines would be marked out for a pitch and we would play eight- or nine-a-side games. We'd always know when it was time to head back as the tide would slowly edge in and eventually encroach over one side of the pitch. It was football on one wing and water polo on the other.

The mood in the squad was good. I began to feel like my goal of moving up the leagues could be realised. However, it soon became clear just how much of a challenge this would be with Barrow. Quite simply, the club were skint. With the people of the town more interested in rugby, it proved a constant battle to attract interest and money to the football club. In my first game, we travelled to face Brighton & Hove Albion, who had just signed former Chelsea, Tottenham and England striker Bobby Smith, now in his mid-30s. They were a good club and expected to challenge for promotion. Albion play in blue and white, the same as Barrow, but we couldn't afford an away kit. So, on a sunny, hopeful opening day of the season, we ran out to face one of the favourites for the league and their superstar signing wearing the strip of the Vickers Armstrong Shipbuilders team. The directors had been forced to go cap in hand to the company down the road the day before to see if they'd loan us their kit. I remember lining up in my maroon shirt and white nylon shorts turned yellow by multiple washes and thinking to myself how crap and amateur we looked. It was no surprise that we lost 3-1.

It wasn't the only time we had kit issues that season. It snowed heavily ahead of a home fixture we had against Crewe around Christmas, leaving the pitch covered. They didn't cancel games back then but, instead, painted blue lines over the snow. However, our largely white shirts would make it near impossible to pick out team-mates, so a call was made to Barrow rugby club to secure their shirts for the game. The thicker blue tops, with the classic rugby 'V' across the chest, were handy in the weather but didn't help us play any better. We lost 2-1.

The tone was set by that opening game at Brighton. The season proved a constant struggle, with wins extremely hard to come by. We took some hidings, too. We lost 6-2 twice, got hit for seven at Oxford and lost 9-1 at Third Division Workington Town in the League Cup. In total, we conceded 105 goals, although we did improve on our league position from the season before – 21st as opposed to 24th. Again, though, everything was framed through the fight for financial survival. It's near impossible to compete on the pitch when you don't even know if the bills can be paid each week.

On a more positive note, I felt I was making strides forward as a player and a person. Despite the losses, the local press often picked me out for praise for my performances at right-half, pointing to my work-rate and spirit alongside Keith Eddy and Dave Holder.

I scored my first goal for the club in our first win of the season –
2-1 at Darlington. I also netted and provided two assists in a 4-0
victory at local rivals Southport, our biggest and most satisfying
win of the campaign. My proudest contribution in front of goal,
though, came in our 1-0 home win over Halifax, not because it was
against my former club but because it represented a culmination of
all my hard work.

Thirty minutes into the game, we got a free kick just outside
the box. One of the lads went to pick up the ball but I demanded
to have it. This was exactly the kind of situation for which I had
spent all those solitary afternoons practising. Instead of two corner
flags stuck in the ground, there stood a real wall, made up of my
old mates Alex South and John Brier, with Pete Downsborough,
the Town goalkeeper, behind them. In my mind, I took everyone
away – the men in the wall, keeper, even the crowd – and imagined
I was in Holker Street alone on a sunny afternoon. I visualised
the moment, strode up and struck it perfectly with the inside of
my right foot, curling it around the wall and inside the post. I was
elated and began celebrating wildly, delighted that all my practice
had paid off. I was soon halted, though, by the sting of the ball
smashing into my back. Pete had picked it out of the net and belted
it at me. Southy soon followed up with a barrage of abuse. They
thought I was jumping around so much because I'd got one over
on them but that wasn't the case.

The unsavoury tone continued through the rest of the game,
with our winger Roy McCarthy and Halifax's Walt Bingley sent
off for a punch-up in the second half. It was only afterwards that
I was able to explain what my celebrations were actually about.
Thankfully, Southy and the rest didn't hold anything against me.

The biggest sign of my growth as a player – and the most
gratifying and humbling moment of my time at Barrow – came

just a couple of months into that first season. Ahead of the seventh game, at Hartlepool United, Don took me aside after training. 'Dave, you're working your socks off,' he said to me. 'You battle harder than anyone else in the team and you get everybody else working. I want you to be my captain.' I was surprised but delighted and immediately agreed to take on the job. I knew, though, that it would ruffle some feathers in the rest of the squad, not least those of the man I was replacing, Tommy Cahill. He was an experienced full-back who had been at Newcastle and played nearly 300 games over a decade at Barrow. I was a 19-year-old kid with just over 40 professional games to my name and had been at the club no time at all.

It wasn't just Tommy; there were other veteran players in the squad with much more prominent CVs than mine who it would now be my job to lead. Malcolm Edwards had been at Bolton and Don Watson at Sheffield Wednesday. The message from the gaffer was pretty clear – 'your time is coming to an end and this is my man'. I did get some stick off the older lads, some in jest, some more pointed and I'm sure there were even more critical conversations had out of my earshot. But I drew confidence from what Don had said to me and remembered what I had read in the book back at my digs. I resolved to lead by example, continuing to set the standard for others to follow. I never thought of myself as big-headed but I'd discovered quickly where the line was for effort and I knew I had the wherewithal to stand for what I thought was right, even with those who were my senior. I strived for positivity, always eager to offer an encouraging word and, on the flip side, any coyness I might have had about dishing out hard truths quickly evaporated. I remained as skipper for the rest of the season and continued with a principled attitude for the remainder of my career. Well, most of it, anyway.

The undoubted highlight of my time at Barrow was the FA Cup tie, played over three matches, against Grimsby Town in that first season. The Mariners were in the Third Division then, having only been relegated from the second tier the season before, but we matched them kick for kick over five hours of football. In the initial tie at Holker Street, I had a great game and an own goal from wing-half Brian Clifton earned us a 1-1 draw and a replay at Blundell Park. Three days later, following a nine-hour journey to the east coast – a result of fog and us taking a wrong turning in Leeds – we were denied victory in normal time only by a dodgy penalty for a supposed handball against Brian Arrowsmith. Having scored that, Grimsby then took a lead that they held deep into extra time, leaving us facing an exit from the competition.

What happened next is one of my happiest moments on a football field. Having seen an initial attack break down, the ball broke to me in the box. Despite a melee of players in front of me, I was somehow able to steer the ball into the net and send us all wild in celebration. Penalty shoot-outs had not yet been conceived, so a third game was required, to be played at a neutral venue of the FA's choosing. It was usually somewhere located geographically between the two clubs, opening up the possibility of Ewood Park in Blackburn or Preston's Deepdale. Imagine our surprise and delight when they chose Old Trafford, the home of Manchester United. I had always dreamt of playing at the ground of the team with which my dad began his career and I had spent part of my childhood following. Now here was my chance.

I'm not sure Old Trafford had ever played host to such a rag-tag bunch before, though. At around 6.30pm on Monday, 23 November, a battered old blue-and-white 18-seater Volkswagen bus carrying 18 misfit dreamers rattled proudly up to one of the most famous venues in world football. We called our chariot 'The Beetle' and, while you needed a sturdy behind and at least one rug to stay warm inside her, she became a symbol of our never-say-die spirit. I was so proud to lead the side out for the game and even prouder of the way we played. The effort was there but unfortunately our finishing wasn't and a more ruthless Grimsby beat us 2-0. It was a disappointing result but an incredible experience and brought a crucial injection of money for the club. With a crowd just short of 10,000, Barrow walked away with £500, staving off the threat of closure for a few months at least. Those three games were a ray of light in what were otherwise dark times.

I've only been sent off twice in my career. The first of those dismissals came at Crewe on Boxing Day 1964. It was a freezing cold day and we weren't in the best of spirits, having lost our previous two games – against Brighton and Oxford – by an aggregate of 11-1. It quickly became another one to forget. We were 4-0 down before the break and facing up to yet another hammering. To make matters worse, all through the game, every time I got the ball, Crewe's left-winger Barry Wheatley was raking his studs down the back of my legs.

We came out fighting in the second half, with goals from Jack Maddison and Bobby Tait making it 4-2. After an hour, though, I'd had enough of Wheatley's dirty trick. I waited until the play had gone to the other end of the pitch, up by the corner flag, and the referee and linesmen were far away. I turned to Barry and lamped him in the face, dropping him to the deck. The only people who saw it were the home supporters near the touchline and they started making a fuss, drawing the referee's attention. The officials had no idea what had happened but they saw Barry on the floor and listened to what the crowd were saying. The ref sent me off. Having got me dismissed, the crowd booed me all the way off the pitch and down the tunnel.

As I sat in the dressing room, I heard boom, boom, boom, boom getting steadily louder up the tunnel. Then 'bang!' – two panels of the door came shooting off into the room, followed by Don's foot. He tore strips off me. 'What did you do that for?! You're the captain, you're supposed to lead by example! And we'd just got back into it!' I was just about to foolishly point out we were still losing by two when I was saved by a steward coming to see what the loud bang had been. He spluttered something about having to pay for the door before he was unceremoniously told to sling his hook. I was left to sit and listen to the muted roars of the Crewe crowd as they scored twice more to seal a 6-2 win.

The sending-off led to an FA hearing in Manchester at which I was given a two-game suspension and a fine of a week's wages. Interestingly, the reports from the referee and both linesmen were identical, which is some feat for an incident they hadn't seen. However, out of adversity came opportunity. Knowing I would be unavailable for home games with Darlington and Wrexham and not allowed to train with the squad, Don told me to go home to Halifax, have a break and see my parents. He also tasked me with a special mission. He had heard that former Burnley, Bolton and England winger Brian Pilkington may be available to sign from Bury. Brian had played more than 300 games for Burnley, helping them win the First Division in 1960, but he was in his mid-30s at that point and struggling to get a game in the Second Division. 'Go and watch their reserves,' Don told me. 'See if Pilkington is fit enough, if he can still beat his man and he still has a desire to play. See if he'd do a job for us.'

It was my first proper scouting assignment. It was clear from watching Brian that he still had the hunger to play and his fitness levels were good. He'd lost a yard of pace, which was understandable, but he still had the ability to give defenders a hard time, especially at the level Barrow were playing. I called Don and passed on my report. The next thing I knew, Barrow had signed Brian, partly on the word of a 19-year-old first-time scout. I took particular pride in the fact that Brian did a fine job for us on the wing over the next season and a half.

As my sending-off at Crewe had shown, I still had the odd moment of volatility on the pitch. Off it, though, I was settling down. Any concerns I had about the negative effects distance might have on my relationship with Larraine were unfounded. Once I'd passed my driving test, I was able to go back to Halifax fairly regularly, often on Saturday evenings after a game, to see her and keep the flame burning.

Back then, you were encouraged to marry young. I think football clubs encouraged it because they thought it would keep their players settled and away from pubs, clubs and heavy boozing. So, on the Saturday prior to the start of the 1965/66 season, with me having just turned 20 and Larraine aged 18, we tied the knot at All Angels Church in Shelf. It was a lovely day with our family and friends. My pal from Halifax, Malcolm Russell, was my best man. We weren't able to have much of a honeymoon, though. Don told me I could have a couple of days but to be back in training on the Monday. Our solution was a short stay in Windermere, just an hour away from Barrow. Larraine moved to Barrow shortly after and I left digs and Ray Brennan to live with my new wife in a house we rented off the club. Unfortunately, from this healthy start, the season that followed was anything but for me.

I had managed to avoid injuries during the first few years of my career, priding myself on staying fit. The only games I missed in my first season at Barrow were the two through suspension. But my second season with the club was a broken one in which I was limited to only a handful of first-team games. I missed the start with a groin strain and then tore ankle ligaments in a training game in November. It was deeply frustrating to miss what was a much-improved campaign for the club, aided by new players like midfielder Mick Hartland and ex-Chelsea forward Jimmy Mulholland. With Brian Arrowsmith taking over as captain, we briefly pushed for promotion before eventually finishing 12th.

The club were finally on the up but the injuries contributed to me growing restless. I had lost a season, delaying my desire to push onwards and upwards through the leagues. With my contract up for renewal, I once again found myself in Don's office. As I knew he would be, he was empathetic to the situation. 'With interest from other clubs, the directors will want some money for you,' he told me. 'But you came up here, you've done a great job for me, you've been a good captain. I'm going to get you a free transfer if you want it.' I told him that I felt like I'd done my bit and that I wanted to try a new challenge. As it had begun, my Barrow career came to an end with a massive gesture from one of the men I respected most.

We may not have achieved all we hoped at Barrow, hamstrung throughout by the financial reality of life at a tiny club playing in front of a couple of thousand people in the Fourth Division, but I look back on those two years fondly. I made friends I've kept in touch with to this day. I often think back to those torturous but joyful journeys on 'The Beetle' and the games on the beach, the tide inching ever closer to the centre spot. I think I gave Barrow my all. I'm most grateful, though, for what the club gave me. I could easily have carried on part-time at Halifax and possibly not had a career at all in 12 months. But Barrow gave me the opportunity I needed, presented me with a challenge, a constant learning curve and an environment in which to grow and thrive. I arrived in Cumbria a boy and left it a leader of men.

Five

The Prime of the Consistent Mariner

(1966–1967)

There's a nervous atmosphere around Blundell Park. In the stands, the growing pre-match murmur of what will eventually be just over 6,700 people focuses on one question: staying up or going down?

It is Saturday, 20 April and the final home game of what has been a long and challenging 2023/24 season. Swindon are in town and all Grimsby need is a point to ensure they will be playing in the Football League again next season. Here is one last chance to roar the boys to safety.

Away from the central stage, in the function suite of the ground's main stand, a fish and chip lunch is being had by supporters desperate to distract themselves from the tension. To aid with this, they are regaled by tales from the past, delivered by an ex-captain, and former hero, a true Mariner.

The questions come thick and fast, the answers received with smiles and laughter by those with rose-tinted childhood memories of this Mariner's playing days more than half a century ago. In a rare moment of silence, a hand rises to deliver another request: 'You played so many games for Grimsby ... which ones do you remember most?'

The Mariner pauses a moment to think. 'Well,' he begins ...

BARROW HAD been the making of me, the club at which I had come of age as a player and a person. My next move needed to be to a club where I could lay down roots and establish myself as a professional. I needed experience to improve and to understand my own game and the only route to that was regular matches in a settled environment with good players around me.

I was already something of a rarity for having had two clubs before the age of 21. This was an era in which players remained with a club – often their first – for the majority of their career. A footballer's wage did not set you up for life after retirement as it does now, so the aim was to stay somewhere for a decade, securing you a testimonial game and its gate receipts that could then be funnelled into a new business. My new club needed to be a keeper, stable and dependable, with an ambition that matched my own.

I'd been told by Don there were clubs interested in me but until offers arrived I was technically unemployed, raising the risk of being left in limbo for the coming season. To up the stakes even more, Larraine was pregnant with our first child, which was wonderful but made it even more of a necessity that I keep the money coming in. To get away from it all, we decided to travel down to Devon for a holiday immediately after returning from Barrow's last game of the season at Luton – a 3-2 defeat in which I played particularly well. Her parents had moved to Exmouth and it offered something of a safe haven to relax and focus on the positive future addition to our family rather than football. While there, though, football came calling for me.

A couple of days into the holiday, the phone at the house rang. It was the manager of Exeter City with an offer to join them. Over the next few days, I also fielded calls from Rochdale and Crewe – both, like Exeter, in the Fourth Division. They had seen my name on the free transfers list and obtained the number for my in-laws' house from Barrow. At the same time, a letter arrived from Ken Furphy, then manager of Third Division Watford, declaring his keenness to obtain my services. 'I was surprised to see your name on the free list following your performance at Luton,' he wrote. 'It makes me doubt my own ability to assess a player.' Finally, Grimsby got in touch, another third-tier side throwing their hat into the ring. They – in particular their trainer George Higgins – remembered well the FA Cup ties between themselves and Barrow in which I had played out of my skin and scored that late extra-time goal to take it to the second replay at Old Trafford.

I spoke to my parents and then sat down with Larraine to discuss it. Ambition dictated that it was a straight choice between the two Third Division sides – but which one? Little could separate the two in the season just concluding, with both in mid-table. So, I made my decision on what had come before. Grimsby may have been a third-tier side at the time but they had spent notable periods in the First and Second Divisions, had never been below that for long and had desires to return to the upper end of the ladder. At that time, Watford had never been higher than the Third Division. So, to the east coast I went, to become a Mariner.

By dint of an FA Cup run and some postponements, Grimsby still had games to play deep into May of 1966 and, so, having agreed to join them, Larraine and I made our way up to Cleethorpes from Devon for the last game of the season against Millwall on the Saturday. I would meet with the manager, Jimmy McGuigan, the following morning and sign my contract. Unfortunately, because of the lengthy journey, and traffic on the Fosse Way, we didn't arrive until after the game, so Jimmy told us to have a nice meal in our hotel and a night on the town. He'd see me early the next day.

As we were eating in our hotel restaurant, suddenly a familiar figure appeared by our table – Rod Green, my old Adonis of a pal from Halifax reserves. He had left The Shay in 1962 and had stints at both Bradford clubs and Gillingham before spending the season which had just finished at Grimsby. He had played against Millwall that afternoon, so it was a surprise to see him at our hotel. 'Now then, Worthy,' he said. 'The gaffer asked me to come down and get a meal and a few bottles of wine, make sure you find your way around okay.' A really kind gesture, I thought. So we did just that, got stuck into some nice food and drink and had a night out in Cleethorpes. I was feeling really positive about everything during my meeting with the manager the next morning. 'Can I just say thank you for last night, Mr McGuigan,' I began, to which he responded with a smile and dismissive wave. 'And it was a really nice of you to send my old pal Rod down to keep us company,' I continued. His face changed to one of confusion. 'You asked Rod to come and have some food and wine with us last night,' I added, less sure of myself. 'I never told him to do that,' he replied, realisation dawning. 'The cheeky sod has pulled one over on us.' Typical Rod, he'd got wind of my arrival and seized his opportunity for a freebie.

Things quickly got back on track and I signed my contract to officially become a Grimsby player. It was another nice little wage hike, reflective of the higher division I'd be playing in. As with Barrow, I received a signing-on fee. This time, in recognition of my growing domesticity and future fatherhood, Larraine and I went out and bought our first washing machine.

It was a step up from what I'd experienced before. There would be no borrowing kit from the local shipyard, no 'Beetle' bus or training on cinders in a car park. For the first time in my career, I was at a club with its own training ground. There were only a couple of showers, so most of us had to drive back to Blundell Park to get washed properly but it was still an improvement. In addition, there was the local King George V sports ground, with a 400m running track for longer, stamina-building training, usually on a Monday or Tuesday.

The crowds were bigger, too. At Barrow we would play in front of gates between 1,500 and 2,500. At Grimsby it was easily double and sometimes treble that. When we really got it together, we started to see crowds of 10, 15, even a rare 20 thousand. With its tight stands, Blundell Park lent itself to a raucous atmosphere, so you felt the presence of every fan. Now, it has opened up a bit, with the construction of the big Findus Stand, but back then it felt like they were right on top of you. I wasn't there long before the history of the club made itself felt. Supporters would talk in hushed, revered tones of the famous half-back line of Alec Hall, Harry Betmead and Teddy Buck, who played more than 1,000 times for the club between them and were the cornerstone of a Town side that remained in the First Division for eight seasons either side of the Second World War and reached two FA Cup semi-finals. Betmead was one of three Grimsby players, along with Jackie Bestall and George Tweedy, to play for England. Having just witnessed the Three Lions win the World Cup, I had visions of two good seasons to propel myself into competing against the likes of Bobby Charlton, Bobby Moore and Nobby Stiles and potentially joining Hall, Betmead and Buck in Grimsby folklore.

It very quickly felt like home, aided by some brilliant team-mates who would soon become lifelong friends. I've already mentioned Rod but, when I first arrived, there was also goalkeeper Harry Wainman, defender Ron Cockerill, tall, prolific striker Matt Tees, centre-half Keith Jobling, Jimmy Bloomer and Bobby Ross and forward Dave Wilson. Later, there would be goalkeeper Chris Harker, full-backs Johnny Duncliffe and Johnny Wilkinson, outside-left Geoff Martin, midfielder Billy Rudd, forward Gordon Walker and many, many more. It helped that a lot of the players lived in close proximity to one another, in houses rented from the club. Bobby Ross lived close to us on Campden Crescent. Just along the road lived the captain of the club – a quiet, unassuming fella who would never amount to anything … Graham Taylor.

As most of the football world will attest, Graham was a genuine, warm and thoughtful person. He played left-back but was predominantly right-footed, so much so that I called his left foot 'The Shovel'. With his right foot, he could stroke passes around fine but with his left, he would scoop it up the line. I was no maestro with my weaker foot but I did put a bit of work into improving it, plus I spent most of my career on the right side of the pitch. Graham was extremely solid and dependable, though. He rarely made mistakes. He knew where to be and when. My game was about energy and drive, getting up and down the pitch. There was a ferocity to it. But Graham was never that. He was a steady, all-round player who would tuck into defence and focus on stopping his opponent making an impact on the wing.

He was from Nottinghamshire originally but grew up in Scunthorpe, where his dad, Tom, was a sports reporter for the *Evening Telegraph* and was known as 'The Poacher', covering The Iron during the 1950s and 60s. I don't know if this was his father's influence but Graham was always very careful with what he said and how he said it.

We had a lot in common because he was a grammar school boy like myself and had fallen foul of his headmaster because of his love for the beautiful game. I remember a story about him going to inform the school that he was leaving sixth form early to join Grimsby. His headmaster angrily declared to him that 'grammar school boys do not become footballers, they play rugby'. I'd heard that before. We also both had an interest in coaching. I very quickly began studying for my badges, shortly after moving to Town, but Graham was already ahead of me and coaching teams in the club and locally. It was very clear he had a keen tactical brain. On journeys to and from away games, we would often discuss tactics – about how we should play in the upcoming game and then analysing how it went afterwards. Occasionally, we'd criticise the choices made by the manager, although always discreetly enough so he didn't hear. We would both have our own goes at management once our playing days had ended, although I think it's fair to say that Graham's went a touch better than mine.

Another area of similarity between Graham and I was pride in our fitness. The two of us and another full-back, Jimmy Thompson, were the fittest lads in the squad and would always be at the front of the pack during long distance runs. We trained like mad, building up our stamina. Quite often, as we pounded away in pre-season training, lap after lap, we would pass the aforementioned Ron Cockerill. Ron was a tall, slim bloke, appearing even grander than his 6ft 2ins because he stood proudly, shoulders back. He would dress immaculately, arriving each morning in a suit and tie. He was a lovely, elegant player, too, with a great touch and an ability to stroke beautiful passes. He could thread them through the eye of a needle. And there was power as well as precision. They nicknamed him 'Cannonball' at Town because of the rockets he'd unleash from range. What he couldn't do, though, was run. He had little stamina. A few laps in, we three leaders would stride past poor Ron, bent double, being sick on the track. 'Morning Ron,' we'd snigger. 'Looking good.' Sometimes, the trainer, George Higgins, would come over and drag him up and poor Ron would have to soldier on, throwing up every few laps, sometimes over poor George's shoulder.

There was ten years between Ron and I and we were chalk and cheese personality wise. I was a scrappy little thing in my T-shirt and jeans, a big mop of hair in my face; he was a towering, cool, dapper gentleman in his suits, his cropped hair slicked back. We got on like a house on fire, though, as did our wives, Larraine and Thelma. On Sunday evenings, the four of us would regularly head to a pub on the outskirts of Grimsby called the Crown & Anchor, where there would always be a band playing. Like myself, Ron liked a song, although, while I would belt out an Elvis or Rolling Stones number, he was more of a crooner, with the slow, mushy love songs. One evening, while the band were having a rest between songs, Ron seized his chance for an audience. He took the microphone and began to sing the Tony Bennett song 'I Left My Heart in San Francisco'. The people there must have recognised us as footballers because they quickly got into it and gave him a big round of applause after. I thought to myself: 'Well, I can't let him have all the fun.'

At that time, the comedian Freddie 'Parrot Face' Davies was on television a lot and I did a pretty good impression, so I got up and did a turn. It must have gone well because every week we went back, the punters there would ask us to get up and do our little act and, in my mind at least, it got busier and busier. The bands would end up stood in the corner wondering if they were going to get back on.

The thing that truly sealed my friendship with Ron and Thelma and Graham and his wife, Rita, was the support they gave to Larraine and me after she gave birth. Gary arrived in the November of that first year, which made Grimsby feel even more like a home but also presented its challenges. Graham and Rita had infant daughters themselves and the latter would meet up with Larraine to take the babies for walks and share stories and advice on parenting. Thelma went even further, really taking Larraine under her wing. They had a daughter, Karen, and two young boys, Glenn and John, so had been through it all before.

Gary would cry a lot and it got to the point where we weren't getting the sleep we needed. Thelma would come and take Gary for the odd night, to let us get some rest for a few hours. It was such a kind gesture.

Ron had been at Grimsby for close to a decade, having been sold to the club by ex-Mariners and then Huddersfield Town boss Bill Shankly. I would only play alongside him for a season and a bit before a cruel injury ended his career. It happened at a night game at Brighton in the October of my second season at the club. Albion were on the attack and the ball broke for Ron to clear. As he went to do so, one of the home players stupidly pushed one of our lads and he ended up colliding with the big man, breaking his leg. He had to be rushed to hospital and stayed there overnight while we travelled back. I took it upon myself to go round to their house and tell Thelma the news, although neither of us knew how serious it would be at that point.

After leaving the game, Ron worked as a car salesman and HGV driver and also tried his hand at a bit of management in the Lincolnshire League. He and Thelma took a lot of joy from seeing their two boys make a career in football, both as midfielders. Glenn is most famous for his time at Southampton, while John continued the Cockerill legacy at Grimsby as a player, coach and caretaker manager. I still see him occasionally at games when I go back and we laugh over old stories of his dad. Ron died in 2010, at the age of 75. Whenever I'm in Cleethorpes, I will make the effort to go and see Thelma, as a continued way of showing my gratitude for everything she and her husband did for Larraine and me. She still lives in the same house she shared with Ron back in our playing days and most days takes the same walk up past the park, across the railway station and up to go along the seafront and back. Ron would never have kept up with her.

It helped my cause at my new club that I went there as a 'utility player'. I'd played in a number of positions already in my career – up front, on the wing, in midfield. I could slot in anywhere, especially if someone picked up an injury. Coupled with my young age, it meant I wasn't a direct threat to the position of any of the senior guys. I didn't ruffle any feathers. It wasn't quite as smooth with the supporters, though. Prior to my arrival, Town had a right-winger called Jimmy Pennington, who had done superbly for them before leaving to join Oldham. He was only a small lad but he was tricky and scored goals. He was a real fans' favourite. My early appearances for the club came largely on the right, leaving me with big boots to fill, and there were a few who clearly thought I wasn't able to, making their opinions heard from the stands. The wing is no place to be when a crowd are against you. In the middle, you're protected a bit from the chatter but in a tight ground like Blundell Park, running along the touchline, you're well in earshot of all the insults and sarcastic comments.

It wasn't all negative. One particularly uplifting early fan interaction made a lasting impression. It came during my very first week at the club. After the flurry of activity following my signing had died down and I settled in a bit, I decided one Tuesday evening to walk the ten minutes down the road from the house to Blundell Park to watch a reserve-team game. As I set off, there was a man just in front of me, walking in the same direction. As we turned the same corners and walked the same streets, it became clear we were heading to the same destination, so we struck up conversation. Claude Hodgson was his name and he told me he had followed Town for years, attending pretty much every game, through good times and bad, and often went down to watch the reserves as well as the first team. When we reached the turnstiles at the ground, I told him to wait there a minute. I nipped inside to the office of

Mrs Edwards, the secretary, and asked her if I could have a couple of tickets for that night's game. It wasn't much to get in, maybe ten shillings, but players weren't charged. I ran back down to my new friend. 'You're a proper supporter, please take this,' I told him, handing him a ticket. He was really grateful, shook my hand and headed off to watch the game. I assumed I'd never hear from him again. Two days later, there was a knock on the door. I was out but Larraine answered. The same supporter was there with a parcel in his hand. 'Hello Mrs Worthington, I've brought this for you and your husband as a thank you for him getting me the ticket the other night.' Wrapped up in the parcel, in greaseproof paper, was a load of fish, more than we could possibly eat between us. It turns out that Claude was a well-established, and well-known, fishmonger on the docks and, so, was thanking us in the best way he knew how. Every Thursday after that, without fail, for the entirety of my Grimsby career, there was parcel of fish on our doorstep. I was there for seven and a half years. The truly remarkable thing is that we moved house midway through that time, about half a mile up the road. We didn't tell Claude but he found out because the fish continued to arrive at our new address, every Thursday like clockwork. All that for the simple gesture of getting him in to a reserve-team game.

I like to think I quickly began to win over more fans with my committed early displays on the pitch. It helped that I scored in each of my first two appearances. In a League Cup tie with Barnsley, I leapt high over a big centre-half and nodded the ball into the corner of the net to help us to a 2-1 win. Three days later, I scored the opener as we beat Walsall 3-1 at Blundell Park in the league. It was great to run over and punch the air in celebration in front of all the fans in the Pontoon Stand. To continue the positivity, in the fourth league game of the season we absolutely battered our local rivals, Scunthorpe, 7-1 at home. Rod Green and left-winger Brian Hill both scored hat-tricks. I cheekily like to tell people I made all seven from the right wing. What made it even better was that Ray Clemence, the future Liverpool and England goalkeeper was between the posts for Scunny that day. After the game, I was one of the last people out of the big players' bath in the changing room. I remember just sitting there in a bit of a daze. As he was passing, one of the other lads peered in and asked: 'What's wrong with you, Worthy?' 'I've never won 7-1 before,' I replied dopily. 'I've lost 7-1 but never won. It's great.'

Unfortunately, that was the high point of my first season. There were other good wins but these were outnumbered by defeats and we finished a disappointing 17th, with Jim McGuigan losing his job at the end of it. I felt for Jim. He was a decent man and a good coach, with some modern ideas for the time, moving us away from the 2-3-5 formation that most teams still utilised and towards 4-4-2. I'll always be grateful to him for spotting in me the ability to play at right-back – the position that I would make my own at Town over the next six seasons.

I think it was something of an experiment for him, initially. Jimmy Bloomer had been playing on the right of defence but he was a bit younger than me and the gaffer felt like he needed someone with a bit more experience to get us through some tough games at the end of the season. I'd watched players like Jimmy Armfield and Ray Wilson for England and seen the way they used their fitness and drive to get up and down the pitch. I wasn't lightning quick but I had some speed and I knew I possessed the stamina to keep going for 90 minutes. On a defensive front, it simplified the job from the one I'd occasionally played in midfield. You had one opponent to deal with – the winger. Going forward, my physical attributes could get me into good areas and I backed myself to supply a decent percentage of good crosses for our two strikers. We'd lost Rod Green and Matt Tees to Charlton by this point but I think my contributions helped his replacement, Dave Wilson, and Gary Moore score the goals to steady the ship and keep us up.

When I found out about Jim McGuigan's sacking I had just got in from shifting bricks around a building site in Devon. The normal life of a football club continues during the close season, but for the players, especially those at my level, summer jobs were a financial necessity. It was nothing like today, where the money at every professional level is beyond that of the average bloke in the street. For the first two summers of my time at Grimsby, Larraine and I headed to the south-west. I would rest up for two weeks and then work for a month and a half until we had to be back up north for the next season. The first summer, I worked at a site in Withycombe Raleigh, where they were building an extension to the local school. I'd help out however they saw fit, shifting bricks about, digging ditches and occasionally driving the big dumper truck, even though I wasn't licensed for it. One time, I tilted it over and got it stuck in a ditch. We had to call over half the site to help drag it out. I wasn't popular that day but, in general, I got on well with the lads on the site, who all loved the fact I was a footballer. It was red hot so we'd work shirtless all day and then head to the pub for a few pints of scrumpy. My mother-in-law scolded me more than once for staggering in on an evening, late for tea.

I took on a very different summer job in my second year at Grimsby. Larraine's dad, Terry, was a bit of an entrepreneur and was often starting ventures that invariably fizzled out. In the summer of 1968, his big idea was a mobile fish and chip shop. He'd taken inspiration from ice cream vans but instead of Mr Whippy, he was Mr Chippy. In the back of the vans, he installed deep fat fryers in which he would cook fish and every lunchtime he and my mother-in-law, Marge, would drive around the factories of Exeter and sell to the workers. When I arrived for the summer, I was able to help out behind the wheel. There was one particular morning when it was myself and Marge in one of the vans, heading off to an industrial site in Exeter, me driving and her in the back frying. It was a red hot day, yet, for some reason, she'd decided to wear a thick woolly jumper under her white nylon work coat. Given the weather, there was a lot of holiday traffic about and we ended up getting stuck for a long time in queues on the Exeter ring road. Slowly, the impact of the belting sun, the exhausts from all the nearby cars and the steam from the fryer started to hit. The van slowly turned into a sauna. After about ten minutes, I heard a shout from behind me: 'David, don't you look behind you!' Instinctively, I glanced at the mirror and caught a glimpse of my mother-in-law, stripped down to her underwear. For a moment, we must have been quite the sight – a Mr Chippy van with steam bellowing out of every window and, inside, a frantic 50-odd-year-old in her bra and pants. I kept my eyes firmly forward for the rest of the journey. When we did finally get to our location, all the fish had congealed from being in the fryer too long and the customers had gone back to work.

That was our last summer in Devon. After that, we spent the majority of our summers in Grimsby and I would find work closer to home. One year, I went down to the seafront and worked on the dodgems near the pier. I was one of two or three lads who would collect money off people and then line all the cars up straight again when the electricity was off between runs. It was an easy enough job, apart from when the fishermen from the trawlers would come back from sea. A lot of them would immediately get on the beer, getting into a state before staggering down to have a go on the dodgems. Sometimes, they'd refuse to pay or to leave after their go.

If there was any serious bother, we would call over to the mechanic in the corner. He'd rise to his feet and pick up a giant wrench, just in case things escalated.

Regardless of the summer job, I would always ensure I kept my fitness up. I would be out running on the streets early in the morning before any shift. I used to feel sorry for the lads who didn't continue training. They'd arrive back for pre-season and be absolutely knackered for the early stamina work. The effort I put in meant I was always able to handle it. I was certainly glad for this approach when I returned for my second season to find who was to be the new manager, one I knew wouldn't take any slacking from his players – Don McEvoy.

It was a surprise to see Don again so soon, although his stock had risen, having managed Barrow to promotion the previous season. I was happy, of course, but it was a bit awkward, too. This was the third club out of three that he'd been my manager. The other lads knew he had made me captain at Barrow and I was wary of being considered a bit of teacher's pet. To Don's credit, I think he was savvy enough to recognise the position I was in. There was never even a hint of favouritism and certainly no suggestion of me taking the armband off Graham. I kept clear of any situations that could harm me. I knew Don and his wife, Doreen, needed help with babysitting after moving to Cleethorpes but, unlike at Barrow, I made it clear I wasn't an option. I did have the advantage of knowing what to expect from the new gaffer on the training pitch, so I was able to warn the lads of what would be expected of us. Ron would have been delighted.

Don was very much his own man but one thing he did carry on from his predecessor was to keep me in the right-back position. I was largely a forward for him at both Halifax and Barrow but, like Jim before, Don recognised the stamina and drive I could bring to the full-back role. I didn't entirely shed the utility man tag. When injury opened up a spot somewhere else in the team, I was occasionally asked to fill it. I only missed one game in the 1967/68 season, playing 50 times including cup games. I didn't realise it at the time but in the December of that campaign I began what would be one of the defining aspects of not only my time at Grimsby but my entire playing career – an unbroken run of 245 consecutive games in all competitions. Spread over six seasons, it set a new club record and helped cement my place in Mariners history.

Six

The Run

(1967–1973)

Game One

Watford 7-1 Grimsby Town (21 December 1967)

My long, unbroken run of games at Grimsby got off to the worst start. Four days before Christmas, our festive spirit was broken by a brilliant Watford, who scored seven but could have had 12. Managed by Ken Furphy, the Hornets were packed with talent. They had Terry Garbett in midfield and on the wing there was Stewart Scullion, who ran us ragged. A 17-year-old Tony Currie, who would go on to play for Sheffield United, Leeds and England, scored three of their goals.

It was an especially painful experience for me and not just because I came into the fixture with seven stitches above my eye, courtesy of a training ground collision with a young trialist. It made heading away near-post corners a risky business but, thankfully, the stitches held.

The real salt in the wound was that it was Watford doing the damage – the club I turned down to join Grimsby. Instead, they signed my mate, Keith Eddy, who had been playing on the opposite side of the half-backs to me at Barrow. It helped set him up for a great career, one I had imagined for myself when I left Cumbria. He achieved promotion to the Second Division with the Hornets in 1970 before playing First Division football with Sheffield United.

He then spent two seasons in the North American Soccer League, playing for New York Cosmos alongside Franz Beckenbauer and Pelé. What I wouldn't have given for the opportunity to play in the same side as the mighty Brazilian, the greatest to ever play the game. I'll never regret joining Grimsby but I do sometimes wonder what might have been had I opted for that day's opponents instead.

If we didn't know before, the result hammered home that Town were in for a struggle that season. It left us hovering near the bottom of the table with just five wins from 21 games.

Game Six
Shrewsbury Town 3-2 Grimsby Town (26 December 1967)

Don McEvoy could never quite get it to work at Grimsby. I knew his approach and was accepting of the modern ideas for training and tactics he had acquired at Lilleshall but others were less tolerant. Don was no politician, either. He was unwilling to humour club directors who felt their money bought them a valid opinion on the make-up of the team and how it should play.

Matters came to a head on Boxing Day 1967. We'd just played out our ninth game without a win, going down 3-2 at Shrewsbury, and were travelling back by bus. Don had not been too downbeat about the result, praising our effort, but it was still a sombre atmosphere, not helped by the presence of one of the directors on board. It wasn't unusual for members of the board to join us for away games. They would sit at the front and always insist they be dropped off first in Cleethorpes. This journey was no different. As we neared home, he addressed the driver: 'Charles, drop me at my house first, please.' I'm not sure what triggered him but the next voice we heard was Don's. 'No you don't, Charlie,' he declared. 'You drop me first and then take the director home.' Poor Charlie didn't know what to do. He eventually made the right call, prioritising the man who paid his wages. At the second stop, Don disembarked with a quick 'good night lads, see you all tomorrow'.

We knew the writing was on the wall for the gaffer, that he'd overstepped the line. But that was Don – he was straight-talking and refused to entertain anyone he saw as a fool, especially when it came to football. The board didn't sack him straight away, allowing him to manage us to another loss, a narrow 1-0 in an immediate return fixture against Shrewsbury. After that, he was gone, ending the third and final time I played under him in my career.

Don went on to Southport, where he managed my old mate Malcolm Russell and Eric Harrison again, and then had a final spell back at Barrow before he retired from the game. He and his wife Doreen came back to West Yorkshire after that, to live in Brighouse, not far from Halifax. He did some summarising of games for local radio but spent most of his time as the landlord of a pub, The Crown. I went to visit him there a few times. Typical of Don, everything was spotless, and his darts and dominoes teams were well drilled. He had many stories to tell of his playing and managerial days and he'd hold court amongst groups of enraptured patrons. It was lovely to see how happy and relaxed it made him. He died in a Halifax nursing home in 2004. I was away scouting in France at the time and was unable to get back for the funeral. Don was a football man through and through. I think he would have understood.

Bill Harvey succeeded Don as manager. Bill was a lovely bloke and a real joker but I don't think he was much of a manager and failed to garner the respect he needed to succeed. There was one big positive of Bill's time at the club. He brought John Macey with him to the club. John was a brave and competent keeper and remains a good friend to this day. We hung on until the final day of the 1967/68 season but ultimately went down on goal average – losing out to Mansfield Town by the agonising margin of 0.008. For all of my lofty aspirations when I first joined Grimsby, I was heading back to the Fourth Division.

Game 79
Grimsby Town 1-3 Doncaster Rovers (5 May 1969)

A year on, we were in no better shape. In fact, we were worse. The poor performances and the deflation of the season before carried through into 1968/69. We also lost some important players, chief amongst them our captain Graham, who left to join local rivals Lincoln. Bill lasted almost exactly a year in the manager's job, getting the sack in January, with us having won six of 27 games. The trainer, George Higgins, was caretaker until March before Bobby Kennedy took over as player-manager. Unlike Bill, Bobby immediately had the respect of the squad because he'd played more than 250 games at a much higher level for Manchester City.

It was clear from training and his early games in midfield that Bobby had plenty of quality. He was a lovely passer of the ball. He'd lost a yard of whatever pace he might have had but he compensated for that by keeping himself supremely fit. It was a quality he expected of others, too, so he stipulated a lot of stamina work in training, such as long cross-country runs through the woods. Initially, it had a positive impact. We became more competitive, putting together a little run of unbeaten games in the middle of the season. It didn't last, though. We won just one of the last nine matches, culminating in a humbling 3-1 home loss to Doncaster. We finished 23rd, with only Bradford Park Avenue sparing us the indignity of being the lowest-ranked side in the Football League. There was no automatic relegation to non-league in those days, so a (thankfully successful) application for re-election to remain in the Fourth Division was put to the Football League. We would improve the next season to finish 16th, helped in large part by the performances of our lightning quick right-winger Stuart Brace. Bracey was a top man and a fine footballer, it is just a shame that his 25 goals in 1969/70 did not contribute to anything greater.

In my opinion, Bobby ran the legs off of us in training. Come match time, we were sluggish and our opponents often sharper. It was demoralising. I was able to cope with the running, born out in the fact I was the only player in the squad to feature in every game, but I hated all the losses. Matters were made worse by a disagreement between the club and me. Having seen how other players supported themselves following the end of their playing careers, I was keen to open a sports shop in Grimsby. I'd even gone as far as to identify a possible location, in a parade of shops on Grimsby Road no more than 300 yards from Blundell Park. I imagined the kids of Cleethorpes coming into the shop with their mum and being as gobsmacked meeting me as I had been when my mother took me to see her pal Stan Mortensen at his shop in Blackpool. However, the Town board dashed my hopes. It was their opinion that it would be too big a distraction from my football.

Part of my motivation for pursuing the shop – and the future financial security it could provide for the family – was that the Worthington household had not long grown from three to four. My daughter, Keely, was born in May 1968 – a ray of light in otherwise cloudy times. The house became a whirlwind of activity, with the baby requiring constant care and Gary now old enough to walk. Almost immediately, he had a ball at his feet in the garden. It was clear early on that he was a right footer like his dad but I made sure he also used his left plenty. I didn't want him having a shovel like Graham!

Game 129
Southport 1-0 Grimsby Town (8 September 1970)
I don't think I was an especially technically gifted footballer. I

certainly wasn't a patch on our Frank, who was now a first-team regular at Huddersfield and earning himself a reputation for flair and the unexpected. In contrast, the eldest Worthington brother was far more conservative. I wouldn't often dribble past people, ping shots into the top corner or even consider trying a step-over. I think the most exciting thing I did on a pitch was a trick I would perform before every game in front of Blundell Park's Pontoon Stand. The move began with me flicking up the ball from a standing start and performing a few keep-ups before kicking it up and on to the back of my neck, where I would let it rest a moment. I then allowed it roll down my back for the big finish – a backheel that propelled the ball back over my head to trap first time under my boot. It started as a bit of fun but soon became an anticipated ritual that drew cheers from the fans. There are still some now, nearly 60 years later, who stop me to say they remember me performing it. I don't let on that I was taught the trick by my youngest brother.

What I was able to put in every week was a shift. People knew what they would get from me – graft, fight, relentless running and a committed, consistent performance. I would be on my knees sometimes near the end of games but I never let it show that I was knackered. Right until the final whistle, every ball was mine to win. It ensured I stayed on the teamsheet week in, week out. It is difficult for those around the modern game – players and fans – to understand the necessity to stay fit and keep your place in the team during my day. It wasn't as much of a squad game back then and my consistency protected my position. Even when I had a less than stellar game, it would always be in the manager's mind 'well, Worthy isn't going to have two bad games on the trot'. These qualities, more than any others, are what led to me captaining sides, firstly Barrow and then Grimsby, with Bobby making me skipper for the 1970/71 season.

The responsibility only added to my determination to do everything I could for the team – something that was drawn starkly into focus in the fifth league game of the campaign, at Southport. With 24 minutes gone and us 1-0 down to a deflected goal, our goalkeeper Harry Wainman took a heavy knock to a thigh he'd injured in training a few days before. He couldn't put any weight on his leg, so had to go off. Teams only had one substitute in those days and never gave that spot to a goalkeeper, which meant an outfield player going in goal if your No.1 got an injury. The lads were all looking around at each other, with Bobby, who was on the field playing as well as managing, seeking a volunteer. To me, it was a no-brainer – I'd played in pretty much every other position before, I'd been a wicketkeeper in cricket and gone in goal a few times during training, plus I was captain. I stuck on the keeper's jersey and did my duty.

As I've delighted in reminding Harry in the years since, I had a great game. Southport threw plenty at me but I held firm. In one especially pleasing moment, my mate Malcolm Russell, then at Southport, ran through on goal. I went out to meet him and dived at his feet, diverting his shot away. Malcolm turned to me. 'You lucky sod, Worthy,' he said. 'Luck? That was a class that, Malc,' I replied, with a wink. Sadly, we weren't able to find an equaliser but I certainly like to think I did my bit.

Game 171
Grimsby Town 2-0 Crewe Alexandra (4 May 1971)
The 1970/71 season was a frustrating one. We regressed and finished 19th in the end and it would have been much worse had it not been for a run of 11 games, in which we only lost once, to finish the campaign. As good as a player as Bobby was, we actually improved when he took himself out of the side to focus

on managing, winning six of the last nine. This culminated with a final-day victory over Crewe at home, thanks to goals from Bobby Ross and Matt Tees, who had re-joined the club mid-season. Our late upturn in form came too late for Bobby, though. The board sacked him almost immediately after that final game.

To me, it proved one thing – we were better than what we'd shown. The team weren't functioning, despite the presence of some fine players. Top of the list was little Dave Boylen. Dave was an apprentice when I first arrived but you could see, even at a young age, that he was special. It wasn't long before he was with us in the first team. He played inside-left but was what, nowadays, you'd call a No.10. He had a great first touch. He would receive the ball practically on the spin, taking it into space before popping it off crisply to a team-mate. He could slide it inside the full-back into the stride of Alan Woodward on the left wing or he'd spot Bracey setting off running on the right and ping a pinpoint ball over the top. At that level, he stood out a mile. He was only a tiny bloke, 5ft nothing, so the opposition would target him every week. Boyley would take some hits but he never complained. He just bounced back up and started picking passes again. My kind of player.

We used to play little practical jokes on him because of his size. When we played away, we would often stay in a hotel overnight on the Friday. I'd often go down early, before the evening meal, to find out where we were sitting. I would then go and find one of those high chairs with a little tray in front that babies sit in to eat and place it in a nice spot in the middle of the table. When Boyley arrived, I'd point over to it: 'There you go, Dave, there's your chair.' He would just shake his head and smile. He got his own back, though. I'd always had the mickey taken out of me for having quite a big nose, which peaked during an away trip to

Crewe in mid-March of that season. During the game, as we were defending a corner with me on the front post, a home fan leant over the hoardings and shouted 'hey, Pinocchio' at me. The nickname stuck amongst my delighted team-mates. On a subsequent away trip, I came downstairs from my hotel room for the evening meal. I was directed to a seat and there, on the place mat in front of me, was a huge fake plastic nose on an elastic band. At the end of the table, a big smirk on his face, was Boyley.

The 1970/71 season was a huge disappointment but the summer that followed it was one of the most enjoyable of my career. We had stopped travelling down to Devon to stay with Larraine's parents but my father-in-law's entrepreneurial spirit must have rubbed off on me. Influenced by his Mr Chippy idea, I decided to take a more traditional route and approached Adas Ices, a local ice cream business that was looking for a driver to take a van around Grimsby and Cleethorpes. They were more than happy to give me the job. So, I spent the days driving around the area, selling ice creams and lollies.

The prime spots were by schools, where you were guaranteed an eager clientele. One lunchtime, I decided to go up to Toll Bar Academy in Waltham. As I arrived and parked up, I spotted another ice cream van further up the road near the gates. I toyed with leaving, so as not to cause a row, but figured that if I stayed far enough away, it would be fine. As the kids filed out of the school, most went to his van, but a few stragglers trickled down to mine. As I was serving, one lad looked up at me and gave a double take. 'Hey, are you Dave Worthington?' he said. I nodded. 'Can I have your autograph?' he continued. So, I signed a bit of paper and gave it to him along with his ice cream.

Afterwards, I watched him scurry back up the road, join the throng of other kids and excitedly start pointing in my direction.

Before I knew it, my van had a huge queue full of autograph-hungry kids and the other bloke's was largely deserted. When all the kids had gone, the other van began slowly making its way down the hill towards mine. I braced myself for a showdown. For a second, Harry Hooper flashed through my mind, shuffling down that corridor at The Shay, singing the song from High Noon: 'And I must face a man who hates me.' Needless to say, my rival was not happy. 'This is my patch,' he shouted. 'I was here first.' I'd dealt with enough abuse on the pitch over the years. I stood my ground. I told him I needed the money, just like he did, and that I'd be back again tomorrow. 'You better not be,' he yelled before speeding away. I went back the next day and parked in the same spot, down the road from my rival. Once again, the kids flocked to me. After a few days of this, he gave up and went in search of a new patch, while I cleaned up. As far as I'm concerned, all is fair in love, war and the ice cream business.

Game 172
Grimsby Town 4-1 Scunthorpe United (14 August 1971)

We began the 1971/72 season under a new gaffer. Lawrie McMenemy was a manager on the up, having won a non-league title with Bishop Auckland before leading Doncaster Rovers to the Fourth Division title in his first job in the Football League. Our chairman at that time, Paddy Hamilton, had a hardware business with a depot in Doncaster and he would often hear the workers there talk glowingly of the way Rovers were playing under Lawrie. When Bobby was sacked, Paddy knew the man he wanted to replace him.

It wasn't to everyone's taste. Some in the community had written us off before a ball had been kicked, no doubt fuelled by the previous years of failure. At a warehouse near the docks, one supporter by the name of Dick Broadbent declared to his colleagues that there was no chance we would win promotion. So confident was he of our impending failure that he said if we did go up he would 'run through the streets stark bollock naked'.

Inside the club, Lawrie made an immediate impression, not least of all because of his size. At 6ft 4ins tall, he towered over most of the squad. He would stand bolt upright, too, with his shoulders thrust back, no doubt a habit drilled into him from his time spent as a Coldstream Guard prior to his brief injury-curtailed playing career at Gateshead. He was too tall for his office at Blundell Park. In my first meeting with him, he got up to leave his desk to shake my hand and he kept going up and up and up.

It was clear from the start that Lawrie was going to be different from all the managers who had come before. He had a presence, an aura of professionalism and confidence. He was strict and held high standards without being oppressive, able to feel like one of the lads, whilst never letting you forget he was the boss. In the years since, people at Grimsby – mainly fans – have asked me when I knew that season was going to be special and the honest answer is week one.

The first home game couldn't have gone much better. Our fierce local rivals, Scunthorpe, came to Blundell Park and we tore into them. All our potential and frustration from the season before came pouring out. We scored four and could have had more. Three days later, we travelled to Lawrie's old side, Doncaster, in the League Cup and scored four again, to their three. We then went to Exeter in the league and racked up another 4-3 victory. What a week: three wins, 12 goals and some of the best, attacking football a team from Grimsby had played in years. On the long bus ride home from Exeter, I remember sitting and thinking to myself: 'Blimey, something is happening here.' Looking around at the happy but slightly dazed faces of my team-mates, I think they felt it, too.

Good teams need goalscorers. That Grimsby side had Matt Tees. Teesy was tall and thin, all knees and elbows. He will not have weighed 10st wet through. But he used his height and all his awkward angles to great effect. In the opening-day victory over Scunny, he netted three of our four goals. One of them was archetypal Tees – nipping in from nowhere to nod in a cross past a baffled goalkeeper. However, whilst he had an instinct for finding the net, he was useless at everything else! He had the clumsiest touch I've ever seen for a footballer. In training, when performing keep-ups, most of us would stay within a tiny radius, the ball under our spell but Teesy would be all over the place, chasing his increasingly wayward kicks. 'One … two … three … damn it! One … two … three … oh, bugger!' He wasn't a natural athlete, either, and did little to remedy that.

When Lawrie was first brought in to meet the squad by the chairman, he reached one corner of the dressing room and had to wade through a cloud of smoke. 'Lawrie, this is Matt Tees,' explained the chairman, pointing to the pipe cleaner of a man with a mop of curly hair, puffing away on his pipe. 'He's your main striker.' Lawrie's face dropped a mile. I'm certain the manager will have been thinking about bringing someone else in to play at No.9 but Teesy never gave him the chance. Including that opening-game hat-trick, he scored in each of our first four matches. In October, he scored in another four games on the bounce, including another two in the return game as we completed the double over Scunny. He was pure magic – a godsend for those of us required to provide chances. All we need do was get the ball into the box and away from the keeper and he found a way to prod it home. There was one game, I can't remember which, where the goalkeeper did catch the ball from a cross but, as he went to throw it out quickly to one of his team-mates, he slammed it into Teesy's backside and had to watch in horror as the ball rocketed past him into the net. A natural goalscorer!

Game 190
Grimsby Town 1-1 Norwich City (26 October 1971)

I'd never experienced much of a cup run before. Most seasons, to that point, it had been round one and done. That year, we carried our good league form into the League Cup. Following our win at Doncaster in the first round in August, we beat Shrewsbury and Gillingham (via a replay at Blundell Park) to make it to round four. There, we were drawn against Norwich City, who were leading the Second Division at the time and had the best defensive record in all four divisions, having conceded just eight times in 14 games. They had Doug Livermore and Graham Paddon in midfield. With his long blonde hair and beard, the latter looked like a Viking. He also had a fierce left-footed shot on him. On the wing was Ken Foggo, who gave me a really tough time. Ron Saunders, who would later lead Aston Villa to the First Division title, was their manager. We were the lowest-ranked side left in the competition but high on confidence and eager to test our newfound belief against a supposedly superior opponent.

The players' excitement was clearly matched by that of the fans. When we ran out of the tunnel for the game, we were met by a sell-out crowd of 22,408. The atmosphere was electric, as good as any I've played in. I was central to the drama early on but not in a good way. Inside 20 minutes, the ball broke to Livermore in the box and he hit a shot that beat Harry Wainman and was heading for the net. As the last man, on the line, I flung myself towards the ball to try and head it but realised quickly I wasn't going to reach.

Instinctively, I stuck out my hand and punched the ball over the bar before crumpling in a heap on the floor. My only chance to get away with it was to play act. So, as I was on the floor, I held my head to suggest this was where the ball had struck me. The referee, Ray Tinkler, who was from Boston and did quite a few of our games, was not fooled. He immediately pointed to the penalty spot. The crowd went mad, hurling all sorts of abuse at the official. In the middle of the storm, Ray trotted through a crowd of players and up to me, still flat out on the floor. 'Worthy, you may have these lot fooled in the stands but not me. Get up.' I gingerly rose to my feet. 'Yep, fair enough ref.' Norwich's 'Viking', Paddon, lashed in the penalty to make it 1-0.

I would make amends during a second half in which we absolutely tore into the Canaries. It was possibly one of the best 45 minutes of that season. Just after the hour, Jack Lewis was fouled out wide and I chipped in a free kick that my fellow defender, Stewart Gray, met and headed home. Blundell Park erupted. I'd never heard noise like it. Unfortunately, despite throwing everything we had at Norwich in the remainder of the game, we couldn't find a winner. We left the field to a standing ovation. I'm certain we could have done a couple of encores.

A week later, we travelled to Carrow Road for the replay. Around 2,000 Mariners fans joined us. Once again, we gave a fine account of ourselves. Norwich took the lead early on but we took the game to them and equalised shortly after when Bracey and Mick Hickman both back-headed my cross for Teesy to smash home. For long periods after, we outplayed Norwich but they had that extra class where it mattered. We couldn't find a way past their defence but they took two of their chances to seal the win. There was a strange mix of deflation but optimism in the changing room afterwards. We'd lost but to a better team that we'd made look ordinary at times. Lawrie was delighted with our efforts. We were staying in a local hotel that night, so he gave us permission to go out for a few beers if we wanted. He didn't need to tell us twice.

There was a good social scene throughout my time at the club. It was a ritual to have a drink or two after home games in the bar at Blundell Park, where we would mingle with supporters. Depending on whether we'd won or not, you'd either get drinks bought for you or an earful. Afterwards, we would often take the wives out into Cleethorpes, to a club – the Beachcomber, Flamingo or Winter Gardens. I can picture it now, Bobby Ross nursing a whisky, a tipsy Teesy giggling away and little Dave Boylen, gripping his pint with both hands. Sorry Davey, I couldn't resist.

That night in Norwich was a good one. It must have been because I ended it on the roof of the bus shelter opposite our hotel singing 'Maggie May' by Rod Stewart at the top of my voice. At one point, I looked up and there was Harry and Boyley at their hotel window, shouting at me to get down. If I'd been sober, I'd have realised the risk I was taking. One slip and that could have been me for the season, possibly my whole career or worse! In that moment, though, I had a song to finish. 'Maggie I wished I'd never seen your face, I'll get back on home one of these days …' At that point, Harry and Davey came charging out of the hotel doors, making the sound of an ambulance siren: Na-na, na-na, na-na. Somehow, they managed to get me down and helped me back up to my hotel room to sleep it off.

In the years that followed, the Norwich cup ties have been two of the games that Town fans are most eager to talk about. Many recall the atmosphere in a packed Blundell Park as we matched a side that would play the following season in England's top flight. Some of them still carry the perceived injustice of the penalty awarded against us. Decades later, in my retirement after scouting, I was accosted by a fan at a Grimsby game who told me he was at the original Norwich tie. 'That Ray Tinkler,' he said. 'I've cursed that man's name for 50 years! How could he give a penalty for that?! It was clear that you'd headed the ball … there's no way you handled it, did you Dave?!' I cleared my throat and sheepishly explained: 'I'm sorry but I punched the ball over the bar.' There was a moment of silence while he considered this. 'Oh,' he said. 'I think I owe Ray Tinkler an apology.'

Game 198
Grimsby Town 2-0 Barrow (18 December 1971)

Just before Christmas, we beat my former club, Barrow, 2-0. Teesy and Mick Hickman scored the goals as we went fifth in the table. It felt like another important result in what was shaping up to be the best season of my life. Little did I know that my world was about to change. Dad had been ill for a while with angina. Where once he would walk miles to get to work in Halifax, he now found he would get out of breath just taking a few steps up the road in Shelf. When he discovered he also had cancer, the decline was rapid. It felt like no time at all before he was gone. He was just 52 years old. It was terrible for all of us. He had been a huge figure in our lives. He was a breadwinner, a provider, a disciplinarian, a supporter, a teacher and a coach.

Later in my life, after I had finished playing, I performed a parachute jump for charity. I was given the option of doing a tandem dive, strapped to an instructor, but was determined to do it alone, inspired by the jump my father had performed at Arnhem during the Second World War. If he could perform the act in such hostile and necessary circumstances, then I could certainly pluck up the courage with comparably so little at stake. Descending through the air that day was one of the many times I have thought of my dad and the example he set to make me the man I am today.

After his passing, Grimsby were fantastic, allowing me time off to return to Shelf to be with the family and support my mum. Frank arranged with his manager at Huddersfield, Ian Greaves, for me to train with their second team for a week, so I didn't lose any fitness. It was nice, especially in the circumstances, to be around my youngest brother. I'd seen the headlines he was making at Huddersfield but to see first-hand the kind of player he was developing into was a treat. His talent was undeniable. And he was a lot more than flicks and tricks. Before I was due to leave to return to Grimsby, Ian pulled me to one side. 'Where do you think your Frank ranks as regards the hardest trainers in the squad?' he asked. 'He won't be that high, I imagine,' I replied. Ian smiled: 'He's top three.' There could be no greater testament to the man – the father – we had just lost.

My dad's death brought about significant change. I wasn't happy leaving Mum and Julie in the house in Shelf, so we decided they should come over and live in Grimsby. Having been knocked back by the club over the sports shop, I had since bought a hairdressers in town so that Larraine could learn to do ladies' hair and we could earn extra money. It came with an empty flat above it – the perfect place for my mum and sister.

It enabled me to finally spend some proper time with my then 14-year-old sister, to discover that she was every bit a Worthington.

She arrived in Grimsby on her own, with two carrier bags full of clothes, a love for football and a determination to make the best of herself. She has done just that in the years since, which took her from Grimsby back to Yorkshire and then to Spain, before settling in Chipping Norton to be close to her daughters, Hollie and Alex. She's had setbacks but is a beautiful and happy soul.

My mum remained in Grimsby for seven years. She never fully got over the loss of my dad but she did rediscover her joviality. She had her vices, too. She continued to play bingo when she could and had the odd dance. She also enjoyed a nip of whisky on the sly.

One Saturday, when Grimsby didn't have a game, I took her, Gary and Keely down to watch Bob play in a lunchtime kick-off at Notts County. Just before the teams were due to come out, I noticed Keely nudge her brother and the two of them begin to snigger: 'Look at Nana, look at Nana.' My mum was turned slightly away from them, leant in low to try and hide while she snuck a sip from the bottle of Bell's she kept stashed in her handbag. It was just for medicinal purposes, of course. She passed away peacefully in 1996. There have been moments in the years since, as I've gone about my life, that I've imagined her watching on, possibly from a downstairs window across the street, rollers in her hair, a look of contentment on her face.

Game 203
Grimsby Town 2-2 Lincoln City (22 January 1972)

I'd rarely played in front of big league crowds during my time at Grimsby. Following our relegation and struggles in the Fourth Division, attendances dropped as low as 3,000. It was clear, though, that we had struck a chord with the public under Lawrie, as the gates continued to rise throughout the season. We topped 15,000 for the first time in late January for the visit of local rivals Lincoln City. With a healthy number of away fans, it made for a cracking atmosphere. Unfortunately for us, Lincoln caught us a bit cold and were 2-0 up just after half-time. However, not long after they'd scored their second, I made a charge forward to join an attack, finding myself near the edge of their box. Jack Lewis passed to me and I thought 'what the hell?' and had a pop, with my left foot, no less. Their keeper was off his line and the shot flew over the top of him and into the net. Blundell Park went mad, as did I. In previous games, when I had set up goals, I had celebrated by launching myself over the tiny fence and into the jubilant supporters om what was then the Barrett Stand. I was in such a daze of joy in the aftermath of scoring that day, I've no idea if I replicated it or not but it's entirely possible.

I had a great relationship with the 'Cod Army'. I think they respected the work I put in on the pitch, my determination for the team matching their own. I'd not really experienced huge affection from supporters at previous clubs. I'd been a kid at Halifax, in and out of the team, and whilst I'd become captain at Barrow, I wasn't there long enough to truly become one of them. We'd had difficult seasons at Grimsby but this only served to strengthen the bonds between the fans and some players when the good times did finally return.

The gaffer was clever in this regard. He understood the power of a big home crowd and how the backing of a community can help a club achieve their goals. Once he had improved the team's spirit with those early training sessions and results, he set about winning over the town. He encouraged us to go out to local businesses and functions to meet the people who paid our wages. We'd go to hospitals to visit ill fans, especially the young kids in the children's ward. He took us to the local newspaper – the *Grimsby Telegraph* – to see it printed and to ingratiate ourselves with the journalists whose job it was to critique our efforts. I had some empathy for them, as I'd started contributing a column of my own – Dave's Diary – to the *Louth Standard*, where I'd talk about life at Grimsby and the world of football in general. As Town captain, my responsibilities were plentiful. It felt like I was out performing as an ambassador of the club every week, be it coaching a group from the Manchester Church Lads' Brigade at Humberston YMCA or helping judge the Miss St Hugh's Youth Centre beauty contest with my team-mate, Harry Wainman, and the mayor of Grimsby. This was the 1970s, remember!

Possibly our most important visit as a team was down to the fish docks to meet the workers there. The fish trade was crucial to Grimsby, with vast numbers of the community relying on it for their living. The people there comprised much of the crowd that turned up at Blundell Park every week. I most remember the state of their hands – all swollen and cracked from the hours they'd spent handling wet fish on freezing cold mornings, all year round. Having grown up with parents who committed themselves to hard graft and understand the sacrifices that need to be made, I came away from that trip with huge respect for the people I met.

This partly explains my friendship with Norman 'Mac' McKenzie. Mac was a local fisherman, a deep sea trawler boat captain well known to what felt like everyone in town. He was a big man with an even bigger personality – bold and often brash but loyal. He would spend weeks on end at sea, out as far into the North Sea as Newfoundland to catch fish to return to the docks. He wouldn't drink while he was on the job but, boy, could he put it away when he was back ashore. As soon as he returned home, he would head down to the Rose & Crown pub at Waltham and start on the whisky. Sometimes, it would be seven in the morning, so the landlord, Danny, left him a key and a bottle on the bar with a note stuck to it – 'Mac's'.

The only vice Mac loved more than a whisky was Grimsby Town. He was fanatical. If he was ashore, he wouldn't miss a game. He had a bit of money because of his line of work, so would get a taxi to away games, no matter the distance. It earned him cult status with his fellow Mariners fans. They would sing an ode to him at games: 'Mac McKenzie is it true, you can't get a crew to sail with you? Bye bye, Grimsby.'

It was through my playing and him being such a huge fan that we became friends. I became his direct line to all things Town. On more than one occasion, on the journey back from an away game, the team bus would stop at a service station and we'd all pile off to find Mac, getting out of the taxi he'd instructed to follow us there and back. This wasn't just to Scunthorpe or Lincoln, either. I was told of an occasion when he informed his wife one Saturday morning that he was 'just nipping out for a loaf of bread' but instead got a taxi to Exeter and back to watch us play. I've no idea if he remembered the bread.

When he was out a sea, I'd get a phone call at home after games, with Mac wanting to find out the result. If it was an evening game, Larraine and I would be woken at 2am by the ringing. 'Hello?' I'd groggily ask down the phone. 'Dave, it's Mac, how have you got on?'

One time, Mac invited Dave Boylen and I to accompany him as he sailed his trawler from its mooring to dry dock. It was a huge ship and Mac was very proud as he gave two footballers a guided tour. There were only two other blokes on board – engineers down in the body of the boat, who Mac could contact via radio. On the orders of the dock master, we had stopped for a while before then heading in. Suddenly, from nowhere, there appears this small, white, wooden fishing boat. We weren't moving quickly but still needed to slow down to avoid hitting it, so Mac gets on the radio to his colleagues. No answer. He tried again. Nothing. We're now getting very close to the small boat and still not slowing down. Mac tried the radio one last time but was again met with silence.

There was no avoiding the boat now. We plowed straight into it and smashed it to pieces.

The three of us stood and watched from the rear of the boat as the last of it disappeared into the dock. Mac, fuming with rage, headed off down below to see what had happened with his crewmates but couldn't find them. Having been at sea for weeks prior, the pair had decided they wanted a pint and nipped off the boat as it sat stationary near the sea wall. They would have got an absolute battering when Mac got his giant hands on them.

I lost touch with Mac over the years but was contacted by his family following his death. They said he had thought very fondly of me and they wanted to know if I would read a eulogy at the funeral. It was a hard thing to do in front of a packed congregation, including his children. I owed it to him, though. He was a great character and a true Mariner.

Game 214
Peterborough United 0-2 Grimsby Town (27 March 1972)

I had been captain at Grimsby for a season and a half under two managers. However, even halfway through that 1971/72 season, Lawrie wasn't entirely convinced that I was the man for the job. One of our early conversations regarded his intention to sign Lew Chatterley, a quality midfielder who had played for nearly ten years at the top level with Aston Villa. With his touch and range of passing, he'd immediately stand out in the Fourth Division, orchestrating the team and setting a superb example to follow. The gaffer had previously had Lew on loan with him at Doncaster, where they had built up a really good professional relationship.

In his tiny office, Lawrie rose from his seat and explained to me that he was planning on making Lew his captain. As you can imagine,

I wasn't happy. Skippering the team was a source of huge pride to me and the idea of that being taken away stung. I don't think I stormed out and slammed Lawrie's door but I made it very clear how I felt.

Lew actually joined Northampton in the summer of 1971 but the move clearly didn't work out as, only a few months later, Lawrie got his wish and he joined Grimsby. We had been doing well with me as skipper but I recalled that early chat with the manager and knew my position was now under threat. Having fought for everything I'd achieved thus far, I was not going to stop now. In every training match after Lew's arrival, I tried to ensure I was on the opposing side to him. Each time we came together for a tackle, I would hit him as hard as I could. Lew was a bigger lad than me but he was a playmaker and didn't have that battler's attitude ingrained in him. If the ball was there to be won, I made sure I won it, by fair means or foul.

I know for a fact that he hated me in his first few months at the club. A week or two after Lew's arrival, Lawrie again called me into his office. 'Worthy, I've seen what you've been doing,' he said. 'I respect that kind of fight. You'll do for me, you're my captain.' We shook hands to seal it. 'One more thing … can you stop kicking my star midfielder all over the pitch now, please?'

Lawrie's great strength was his man-management skills. He won't like me saying that he wasn't always the greatest tactician but, for me, he didn't consider the structures of the game in minute detail, certainly not in the manner I'd seen Graham Taylor begin to do during our time at Grimsby. What Lawrie did understand was people and what buttons to press to get them to perform to their best. He quickly identified me as a fighter, someone who needed challenges with which to prove people wrong.

There was another similar player in that Town squad – Mick Hickman. Mick was a midfield player and an absolute workaholic.

He only missed a handful of games that year and chipped in at both ends – he scored 13 goals for us and put in god knows how many tackles at the other end. More often than not, it was Mick and I putting in the most yards for the side during a game and Lawrie was smart enough to harness that in more ways than one.

In a home game with Cambridge in April 1972 – my 250th overall for the Mariners – played on an absolute mudbath of a pitch, we were struggling to get a grip. True to form, though, Mick and I were running hard. We led at half-time through a Teesy goal but Lawrie wasn't happy. He immediately began tearing into me, saying I needed to work harder, that I wasn't putting it in. Then he turned his attention to Mick. 'And you,' he yelled. 'Stop dawdling around in midfield and start running.' I don't know about Mick but I was livid and had to bite my tongue to stop myself pointing out all the runs other people hadn't made and the tackles they'd missed. I went out fired up for the second half but quickly realised the rest of the side were right there with me. We conceded an equaliser but, for the entirety of the second half, the effort from the whole side was noticeable. We got our reward in the very last minute, when Mick – perhaps releasing his own pent-up fury – got his head to a Teesy flick-on to hammer in the winner. He was immediately buried under a pile of mud and bodies as we rushed to celebrate. It was a huge win, as it took us top of the table with just eight games to go.

The following week, in training, I was stretching on my own and felt a tap on my shoulder. It was Lawrie. 'I didn't mean what I said about you and Mick not working hard enough in that first half,' he told me. 'It was all for the others. You two work your socks off every week but if the rest of them see me bollocking you after what you've put in, they'll think, "Bloody hell, if those two grafters are getting it, I better work harder myself."' It was a brilliant bit of psychology from the best man-manager I ever played under.

Game 224
Grimsby Town 3-0 Exeter City (2 May 1972)

We went into the final game of the season top of the table and two points ahead of Southend, the only team who could still catch us. If we secured at least a draw at home to Exeter, we would be champions. The game was rearranged from earlier in the season, when heavy fog had caused it to be abandoned. Poor weather was one of the pitfalls of playing at Blundell Park, situated right next to the Humber estuary. On that particular night in March, a thick bank of fog crawled in off the sea, over the stand and descended on the pitch. It was like something out of a horror film. You couldn't see one side of the pitch from the other. The referee had no choice but to call it off. I think the only happy man in the ground was the chairman, rubbing his hands together at a 10,000 crowd and the prospect of an extra, rearranged game to fill the coffers.

I think the club could have sold out that final game three times over. The official attendance is recorded as 22,484 but it was definitely more. All four stands heaved with supporters, the cinders around the edge of the pitch packed with seated kids, while some brave fans had clambered up on to the roof of the Barrett Stand to give themselves a real bird's-eye view. The atmosphere was fantastic – a crackling mixture of nervous apprehension and joyous hope. And that was just in our dressing room beforehand!

We needn't have worried. We took the game to Exeter, as we had against every opponent at Blundell Park that season. Teesy took the roof off the place midway through the first half by giving us the lead with a header. Mick and Lew made sure with goals in the second half. For the final half-hour, with the result and title assured, we showboated, stroking the ball around, lapping up the constant chant of 'Champions! Champions!' from the stands.

At full time, the fans charged on to the pitch as the players quickly headed to the dressing room. There, the celebrations began, with everyone, including the chairman, enjoying a glass of champagne. I was delighted for Paddy. He loved Grimsby and had often had to dip into his own pocket during darker days to keep the lights on and the wages paid. That day, he was able to enjoy himself, knowing a bumper crowd would cover the costs for a while. Years later, I came across a picture in my scrapbooks of those celebrations, taken by a photographer from the local paper. It appears as though the entire team are there but, as I scoured round the image, I noticed a significant absentee – the club captain. Suddenly, I remembered why. At full time, instead of darting for the tunnel, in my delirium I had sprinted the other way and flung myself into the crowd. While the lad from the *Grimsby Telegraph* was lining up his shot of the rest of the lads with their champagne, I was being flung about in the Barrett Stand by a bunch of ecstatic Mariners supporters.

A few days later, the squad gathered again, this time with their captain, at the town hall for a civic reception. It was a much more civilised affair, although once again we enjoyed a fair bit of champagne. A huge crowd gathered outside the town hall and lined the streets nearby afterwards for an open-top bus parade. They erupted when I stepped out on to the balcony to show off the Fourth Division trophy. It flashed through my mind that it could have been Lew Chatterley stood there, lapping up the cheers had I not fought him so hard in training earlier in the season to retain the captaincy. To be honest, if Lew had stepped out with the trophy, I would probably have slid in and tackled him from behind to get it off him!

There was one last important event before the close season. One morning, the whole squad gathered to pay a visit to a warehouse at the docks. There, we met with the company's employees and a small team from the local ITV news, complete with a cameraman. Suddenly, from around the corner, there came a sight I will never erase from my memory – a short, slightly chubby bloke with long, curly blonde hair jogging towards us, completely naked. It was the (at that moment) appropriately named Dick Broadbent, making good on his pre-season promise to streak around the streets if we got promoted. We had to applaud him – it took some balls! Thankfully for him, his workmates confined his run to just the warehouse, although ITV ensured all his glory got a much wider audience.

As another close season rolled around, we prepared to all head our separate ways for a bit of relaxation and our summer jobs. However, a bit of good fortune ensured we were able to combine the two. Linfield, the Irish club, had been due to travel to Spain to play a series of friendly games but had been forced to pull out for financial reasons. Grimsby had been invited to take their place. So, for a couple of weeks, the 1971/72 Fourth Division champions got to soak up the sun in Salou, around 40 miles from Barcelona. It was an area I would come to know well later in my life but this was my first visit to the country and just my second trip abroad, after a holiday in France a few years earlier. It was certainly the first time I'd flown anywhere.

Salou is now a thriving holiday destination but back then it was three hotels, a beach and little else. We pretty much had the run of the place. As you can imagine, with a bunch of young blokes away together, high on life, it became a bit of a stag do atmosphere. On the coach, Alan Campbell would sing, usually 'Is this The Way to Amarillo', with the rest of us as backing singers. We'd parade down in club kit most days and mess about around the pool, competing in races and diving. There was a fair bit of drinking done, too, although not to great excess – we still had work to do.

Our four opponents were CD Tortosa, Gimnastic Taragona, SD Huesca and Terrassa FC, mainly fourth-tier sides on a par with ourselves. We planned to approach the games as friendlies, at a leisurely pace and with minimal competitive edge. Even if we'd wanted to go in hard, the fact they were played on compacted sand pitches meant a sliding tackle would likely mean losing the skin off your leg. The high temperatures played a part, too. The sweat would roll off you standing still during the day, so kick-offs were at 10pm, when it got a bit cooler. It was a far cry from the swirling wind, rain and sub-zero temperatures of Blundell Park.

Three of the games were played in the intended spirit, but one – I can't remember which – had an edge to it. A few of their early tackles crossed the line and brought out our own fighting instincts. The referee didn't help by giving them everything, including a goal that was blatantly offside. In general, though, it was a great trip and we all returned to Cleethorpes tanned and sporting a sombrero.

Game 245
Grimsby Town 0-2 Charlton Athletic (14 October 1972)
All good things must come to an end. Life back in the Third Division had begun well, with six wins from seven games in September leaving us second in the table, leading to dreams of back-to-back promotions. Reality bit the following month, though, with four losses in six. It was also during that October that my proud run of consecutive starts was curtailed. The last of the games was a disappointing 2-0 home loss to Charlton Athletic. An injury after that in training – and I can't remember exactly what it was, only that it must have been a relatively bad one – caused me to sit out a return to my first club, Halifax Town. My spot at right-back was taken by Alan Campbell, who stayed there for the next five games as I remained on the sidelines.

In total, my run comprised 245 games, 224 of them in the league. At the time, it was a club record, although it wouldn't stand for that long. In 1976, Grimsby signed Joe Waters, who had played with our Frank at Leicester and would go on to become a Mariners captain and legend, helping them to two promotions. He also broke my record, making 226 league starts on the bounce and many more with cup games included.

I returned to the team in December 1972 but a second injury later in the season restricted me to 34 appearances. It was a decent campaign for the club overall. We carried over some of the momentum from the previous season and flirted a few times with getting into the promotion mix but ultimately finished ninth. Little did I know that the final game – a 1-1 draw at home to Plymouth Argyle – would be the last I would play for the club.

Lawrie was on an upward trajectory and Grimsby weren't moving with him at the same pace. It wasn't much of a surprise to those of us who had played under him that other clubs came calling. In the summer of 1973, he left to become assistant boss at First Division Southampton, with assurances he would soon succeed Ted Bates as manager. It didn't start very well for him, with the club suffering relegation, but he would later secure hero status by winning the FA Cup as a Second Division side, beating Manchester United in one of the biggest final shocks in English football history. He would then lead them to promotion and second place in the top flight in 1984 – still the club's highest league finish.

There were other departures from the club. Teesy left to join nearby Boston United, where he finished his career. Soon after, Stuart Brace joined Southend. A part of me hoped Lawrie might take me with him to Saints. He did return to Grimsby for a player but it was for the man he originally wanted to be his Town captain, Lew Chatterley, which made sense considering the level at which he had previously played and the quality he possessed. Lew later became a coach, serving not only as assistant to Lawrie but others, too, including Alan Ball and Graeme Souness. Lawrie did eventually have a Worthington with him, signing Frank in 1983. Our kid was brilliant for him on the pitch, helping them to that second-placed finish, but I think Lawrie struggled with the noise and rebelliousness that came with him off the field. Frank was into his mid-30s by then and not one for being told to toe the line. The two fell out and Frank moved on.

At the beginning of the 1973/74 season, I faced my own clash of personalities with a manager. Ron Ashman was the man the Grimsby board chose to replace Lawrie. He had been a good player at Norwich and then boss of our rivals, Scunthorpe, where he had helped bring through a young Kevin Keegan. As with every new manager in my career, I was determined to knuckle down and impress but it was clear early on that I wasn't for Ron. I don't know whether he wanted to assert some authority or make a clean break from Lawrie but he didn't want me in his team, let alone captain of it. That summer, he signed Hull full-back Don Beardsley, who started and ended that season at right-back, playing all but one game. I, on the other hand, initially sat on the sidelines – my first period out of a first team when fit to play since my Halifax days as a kid.

Things were exacerbated by a disagreement with the club's board over expenses. I felt they should reimburse me for petrol money spent travelling to attend all the various functions as an ambassador of the club. I was out at least once a week, all around Lincolnshire, to talk to fans, attend awards dos and visit schools to coach kids. The cost was beginning to rack up and I had a young family to feed. But the board refused and it left a sour taste in my mouth.

All of my frustrations came to a head one day in training in an act of childish rebellion. Midway through the session, I stuck my hand up to get the boss's attention. 'Gaffer?' I asked. 'Can I go wee, please?' He looked a bit irked at me. 'Yes, go on,' he replied. So I threw my arms up and yelled: 'Weeeeeee!' It wasn't very mature but I was fed up and wanted a bit of a laugh to lift my spirits. It raised a few smiles amongst the lads but Ron was furious. I'd embarrassed him. 'See me in my office after training,' he growled. As I walked in to see him, he was on the phone, which he promptly handed to me. 'I've got George Mulhall from Halifax on the phone,' he said. 'He wants to talk to you.' Ron sat and watched as George and I spoke and agreed on the terms for a one-month loan move back to my first club. It was as quick and simple as that.

It was nice to be back home for a bit and I was glad to be playing again. I ended up making five appearances in the month but it quickly ended and I was on my way back to Cleethorpes. George told me that Halifax would like to sign me permanently but they couldn't raise the money. Once more, I was left in limbo, ostracised by a manager who didn't want to pick me and a problem to a board unwilling to pay me money I felt I was owed. I was 28 at that time – not a young man in football terms – but I knew I still had plenty to offer on the pitch. It had been my goal to reach ten years with Grimsby, to secure a testimonial with the club, but that was now in tatters. It wasn't long after I returned from Halifax that I received a phone call at home from Stuart Brace. He'd left Grimsby to join Southend early in the 1973/74 season. 'Worthy,' he said. 'How do you feel about moving down south?'

When I reflect back on my seven and a half seasons at Grimsby, I rarely think of the last few months I spent there. The ending was not as I'd wish but that doesn't detract from all the happy years spent before then. We weren't always successful on the pitch – in fact, for the majority of my time, we frustratingly underperformed – but I was rarely anything but happy. I built a family in the town and was welcomed, with open arms, into another wider one of players, staff and supporters. Mariners.

Whenever I return, which I do often to watch games, I'm always greeted by handshakes and smiles from fans who either saw me play or have been told about my efforts by fathers and grandfathers. They speak of a trick performed before games, of a lunatic throwing himself into the crowd and of an ultra-committed full-back who could run all day and never gave up. It swells my heart with pride. Together, we will always have that glorious season under Lawrie in the early 70s when everything came together and we finally gave the people of the town something to truly cheer.

In my mind, I can still see that team in full flow: Harry Wainman pulling off saves, Graham 'Baz' Rathbone taking no prisoners at the back, little Davey Boylen killing a ball dead on the spin before finding Stuart Brace, with him tearing up the wing to cross for Matt Tees to rise higher than anyone to nod in. When I flick through my scrapbooks, I always pause on the photograph taken in the changing room after we had beaten Exeter to seal the title. I take in all the mud-spattered happy faces, sweat and champagne-drenched hair clinging to their foreheads. Lawrie stands tall and proud next to the delighted chairman, Paddy Hamilton. I wasn't there to witness the scene first-hand, too busy celebrating with the fans on the other side of the pitch, but this is how I like to remember everyone, in their prime.

Seven

South End

(1973–1976)

Wednesday, 13 October 1993. Rotterdam. There are 65 minutes gone of a crucial qualifier for the 1994 World Cup. England had come into the game needing just a point to effectively secure their place in the USA but trail 1–0. Defeat and the ignominy of watching a tournament from home next summer looms for the Three Lions. In the ground, smoke from orange flares and the noise of jubilant Dutch fans fill the air.

On the England bench, injustice rages, with home captain Ronald Koeman at the centre of the controversy. Having somehow escaped a red card for pulling back David Platt and denying him a clear run at goal, the defender has then rubbed salt into the wound by scoring the opener – a free kick from a similar spot to the offence at the other end of the pitch for which he should have been dismissed.

Graham Taylor, the under-pressure England manager – respected, reviled and ridiculed in equal measure during his tenure – can barely keep his emotions in check, rising continually from his seat to yell at his players, the officials, the whole unjust world. After his latest tirade, he returns to his seat, a job still to do, albeit now a near impossible one. He turns to his staff. 'We should probably get Wrighty on shortly,' he declares. 'What do you think, Worthy?'

AS MY Grimsby career was unravelling, I took my family to Lincoln, to visit my old Grimsby captain, Graham, and his wife,

Rita. Graham had left the Mariners in the summer of 1968, moving to the Imps, whom he represented until a serious hip injury ended his playing career in 1972. He subsequently became their manager – the then youngest in the Football League, at just 28. We had remained in touch, as had our wives, a bond forged between them through the shared joys and hardships of having children.

During our visit, Graham led us all on walk near to his home in North Hykeham. As we strolled along, he began pointing at some of the houses. 'That's one of the club's places there, Worthy,' he said. On the next road: 'That's another of the club's places, there.' This happened two or three more times before I was forced to intervene. 'Why do you keep pointing out these houses, Graham?' I asked. 'Because I want you to pick one to live in,' he replied.

Later, back at his home, he laid out the plan. I was to join him at Lincoln, to become his player-coach. Together, we would, perhaps, form a formidable duo, in the mould of Brian Clough and Peter Taylor, who had recently led Derby from the second tier to the First Division title. He remembered our long tactical conversations on journeys back from away games, he knew I was taking my coaching badges and he felt we had the perfect mix of know-how, insight and ability. It was a brilliant opportunity, one I was eager to seize, not only to rescue me from my current career malaise but to lift me to previously uncharted heights. The Grimsby board felt differently. Fearful of the blowback from negative headlines and fan reaction, they refused to entertain the idea of a popular, albeit marginalised player joining a local rival.

Graham would come calling again, a year on from our first conversation, but by then circumstances had changed. I was settled and only 12 months into a new club commitment I felt it ungentlemanly to break. In my place, I recommended a team-mate of mine. Dennis Booth was a real character, a funny man, gifted at mimicry. He did a fantastic Norman Wisdom. I understand he also later perfected a spot-on and very affectionate take of Graham, the man who became his new boss at Lincoln and whom he followed to Watford. They would achieve great things together – numerous promotions and so nearly a top-flight title and an FA Cup.

Graham's success was fully deserving of a man for whom I had the upmost respect, both as a player and a person. Sadly, his England experience tarnished his reputation, opening him up to undeserved mockery by a cruel and unforgiving media. It was a sign, though, of just how respected and loved he was within football that his funeral in 2017 was so replete with the game's great and good. I was pleased I could be there to say my own goodbye to a dear friend.

Football careers are full of 'what ifs?' On the pitch, every tackle made, cross delivered or goal scored has the capacity to sculpt a professional path. Off it, every move, each choice of club, forges the route of your job and the life around it. I sometimes wonder what might have happened in my career had I been given the chance to join Graham at Lincoln? Would I have followed him to Watford, Villa and then England? Could I have been sitting alongside him and another old colleague, Lawrie McMenemy, on the bench in Rotterdam that fateful night and suggested the one tactical tweak or substitution to alter the history of English football for the better? It's grand thinking but human nature, especially when old age ushers in a wistful nostalgia. In football, when one door closes, another opens. You can only hope that each fresh gateway takes you to opportunity, fortune and glory and not a dead end. When I took the call from Stuart Brace in December 1973, offering me the chance to join Southend, I perceived it as the former. It proved, ultimately, to be the latter.

'The gaffer needs a captain,' Bracey explained to me during his recruitment call. The gaffer in question was Arthur Rowley, a brilliant player in his day for Leicester and Shrewsbury. An unmatched striker in the history of English football, he still holds the record for the most goals in the Football League – a massive 434 in total. It was gratifying to know an ex-player of that calibre rated me enough to pursue my signing and a huge relief to know I would not rot in Grimsby's reserves before being shoved into unemployment. Money wasn't an issue. Southend could easily afford the £7,000 fee Grimsby were asking and the contract proposed to me included a wage higher than any I had previously pocketed. My family and I would live in a club house in Leigh-on-Sea. There would also be little objection from the Town board over the move. I would largely be out of sight, out of mind, no longer an awkward problem for Ron Ashman.

The big sticking point was personal. How would my family feel about the move down south, so far away from the home we had made in Cleethorpes. Just a few months earlier, we had welcomed our third child and second daughter, Danielle. With her so young and delicate, upending everything felt wrong. There was also my mum and teenage sister to consider, along with the hairdressing business. It had been less than a year since I ushered them over from Halifax in the wake of my dad's death. Circumstances beyond my control would ultimately dictate an answer, albeit a far from ideal one.

The house Southend had earmarked for me was occupied by Peter Taylor, the future caretaker manager of England but then still a young and exciting winger who the Shrimpers had just sold to Crystal Palace. 'Spud', as most knew him, had been unable to find a suitable place in London into which he could move, thus delaying my permanent residency in the south. It resulted in me making a weekly 200-plus-mile, five-hour commute from Cleethorpes to Essex and back. The only saving grace was that Southend had been granted permission to play home games on a Friday evening as a result of the close proximity of so many prominent London clubs. I could leave my home early on Monday morning to travel down for training, stay until after the game on Friday and then return for a weekend with the family. There were some lonely times on the motorway but it certainly beat the frustrating isolation I had been experiencing at my previous club.

My new gaffer, Arthur, did his best to make me feel at home. I wasn't sure what to expect ahead of our first meeting. I recalled this giant of a striker from my youth, nicknamed 'The Gunner', who would terrorise top-flight defences. As a professional of such calibre, he demanded respect. I expected an assertive, charismatic man with a powerful authoritative voice. He still looked the part but when he opened his mouth, what came out was jarringly incongruous. 'Nowwwww then Daaaaaave, you alllllllriiiiight,' came a drawn-out, monotonous Midlands tone. 'Iiiiii remember playing against youuuuuu when youuuuu were just a nipper. Shrewwwwwwsbury against Halifax. Iiiiiiit was a prooooooper mudbath. Iiiiii scooooooored but then youuuuu got one back. Weeeee won.'

He went on to explain to me in greater detail what Bracey had told me over the phone. 'Weeeee neeeeeed a leeeeeader,' he told me. 'Soooooomeone who can give it a bit when the chips are dooooooown.' The team's current skipper, Dave Elliott, had been signed from Newcastle a few years prior. He was a midfielder and a really good player, probably the best in the team. He was a lovely bloke, too, but quiet. In the brutal cut and thrust of the Football League, a captain needs to be able to make his voice heard above the din and fire rockets, even raising it at his mates, when needed. I had learned this at Barrow and had no qualms about being that man, even if it meant bruising some egos. Taking the role from Dave set us off on a bad footing but he was a decent enough man to move on past it.

It wasn't just the way the manager spoke that surprised me. I expected the Southend squad to be full of Londoners – lads who had dropped down, having failed to make the grade at West Ham or Tottenham. I imagined walking into training to be greeted by a succession of 'all right, geezer' from Cockneys taking the mickey out of me, the lone northerner. When I was introduced to the players in the gym, the first responded with: 'Yee aareet Worthy, mate.' The next strode up and stuck out his hand: 'Aareet Worthy, you canny, lad?' An unmistakable north-east twang. I was surrounded by Geordies, Mackems and Smoggies.

There was Alan Moody from Middlesbrough and Chris Guthrie, Willie Coulson and Terry Johnson from Newcastle. Dave Elliott, who I succeeded as skipper, had played for both Newcastle and Sunderland, having been born in County Durham. Alan Little, who joined Southend in 1974 and would later go on to manage both Southend and Halifax, was from that part of the world, too. There was also another old Grimsby team-mate, Gary Moore, who was enjoying a far more prolific time of it in front of goal than he had with the Mariners.

I quickly discovered just why there was such a big northern presence in the squad. Arthur Rowley was close friends with the then Newcastle boss, Joe Harvey. If Joe had a young player who wasn't quite good enough for his side but would do a decent job in the Third Division, he would ring our gaffer and offer him the chance to sign him. It proved to be a very fruitful link. The one that most stands out in my mind is Willie Coulson. He had long blonde hair, so he stood out anyway, but he was also a strange shape for a footballer, with a leg splaying out from the knee as if it had been broken before. It made him an awkward mover but he had a clever brain and his left foot was a wand, spraying passes with aplomb from the middle of the pitch.

There was an even split of northerners and southerners in the squad. Rather than creating detrimental cliques, it worked to our benefit. It gave us even teams for games of cricket in the club's indoor gym. Boothy would be the organiser, ensuring we were all there on time. During the games, if someone was out cheaply he would appear from nowhere: 'Ohhhh, Mr Grimsdale! Mr Grimsdale!' Ever the joker. Don't let that fool you, though; these were highly competitive games. We fashioned proper rules – four if you hit the side walls without a bounce, six if you hit the one at the back. There was running between the wickets and a lot of arguing over the validity of an LBW. Our meeting time of a morning became earlier and earlier so that we could get a game in before turning our attention to the day job. There were some decent cricketers in the squad. Neil Townsend was useful and Al Moody thought he was. I was no Alan Knott but I found I was still spritely enough behind the stumps.

The gaffer was a keen cricketer himself, having played a bit of minor counties for Shropshire, although he never took part in any of our games. I think if he'd appealed for LBW we would have been there all day! Arthur was very hands off when it came to training, rarely showing his face during the week. He had come from big clubs, where managers often remained away from the day-to-day grind, which was handed over to a trainer – in our case John Lattimer. Arthur would occasionally watch on from a doorway but spent most of his time in his office. He gave team talks ahead of games but they weren't particularly sophisticated, more a reminder of what he expected from each position. I think I would have been on more coaching courses than him.

Despite his career and record goals tally, Arthur was uninspiring. My previous manager, Lawrie, was a manager who roused his players, who got involved, gave respect and earned it back in bucketloads. You ran through brick walls for such inspiring leaders. In contrast, Arthur was detached, dour and a little self-regarding – the number plate on his car read 434 GLS in honour of the record number of Football League goals he had to his name. In my mind, the incident that best sums him up came after a game away to a good Preston North End team in November 1974, during my second season with the club. We were brilliant on the night, winning 4-1. Peter Sylvester, a really nice but somewhat shy lad, had a superb game. He fluffed a clear early chance but, after that, scored three of our goals.

After full time, we danced into the dressing room absolutely elated, none more so than Pete. We found Arthur there, waiting for us, barely a flicker of emotion on his face. He directed his first comment to our hat-trick hero in his typical monotone way: 'You misssssed the eeeeeasiest chance.' The joyful look dropped from Pete's face. Here was the league's highest-ever goalscorer putting him down for the one opportunity he'd missed rather than the three he'd taken. Instead of using his status to endorse his striker and lift him further, the manager totally deflated him and us.

I don't know if Arthur felt some resentment over being at lowly Southend, having spent so long at the top, but he displayed a distinct lack of enthusiasm for the job. In fact, the only subject on which you could muster some zeal from him was horse racing. If you ever went to see him in his office, he would invariably have the *Racing Post* laid out in front of him. The subject on your mind would quickly be brushed aside so he could gesture to the page in front of him: 'Twoooo-thirty at Cheltenhammmmm tomorrow, get yourrrrr money on this one.' Cheers, boss.

While we were all well informed about the goings-on at Ascot and Goodwood, we made little progress on the pitch during my two and a half years at Southend. There were highlights, the stand out being two FA Cup third round ties played against First Division QPR in January 1975. This was Rangers' finest-ever side, managed by Dave Sexton and boasting players including defenders David Webb and Frank McLintock, formerly of Chelsea and Arsenal, respectively, England captain Gerry Francis in midfield and the lightning-quick mind of Stan Bowles alongside Don Givens in attack. We felt the full force of their brilliance early in the initial tie as they took a 2-0 lead at Roots Hall but, with 25 minutes to go, something clicked in our team. In the space of four minutes, we pulled it back to 2-2. Bracey set up Chris Guthrie for the first, with Dave Cunningham getting the second. I remember most vividly the final 20 minutes, when it was us laying siege to the Rangers goal, roared on by 18,000 fans. We could even have snatched a famous win had the referee awarded a clear penalty for a foul on Dave Elliott. We gave it our all in the replay but two Givens goals did for us at Loftus Road.

These were rare moments of optimism and encouragement. I felt I contributed in the best way I knew how – I ran my socks off every week, giving it my all, and that once more seemed to chime with supporters. We had some good players, too. Willie could ping a great pass, Bracey still had yards of pace and scored goals and, up top, Chris Guthrie was a real handful. Pete was handy in attack, too, but I always felt he could have scored more had he had a bit more of a devil in him. He wasn't nasty enough on the pitch. That was maybe true of others, too, in a more detrimental way to the side. We had a player who was one of those that would rid himself of the ball to a team-mate at inopportune moments to avoid looking culpable for mistakes. If he was under pressure and about to be tackled, he would flick the ball to you, even though you had men around you, leaving you to deal with sometimes impossible defensive situations. Ultimately, the table doesn't lie and each season our finishing position was worse than the one before.

My happiest period of that two and a half seasons at Roots Hall actually had little to do with Southend. At that time, lots of players from across the world were heading to the United States to play in the North American Soccer League, which had been formed in the late 1960s. The league was played during our summer, meaning plenty of players from England could use the close season to earn a bit of extra money and grab the unique experience of playing in the USA. I had wanted to take up the opportunity in the summer of 1973, having been contacted by ex-Lincoln player Ken Bracewell, who was an early traveller to play in the States and then manager of Denver Dynamos.

However, with Ron Ashman replacing Lawrie, the Grimsby board were having none of it. The following April, as my first half-season with Southend was coming to a close, Ken approached me again with an offer. This time, I prepared my sales pitch to the club. Pete Sylvester had it in his contract that he was allowed to go to Baltimore Comets, so I used him as an example and laid it on thick that Denver would be paying me, so it would save the board my summer wages. They agreed. I was off for an adventure.

I was like a little kid, barely able to contain my excitement. I'd been to Spain with Grimsby and France in the car with Larraine but neither of us had experienced a foreign trip like this. The kids had never left England before. Southend's final league game of the season was at Tranmere on 26 April, a Friday night. I returned in the early hours of Saturday morning and the five of us were on a plane from Heathrow to New York the same day. From there, we got a connecting flight to Denver airport, where Ken met us.

'Right then, we'll get you all to the house and get you settled in,' he said, much to the relief of Larraine and me. 'And then I'll see you at training tomorrow.'

The quick turnaround was one thing to test my stamina but the altitude was something else entirely. Denver is called 'Mile High City' for a reason. Having been honed on sea-level Cleethorpes and Essex air for the last few years, my lungs were going to need to adjust quickly. I found it hard to get my breath in the first few sessions but every day felt easier. I've never been more grateful for the stamina I'd built up during my career. Other adjustments were harder. Games were played at Mile High Stadium, the home of the Denver Broncos American football and Denver Bears baseball teams. The gravel diamond for the latter stretched partway over the football pitch. If you liked the skin on your legs, it was not an area on which to attempt slide tackles. We also had to line up before each game and sing the American national anthem, hand on heart. Even now, 50 years later, I can remember all the words.

To someone who had spent an entire career within the relative simplicity of the Football League system, the American set-up was bafflingly complicated. There were 15 teams in the 1974 NASL, split into four divisions – Central, North, East and West. Central had three teams, the others four. The split was understandably geographical, with such vast distances between some teams. But why would we play some teams once, away from home, but not at our own place? The scoring system was strange, too. You got six points for a win and a point for every goal scored in a game up to three. So, a 3-0 win or higher bagged you nine points. There were periods in the season just gone at Southend when it took us nearly two months to accrue that many. Draws were frowned upon. If a game finished level, there would be a penalty shoot-out to decide the winner. In the end, I gave up trying to work it out and focussed on playing well and enjoying the experience. It was a smart decision because Denver had a dreadful season, winning only five games and losing three times as many to finish bottom of the Central Division. By the end, the dwindling number of fans that came to watch stopped calling us Dynamos and began referring to us as 'Damp Squibs'.

I may not have enjoyed much of my time on the pitch but off it was a different matter, helped largely by a great bunch of team-mates. The vast majority had come over from English clubs, primarily Oldham and Rochdale, giving it a bit of a home away from home feel. Defender Ian Wood was a Latic, as was midfielder Ian Bell. Goalkeeper Mick Poole, defenders Stan Horne and Jim Grummet and forward Lee Brogden all came from Dale. Andy Lochhead was another from Oldham, although he was at the back end of a career that had seen him score goals and terrorise defences for Burnley, Leicester and Aston Villa.

Andy was a big, bald fearsome Scot, a man who refused to take a step backwards for anyone. In one game, there had been some niggle between the two sets of players. I had a battle on with my winger and in one challenge I went sliding in and took the ball and the man, sending him flying towards the dugouts. The next thing I knew, a posse of men were all over me – coaches and subs who had shot off the bench to defend their felled colleague. I was flat out and outnumbered. Suddenly, from nowhere, Andy appears like a wrecking ball, barging and throwing haymakers. He took them all on and would have won, too, had he not been pulled away by team-mates and the officials. He retired shortly after that season to become a pub landlord in Worsthorne in Burnley, where he'd played most of his career. Years later, I went to Turf Moor to watch Gary play and I popped in to see him. We spent a good hour or two reminiscing about our time in America and some of the poor defenders he terrorised.

There were only a handful of American players in the squad – in fact, they were outnumbered by foreigners in the league in general. The game hadn't yet taken off in the USA, so their players were miles off the level of those from other parts of the world. We had two notable foreign stars – Brazilian forward Iris DeBrito, who had played with Pelé at Santos, and South African winger Kaizer 'Boy-Boy' Motaung. Kaizer was quick and had an eye for goal. He was an NASL legend and a hero back in his home country. In 1970, back in South Africa, he set up the club Kaizer Chiefs. You've maybe heard of the Leeds rock band that adopted the club's name. Soon, the league would attract bona fide superstars from abroad. Brazilians Pelé and Carlos Alberto, German duo Franz Beckenbauer and Gerd Müller, Dutch maestro Johan Cruyff and England World Cup winners Bobby Moore, Gordon Banks, Alan Ball and Geoff Hurst would all have stints in the States. But my generation of rag-tag, lower league misfits were the pioneers.

The overall experience was superb, for all of us. The players' families were all accommodated in the same area of housing, so even when we were away for games across the country, the wives and kids could hang out together and have barbecues on a weekend. During the week, all five of us could head up into the Rockies on days off for picnics in some of the most stunning mountain scenery you can imagine. It required a ski lift up to get to the very top, which presented a bit of an issue, with Danielle being just a few months old. I would sit on one seat with Gary and Keely, while Larraine sat on the next, grasping Dani as tightly as she dare.

Gary was seven and already starting to show promise as a footballer. He would often come to training and stand by the side of the pitch, dribbling and juggling a ball with either foot – all those early years of practice had paid off to such an extent that he had developed into a left-footed player, despite being natural with his right. One day, after training, I was approached by a man who had earlier been marveling at my son's ability. He introduced himself as Artie Wachter, a former player, referee and now coach. 'I've got a football academy up in the Rockies,' he explained. 'I was wondering if you might be able to bring your boy along to show some of my students what they teach kids back in England?' His school was a couple of hours away, so we were unable to do the journey back and forth for a week but I agreed to let Gary stay with Artie for a few days and help him educate the American kids. It was his first coaching job, and he was not yet out of primary school.

It was only later that I discovered Artie's full story. He had grown up on the streets of New York in the 1930s and quickly developed a lifelong love for sport, including soccer, which he helped promote wherever he could, including in Bavaria during the Second World War, playing there with locals. Through his work as a player, FIFA official and coach, he was inducted into the United States Adult Soccer Association hall of fame. In preparing for this book, I looked up Artie's name on the internet and found a piece about him still playing softball at Robson Ranch in Arizona at the grand age of 92. Now, there's a man after my own heart.

As we were preparing to return home from our summer adventure, I received a telegram from my mum. It read simply: 'Great news about Bob!' My brother and his wife, Louise, had been expecting their first child, so I assumed she had given birth and I would return to celebrate a new niece or nephew. I called my mum to check but she told me it wasn't anything to do with the baby. She was excited because Bob had agreed to leave Notts County after six years and sign for a new team – a Third Division outfit in Essex called Southend. For the first time at a professional club, two of the Worthington brothers would be playing first-team football together.

A lot of time had passed since we participated in those formational kickabouts in the triangular car park of the Duke of York as young boys. I had played little football with Bob since then, certainly nothing competitive, although I did have a small role in his early journey through the game, courtesy of my argument with the rugby-loving headmaster of Hipperholme Grammar School. In response to his attempts to stop me playing football and to head off a similar butting of heads over Bob, my parents had withdrawn him from the school and sent him instead to the more football friendly Sowerby Bridge Grammar – his first transfer move and a successful one at that.

While I was making a name for myself locally at Lightcliffe as a 14-year-old, he and Frank were in the same Ryburn United team – Bob a centre-back, tall for his age and domineering, making the tackles at one end to then set up his younger brother to make their peers look foolish at the other. The club were sponsored by a local businessman, Mr Siddall, who came up with the novel idea of his team playing in a distinctive all-black kit. They would bring a white shirt with them every week for the referee to wear so as to avoid a clash. All three of us brothers had been at Halifax at the same time but never in the first team together. As children, football brought us together but as adults it largely kept us apart. Rarely during our playing days were we in the same place. As I was playing out the prime of my career at Grimsby, Bob was at Middlesbrough and then at Notts County, with Frank at Huddersfield and Leicester.

Bob and I differ in personality. He is a quieter and more studious man. I don't think he craves the glare of the floodlights as much as Frank or myself. Get him in front of a warm, friendly crowd, though, and the Worthington sense of humour emerges.

He can be full of fun. He was a good impressionist and would entertain the family with his takes on comedian and magician Tommy Cooper and the prime minister of the early 70s, Harold Wilson. At Halifax, he would do a spot on Harry Hooper, limping down the corridor, a stub of a cigarette in his mouth.

It was great to live near to and play alongside him at Southend. I was much more settled in that second season, with Larraine and the kids having moved down to join me in Essex. Having my brother around gave the club even more of a family feel. We shared a similar existence on the pitch, too. He had developed into a full-back himself, playing on the left side of defence, albeit in a different manner to myself. His extra height and his background as a centre-half meant he was more defensive-minded and less attack-minded than I. But he could hit a lovely pass with his left foot and could certainly hit a winger if he gave him any bother. It remained both strange and thrilling when the gaffer pinned up teamsheets reading 'Webster, Worthington, Worthington' at the top.

Unfortunately, Bob's stay at Southend was short-lived. Midway through the season, my brother suffered an injury during a game – one bad enough to potentially keep him out of the following fixture. He made it clear to Arthur that he was struggling but the manager was insistent and convinced him to play. Bob's winger gave him a torrid time, taking full advantage of his inability to turn and move properly. Afterwards, Arthur gave him a huge rollicking in front of everyone in the dressing room.

The incident played a big part in souring Bob's love for football. He would briefly go on loan to Hartlepool before leaving Southend and the game to return north to be with his family. In the years after his football playing days had ended, he gravitated back to rugby, playing union locally for Baildon, Old Brodleans and Huddersfield YMCA. He used his large frame and fitness to really good effect, while that peach of a left foot could ping kicks between the sticks from halfway. He never recovered his passion for the beautiful game. In recent years, he has watched his grandson, Eric, play locally but has admitted to me he rarely watches matches on the television. I'll tune in to whatever game is on, constantly chasing even the smallest vicarious hit of the footballer's life but Bob is content to let his involvement with the game remain firmly in the past.

At Southend, it wasn't long before Arthur Rowley would start to have issues with the other Worthington in his squad. It quickly became clear in the 1975/76 season that disaster was looming. After winning the first league game, we picked up just five points from the next nine. The fans, who had witnessed and largely stomached the steady decline under Arthur, began to turn against him. Aware I had been doing some coaching with the club's youth team, letters began to arrive at the *Southend Evening Echo* stating that Rowley should be sacked and I should replace him as player-manager. At games, a chant started up and grew in volume: 'Rowley out! Wor-thing-ton! Rowley out! Wor-thing-ton!' It was never addressed between us but an awkwardness entered our working relationship. Sadly, the inevitable happened at the end of that season and we were relegated to the Fourth Division. It was disappointing, but I had been here before and I was fully prepared to continue on with the club. The choice, though, was taken out of my hands.

I never discussed with Arthur whether the fans' growing clamour for me as manager played a part but at the end of that season, the club released me on a free transfer. If Arthur had played a part in my release, it provided him with little respite. He followed me out of Roots Hall soon after, sacked by the board. He dropped into non-league management, while I never again played a Football League game, my final appearance coming in a 2-1 defeat at Sheffield Wednesday. At least my mum and Larraine and her parents were there to witness it, although it didn't make pleasant viewing during and after the game. At full time, Wednesday fans flooded on to the pitch to celebrate their survival from relegation on that final day and I found myself momentarily at their mercy. I was dragged to the floor and forced to curl up in a ball in the centre circle to protect myself from the blows a few rained down upon me. What a way to end my professional career.

The end comes to every footballer eventually. I'd expected to continue for a few more years yet, being just 31 years old and having looked after myself. I thought I still had plenty to offer, even if just at Fourth Division level. Close to 500 games teaches you a lot about a sport, certainly enough to see off even the wiliest of fourth-tier wingers. However, the phone remained silent. No offers came. I put a few feelers out to former team-mates and managers but clubs saw little remaining worth in a full-back of my values and vintage. On reflection, I don't like to think that I retired as a full-time player, more that football took the premature decision to retire me.

With the luxury of hindsight, I recognise all that my playing career gave me – a discipline and professionalism to complement my inner drive and determination, an association and affinity with four brilliant clubs still enjoyed to this day, lifelong friendships with all manner of wise, occasionally wacky and often wonderful colleagues. It also provided a wealth of knowledge into which I could tap, maybe not in the immediate future but at a later date and to life-changing effect.

In the rawness of my release, though, I felt cheated. For something that provides so much joy to people, football can be ruthless, cold and uncaring at times. Just two years earlier I had been hopeful of a testimonial at Grimsby that would have set up an optimistic and hopeful transition into the next phase of my life. Leaving Southend brought with it uncertainty and fear. I didn't know where the money was going to come from to support my family, how I would replace the routine that had formed the backbone of my last 15 years and what I would feel each Saturday without the glare of the lights, roar of a crowd and ferocity of the battle? For the first time in my adult life, stripped of the only existence I'd ever known, I was stepping into an uncertain future.

The transition from footballer to ex-footballer was challenging. My identity was wrapped up in being a professional player – from the legacy handed to me by my dad, through all the work I'd put in to achieve my own place in the game and the near-500 matches that followed. I didn't care so much about the fame – although even at my level it did have its advantages – but if I wasn't running, crossing, tackling, striving to be stronger, quicker, better, what was I?

While I attempted to figure that out, the more pressing matter was how to support my family and put bread on the table. Having moved back to Halifax, with its familiar, friendly faces, I found work with Larraine's family, working alongside her father and brother in a business selling Calor gas heaters. I was the delivery driver, transporting gas cylinders across Calderdale. It was good, honest work. But it wasn't football.

I yearned for the beautiful game, continually prickled by its absence from my life, like a phantom limb. In the pub, the chatter would invariably turn to that week's results. In the paper, I would read of peers no better or equipped than I still playing each week. Some would occasionally call and tell of games, goals and tales from the training ground. It made me miss the game even more, the day-to-day involvement, camaraderie and sights, sounds and even smells of the changing room. I pined for Eric Harrison head-butting a cupboard, Harry Hooper's singing and Matt Tees giggling within a plume of pipe smoke. It was hard to get my head around the fact

I would not experience that environment, in which I had grown up and lived in all my adult life, ever again.

Only a few months later, salvation called. 'Hello Dave, this is Bill Leivers,' said the voice at the other end of the phone. I knew of Bill from his time at Manchester City, where he had been a committed right-back from a similar mould as myself. As he explained, he was now on the board at Cambridge City and looking for a new manager. 'I've spoken to Lawrie McMenemy,' he continued. 'He tells me you're eager to get back in the game and feels you could do us a job.' God bless you, gaffer!

Cambridge were a non-league club, a long way from the big time. If I got the job, I would once again be uprooting Larraine and the kids to move back south, having only brought them back up north 14 months earlier. Houses would once again need to be sold and bought, schools sought, friends found, routines rejigged. I would also need to explain to my in-laws that they would require a new delivery driver.

While not happy about it, my in-laws were able to source a replacement driver pretty quickly, which helped smooth my exit from the business. It took a long conversation with Larraine but, ultimately, she understood my desire and that a life in football required such sacrifices. Now, managers are sacked seemingly every 20 minutes but back then you could be confident you would stay long enough in a job to settle somewhere. Plus, we were still relatively young – I was 32 at the time – and the kids were getting to an age where they could adapt quickly and make new friends.

A few days later, I was ushered into the boardroom at Cambridge's Milton Road ground for an interview with Bill and the rest of the board. They explained the history of the club and the gravity of the situation they faced. During the 1950s and 60s,

City had been an up-and-comer, attracting an average attendance of around 3,500 – one of the highest in non-league football – but their cross-city rivals United's election to the Football League in 1970 had hurt this, with gates dwindling into the hundreds. A recent relegation saw them now playing in the Southern League's Division One North – the eighth tier of English football.

Money would be extremely tight and I would be expected to play a role in raising it. Players would need to be found to even field an XI. The challenge was big but one I was eager to take on. I had spent a career at clubs with restricted finances, had fought in adversity, led from an early age. I explained the determination and energy I had brought to my teams and the same level I would expect from my players. I would be an ambassador for this on the pitch, taking on the role of player-manager.

After the interview, Bill led me out into reception. 'Were you planning on driving back up to Yorkshire this evening?' he asked. 'Only, I was wondering if you wouldn't mind just waiting here a while? Shouldn't be too long.' I agreed and took a seat as he disappeared back into the boardroom. He emerged again an hour later with a smile and an outstretched hand. 'Dave, we've all agreed and, if you want it, the job is yours.' Within a week, I was back down south and fighting football fires. I couldn't have been happier.

With a month to go until the start of the 1977/78 season, Cambridge City had just seven players on their books. Eight if you included their new player-manager. There were some decent ones – Martin Murray was a runner and battler like me, Tony Rule would play anywhere for the team and Alan Doyle was the star man up front, a proper goalscorer. We needed bodies through the door, though; ideally ones who knew how to kick a ball. With next to no budget to work with, I was confined largely to local lads who had been released by other clubs – the likes of Luton, Northampton, Colchester and my old side, Southend.

I would like to be able to say it was another early scouting experience but such was our desperate need I was denied the luxury of anything so discerning. I was fortunate to have played against some of them, so at least I knew a little of their capabilities. I tapped up contacts, too, phoning Lawrie at Southampton and Ron Atkinson, who became Cambridge United boss during that time. Utility man Mel Green and forward David Lill both joined after having left our rivals. Winger Pete Martin, who I'd faced when he played for Barnsley, also came in. I was fortunate to have two good, knowledgeable men beside me in trainer/physio Bill Brignall and youth coach Eric Simper, who knew which young players could potentially do a job for the first team. Thankfully, our combined efforts meant we scrambled together a squad of players for the start of the season.

A lot about management was new to me but one area I knew inside out was pre-season training. I had spent my entire career keeping myself in peak shape and reaped the rewards. I wanted my players to be the same. They may not be the most talented but I could ensure they were the fittest, which could well be the difference in tight games and over the course of a competitive season. Being part-time and only having the players on Tuesday and Thursday evenings complicated matters but we did what we could, driving them on gut-busting, stamina-building runs in the first session and then working on touch and tactics in the second. Some of them found it hard, travelling from as far as north London to be there, only to be set off on repeated 400m laps. Invariably, if they had to miss a session, it would be Tuesday.

Lessons gleaned from managers I admired during my playing days proved invaluable. In one early game, we went to Gloucester and won 3-2. The players were jubilant after, laughing and joking with each other. I came into the dressing room and channelled my inner McMenemy, kicking off at them, ensuring I directed most of my ire at players who had worked hardest. I didn't say much but just enough to leave them to think on it. A team can often take truths best when they've won, the victory acting as enough of a shield so they don't lose confidence. The following Tuesday, I went to the players I'd targeted and explained my methodology, as Lawrie had done to Mick Hickman and me at Grimsby.

It was a constant challenge. Off the pitch, I was required to sell lottery tickets for the club to keep money coming in, so I would busy myself in the week trawling around shops, pubs and clubs, either dropping them off or courting new agents to sell for us. On the pitch, early results were mixed. It didn't help with the supporters that one of our early defeats was at King's Lynn in a local East Anglia derby. In hindsight, my pre-season promise of an attacking side – one that may concede four but score five – had set an unrealistic expectation and we took just nine points from the first eight games, scoring eight goals and conceding the same in the process. I also experienced the difficulties that come with managing the expectations and egos of footballers.

Midfielder Drew Noble was a decent player but I felt he wasn't producing to his potential and, so, I left him out. He wasn't happy and made noises in the local press. Similarly, forward Steve Mahoney made clear his anger at the club for not adequately compensating him for the journeys he made for training and games. I knew his frustration, having had a similar disagreement with Grimsby, but I was now on the other side. I felt obliged to defend the position of my hard-up employer, despite my empathy to his situation.

Management often centres on hard decisions. I realised, soon after taking the job, that I needed a new goalkeeper. The team's long-standing No.1, Gareth Johnson, was a smashing lad and a fine keeper, a real favourite with his team-mates and the crowd. He was brave and never shirked a challenge but was a bit on the short side for a keeper at that level. He could be easily bullied by big, burly forwards and it cost us a few goals. I called Lawrie and explained the situation to him. 'I've got just the lad for you,' he responded. 'We've got an American kid here at Southampton. We can't register him for the first team but he's been super for us in training.' The following weekend, Cambridge had a new No.1 called Winston Du Bose. He was everything Lawrie had said – 6ft 5in, cool, composed and commanding. He revolutionised the side. The defence grew in confidence. We began to string results together and rise up the table, entering the promotion race.

The move, though, was not without its critics. One local journalist took against me dropping Gareth and made regular barbed comments about me in his reports. It got to the extent that I phoned him at the paper and arranged a meeting. It descended into a bit of a row in his office but I felt I had to stand my ground, even though it did little to stem the negativity about me in his writing. I think I was, ultimately, proved correct with Winston. He did a sterling job for us that season and returned to the club the next. Barring a brief spell with Oldham in the late 80s, he played most of his football back in the United States, in his home state of Florida, and amassed 14 international caps for his country.

Ultimately, we fell short of promotion, finishing ninth as Witney Town and Bridgend Town went up. I felt progress had been made, though. The players had responded to what I asked and I believed that, with a bit of investment to improve some areas, we could go again harder the following season. Instead, things began to unravel. A deal was agreed to sell star striker and fan favourite Alan Doyle for £1,000 to Wealdstone. However, an administrative error with some paperwork at our end meant that Alan ended up departing for free, leaving us without our main goalscorer nor a crucial cash injection.

A few weeks later, after a handful of games in the new season, I went to see the chairman, Donald Few. My wage cheque from the club had bounced. He was hugely apologetic, telling me to go to my office, where he would come and find me. When he arrived, he was carrying empty money bags. He proceeded to lead us to the clubhouse, where he began emptying coins out of the bar's fruit machines. From there, we walked round the corner to the bank and cashed the money for notes that he then handed to me. I was stunned. Later that day, I sat with Larraine and related the story. We both agreed it was too insecure a situation. I would resign and we would return north once more, where I could maybe find a club to continue my still fledgling managerial career.

It was a frustrating situation, made all the more galling by the fact that a month earlier I had come within a whisker of getting the job at Fourth Division Barnsley. They had invited me up for an interview to succeed Jim Iley as boss and I felt it had gone well. My suspicions were confirmed when I received a call the following day from the club secretary. 'The directors were all highly impressed with you,' I was told. 'I think you might get the job.' I was thrilled. 'There's just one thing,' continued the secretary. 'The board want to speak to a late applicant before making a decision.' I paused. 'Who are they speaking to?' I asked. 'Oh, Allan Clarke, the Leeds striker.' I knew there and then it was done. Who would Barnsley want as their new man? Dave Worthington, ex-Grimsby Town full-back and formerly of non-league Cambridge City or Allan 'Sniffer' Clarke, England international, prolific Leeds goalscorer and student of Don Revie? Needless to say, Clarkey got the job and a go at managing in the Football League while I headed once more into the professional football wilderness.

Eight

Hauling Myself Up
(1976–1994)

These are dark days in the country, a time of political and social unrest. Britain is divided between support or condemnation for trade union strikes, culminating in the 1978/79 'Winter of Discontent' – where industrial action and freezing cold temperatures threaten to cripple society. The threat of violence from the IRA remains.

In Yorkshire, industrial tensions are felt most keenly within the mining sector. 'The Ripper', later discovered to be Peter Sutcliffe, is still at large, with people – especially women – fearful of walking foggy, unlit streets at night.

Football in England is also entering its darkest period. The optimism and national unity that greeted the World Cup win of 1966 has given way to tribalism and violent clashes on the terraces and streets between rival 'firms', acting under the banner of fandom. Racial abuse of the increasing number of black players entering the game becomes more common. The infrastructure of the sport is also beginning to show its age, with stadiums built decades before in dire need of modernisation. The groundwork is laid for disaster. In Halifax, a former footballer and manager sits behind the wheel of a van, searching once more for a purpose on the cold, wet, grey roads of West Yorkshire …

THE INITIAL months following my return north were spent once more on the familiar roads of Calderdale, behind the wheel of a truck laden with Calor gas cylinders. The business had continued to grow under the management of my in-laws, who graciously welcomed me back into the fold, providing the means with which I could support my family. It was a profession but not a purpose. Each morning, I rose before the sun to traverse the gloomy, winding hillside roads of Halifax and Huddersfield, loading and unloading in the gravel yards of homes, farms and factories. I returned in the dark, slumping into a seat at the kitchen table to eat and rest before going again the next day. Different roads but all the same.

We quickly found a new house in which to live, on the end of a terrace in Greetland. The kids rolled once more with the emotional punch of moving home and school, slotting back into life up north, resilience personified. I threw myself into the one mission in front of me – to provide for my family. Football continued in my absence. Once more, I was on the outside looking in. I was just another ex-professional footballer, missing the connection they had once had with the game that defined their life. I watched on as Bob Paisley led Liverpool to a record-breaking First Division title, Nottingham Forest sealed back-to-back European Cups, Trevor Francis became the first £1m footballer and our Frank top-scored in the top flight with 24 goals for Bolton. Grimsby earned promotion to the third tier and Cambridge City slumped to 17th in the eighth. I was powerless to impact either. Teams won, teams lost, went up and down and the whole cycle began again. I spent my days on the road and evenings in the pub virtually alongside the house, its name – The Sportsman – unwittingly mocking my longing for a former life.

Distracted by my obligations and woes, I sensed little of the discontent developing in my marriage until it was too late. Larraine's unhappiness came to light during a family holiday to Spain. Planned as a chance for us to relax and spend time together, it instead had the opposite effect. She informed me that she had met someone during the trip with whom she felt a connection. She would soon move to Spain to pursue the new relationship. Back in the UK, I attempted to pick up the pieces.

I was lost; thrown suddenly into the life of a single parent to three children, with little experience and skills upon which to draw, I did the best I could, aided by my mum, who had moved back to Yorkshire only a few months earlier, and Larraine's parents. Keely was magnificent in the early months, taking on responsibilities in the house beyond which a child should be expected to perform. She would cook and help clean and care for her siblings and for me. She became a glue holding the home together.

Emotionally, the toll of the new life into which we were thrust was great. The children had opted to remain with me in Yorkshire but, at times, they still yearned for their mother. Still unable to fully comprehend it myself, I struggled to explain to them, when they questioned it, why she had left.

I was ground down by the continual worry for their upkeep, safety and state of mind and the requirements of work, made even more problematic by it being so closely tied to her family. To their credit, her father and brother offered at least an outward appearance of neutrality and empathy for my position. Her mother made her loyalty to Larraine much more apparent, including pleas for me to take her daughter back when her relationship in Spain faltered. In my mind, though, the damage was done. There was no coming back, no marriage left to revive.

In June of 1981, I attended Bradford Crown Court to give evidence of my suitability to gain full custody of our children. I laid out clearly and concisely my practical, financial and, most importantly, emotional credentials. Larraine did not attend to contest her rights. In the 1980s, it was extremely rare for fathers to be granted full custody of children in the event of a divorce. It was far from a given in my case, even though I knew where they would be better off. Having heard my case, the judge had little hesitation. At the conclusion of his ruling in my favour, he declared: 'Mr Worthington has proven to us he is fully capable of providing the care and support his children require.' I would unlock and embrace the true emotions of that day in the years to follow. In the moment, though, in the midst of the mess and challenges facing me to fix it, I felt only relief and a responsibility to live up to the judge's ruling. It took all of the stamina, determination and resolve I possessed to do so.

It began with a change of job. Like so many of our peers, my brother, Bob, had turned to sportswear to support himself in his retirement, opening the imaginatively titled Worthington Sports. Over time, a number of other local professional sportsmen would work in the business – Yorkshire cricketers Phil Carrick and Steve Rhodes and two ex-Wakefield rugby league icons, Neil Fox and David Jeanes, as well as my former Halifax Town team-mate Malcolm Russell. I joined them as a rep, visiting local sports clubs and schools to promote and sell our merchandise.

It was invigorating to begin with, a new challenge with different skills to learn. I employed some of the same persuasive methods I had utilised as a captain and, briefly, as a manager. Making a sale provided that momentary thrill of victory. The social side was certainly enjoyable – akin to being back in the dressing room. Meetings would be held at the Stansfield Arms pub in Apperley Bridge, over the road from Woodhouse Grove School, where Bradford City trained. Invariably, it would quickly descend into drinking, mickey-taking, laughter and the sharing of old war stories from our respective time on sporting fields up and down the country. I only wish I could have remained in that initial positive state of mind.

As days became weeks and months, I realised that I had swapped one form of ill-suited work for another. The days were long, breaks in them snatched. I would be out early to visit schools and in late after trips to leisure centres, my interactions with the kids restricted to hasty morning goodbyes or sneaked, sorrowful glances into darkened bedrooms as they slept. Weekdays became a blur through a windscreen – dull Yorkshire skies over a never-ending stretch of road. The exhaustion crept up and overwhelmed me. Having spent a healthy life at the front of the race, physically fitter and stronger than most, I was now flagging, scrambling to keep pace, my mind and body drained by the turmoil around me. When bailiffs came calling, threatening to take our belongings to pay off my mounting debts, it felt like the final straw, a betrayal of the cherished ideals and values set for me by my parents. For the first time, I perceived myself undeserving of all they had given me.

One evening, whilst driving alone on the motorway to an event in Bradford, I saw a bridge up ahead and contemplated pressing my foot down and driving the car headlong into its broad, concrete pillars. It was only a fleeting thought, a solitary fatal impulse, but it was indicative of how beaten I had become by the circumstances of my life that, even for a moment, I could contemplate ending it. As suddenly as it had entered my mind, the urge left, barged aside by one overriding image – my three children. I eased my foot off the accelerator, moved into the inside lane and left the motorway, casting one last glance in my rear view mirror to the bridge disappearing over the crest behind me.

I cannot remember where I stopped the car, only that I remained there for a long time, shaken but very still. Gary, Keely and Danielle dominated my thoughts. In their short lives, they had dealt with enough upheaval. Their mother had left. How could I now even think of deserting them, too? Sat in the dark, alone in my car, I resolved to be better, to rediscover the man my parents had taught me to be – determined, resourceful, resilient, optimistic. I would work as hard as I could to create a better life for my kids and me. To my unending joy and pride, they showed me the way.

Keely remained a paragon of stoicism, filling in to cover for my inadequacies around the house and acting as a shepherd for her siblings. She drew from home economics lessons at school, making meals for us all, including showing me for the first time how to make proper Yorkshire puddings. Being so young, it was difficult to discern the impact of events on Dani. I think for a long time I underestimated the challenge they had posed to her young self. Years later, to my sadness and regret, she admitted to me that she remembers nothing of the first seven years of her life, perhaps blocked from her memory in an act of self-preservation. As she headed towards adolescence, aided by a settled and positive environment around her, she emerged from this protective cocoon a tough, well-adjusted and, most importantly, happy person.

Only when the children were ready and we had a degree of stability did I feel comfortable focussing on my own needs, including a new relationship. I met Brenda in The Sportsman, sparking up conversation with her after she had captured my attention across the bar. She was a dancer in the Halifax Catholic Amateur Operatic Society, a bubbly, giggly character who loved to be out enjoying herself. She was just what I needed in my life at that time. A romance quickly blossomed between us. She took my situation in her stride. It helped that she had gone through her own divorce, coincidentally from another man called David, with whom I had worked at Halifax Town Hall as a teenager before my football career had taken off.

My own drawn-out divorce was still ongoing – a process that eventually required me to sell our house to pay Larraine her share.

I was fortunate that I could source an eager and easy-going buyer. Midway through the 1981/82 season, Leeds United had signed our Frank, hoping he would score the goals to keep them up. He got the goals, and my house to live in, but Leeds still went down. Brenda had no children of her own but took to mine with ease and empathy and a real sense of fun. I remember their first meeting – a trip out to the Alhambra theatre in Bradford for the live tour of *Tiswas*, the Saturday morning kids' show hosted by Chris Tarrant. The highlight saw us volunteer to go up on stage and be part of the show, playing silly games to make each other and the audience laugh. It proved the perfect introduction and laid the groundwork for a lasting familial bond between them.

Professionally, I remained unsatisfied and unfulfilled. That huge, empty space, once occupied by football, remained as a dull ache. I was striving for something to fill the gap – a near impossible task. Personally, I desired a new goal, a fresh challenge into which I could sink my teeth, strive and grow, something that could stir my inner drive as football once had. The answer came with the somewhat instinctive purchase of a 7.5-tonne van, the kind you see parked on driveways being loaded with furniture when people move house. From there, I began seeking out removal opportunities, starting with small, single jobs before acquiring a contract ferrying carpets to Bradford and Huddersfield from Witney and Abingdon in Oxfordshire. I was a one-man band, inexperienced but eager to build something meaningful.

One job led to another and another – white goods, kitchen units, more carpets. A company in Slathwaite, near Huddersfield, suggested they could have more work for me shifting wool bales if I had a flat-bed truck at my disposal. I scraped together the money and bought one, content to speculate in order to accumulate. I acquired more vehicles, hired staff and added a professional sheen to my endeavours. My vehicles became a more regular presence on the roads around Halifax, with their distinctive paint job – 'Dave Worthington Transport' – emblazoned on the side, complemented by a thick red, black and white stripe in honour of my favourite football team from over the Pennines.

I wasn't an overnight success. The process was gradual, occurring over a number of years and involving a steep learning curve to educate myself in the requisite skills of a business of which I had previously known little. Again, my experiences in football came to my aid. I was eager to learn, never too proud to ask for advice, an indefatigable sponge, soaking up information I could then put into practice. When help was absent, trial and error became the solution.

Initially, I was required to do plenty of driving, sometimes for hours on end to Scotland and back. I would often find myself up in the freezing Highlands as night came, tired and in need of rest. I learned quickly to take plenty of blankets with me so I could lay across the seats of the van and sleep in some degree of warmth. In the morning, I would emerge from my makeshift bedroom into the most stunning of locales and wash myself in a nearby stream before setting off home. Later, I would acquire a van with a small sleeping pod that could be accessed through an opening above the driver's seat but those early days were much more rough and ready. In my previous job, tied to a schedule not of my making, the roads had felt restricting, like I was on permanent rails. Working for myself, I was liberated, on a route towards endless possibility and some kind of freedom.

Such was my rapacious desire for growth, I found myself unable to refuse opportunities. I got word that Benn's Removals, a transport company with 130 years' worth of trading history, was up for sale. The Brownridge family, who owned the business, including its fleet of distinctive orange vehicles and base of operations – a site with a petrol station and large four-bedroom residence – were looking to sell it all and retire. I didn't immediately have the money that they were asking but dug deep, secured bank loans, received some financial help from Bob and a family friend, Dave Lister, and eventually struck a deal. The house on site became our family home, in which I set up an office. From there, I took on a more managerial role, directing operations and spending the majority of my time on the phone rather than a road. In just a few years, my impulsive van purchase had become a small fleet.

It gave me more of the life I desired. I continued to strive to ensure my children were comfortable but I was now able to see and share in the fruits of my labour. The kids were happy, settled. Brenda became an important figure in their lives, providing support, love and a positive female role model in the absence of their mother. She was wonderful for me, too. Our relationship had begun in tougher times, with us both picking up the pieces after the breakdown of our first marriages, but we grew stronger together, the union becoming a cornerstone of our new life. We made it formal at a church ceremony in Elland.

Through all the ups and downs, football remained a lifeline. I was no longer a professional but I could not entirely forgo the game. Local league games gave me my regular fix. On any weekend I could spare, I appeared for amateur sides on mudbath pitches, much as I had as a 16-year-old prior to joining Halifax, a little more jaded with a little less to prove, but still capable. I was only in my mid-30s, still fit enough and with plenty to offer at that level. I had a spell playing for Huddersfield club Bradley Rangers in the Yorkshire League, alongside another ex-Halifax player, Mark Harrold. My old mate, Rod Green, had returned to the area and was managing local Halifax side Stump Cross. He convinced me to play for them for a time. Rod hadn't changed a bit, still the same cheeky bloke who had connived his way into a few bottles of free wine on my first evening in Grimsby.

The games were typically ferocious, with younger opposition players eager to demonstrate how unimpressed they were by anyone with Football League appearances to their name. It required all the experience of my near-500 games to sense when and from where the latest wild challenge would fly. I enjoyed the battle. It wasn't Blundell Park under floodlights with 20,000 fans roaring me on but it was enough to scratch the itch. I may have lost my once-cherished status and a yard or two of pace but the fire in my belly burned brightly.

Such was my hunger to eke out the last remaining vestiges of my playing days, no matter the level, I accepted an invitation from Bradford City boss George Mulhall to help him out in some reserve-team games. City had three kids on the books whom he felt had a real chance of making it in the game: winger Mark Ellis, defender Peter Jackson and a midfielder by the name of Stuart McCall. They were all talented for their age but, in George's words, 'headless chickens'. It was my job to sit in midfield and set an example. He needed someone with the fitness still to play and, more importantly, the experience and wisdom to talk to the three, praise them or give a rollicking when required. It was only half a season but I like to think I helped, although they themselves did most of the hard work to make a success of their respective careers. The trio would all play more than 200 first-team games for City.

Mark or 'Mega' – as in megastar – achieved two promotions with the club but saw his promising career curtailed by a serious injury in his mid-20s. Jacko was Bradford's youngest-ever captain and a hero at the club, a status he also holds at Huddersfield, where he played and managed. Stu achieved huge success, playing in the English top flight with Everton, winning ten trophies in

Scotland with Rangers and 40 caps for the Scottish national team. He subsequently managed Bradford on three occasions as part of a lengthy coaching career. I've bumped into all three in the years since and we've reminisced about those early years when I taught them everything they knew! That time at Bradford was made even more enjoyable by the presence of my sister, Julie, around the club. Having returned to West Yorkshire, she had taken up a secretarial job at Valley Parade, completing the full set of Worthington siblings to make a living from the game.

Soon, I was joined on the muddy fields of Halifax by another Worthington, eager to prove himself to the football world. I had continued to tutor my son in the game throughout his youth and his quality quickly became clear. His close control was superb, his left foot honed. He maybe wasn't the quickest or strongest kid but there were ways to compensate for that, by listening and learning, developing an in-game awareness and an understanding of where to be and when. Gary was a good student. I had begun to play regularly for Elland Athletic, with Gary featuring in their junior set-up, but he would soon step up. Aged 13, he was slowly eased into the first team, featuring intermittently on the left wing. Knowing he would be immediately targeted by burly, snarling full-backs twice his size, especially those that recognised his lineage and ability to make them look foolish, I armed him with a simple rule: one touch. When the ball came his way, his first job was to lay it off to a team-mate immediately; one easy cushioned pass inside. This would reduce the chances of a coming together with a big defender. After that, he could move in behind and seek possession again to try and torment a back-pedalling opponent. It worked well, keeping him largely out of trouble and allowing him to shine.

I wish I could say I was able to revel in the talent he displayed in those games but the protective father part of me won out. I would spend most games on high alert to the threat of him getting crunched. There were some tough teams in the league. Mixenden, from a notoriously tough part of Halifax, were one. I didn't mind them targeting me – I could handle it and give a bit back – but the notion of a green, unprepared Gary facing such treatment was unpalatable. I understood then how my own father must have felt watching his teenage son attempt to ride big blows from local league brutes. Equally, I could share in the pride he, too, must have sensed when his son dusted himself off, got up, smiled and got on with his job. Little did I know but on the touchline during those games stood another keen and knowledgeable observer who would soon help take my son out of the bear pit and into the big leagues.

It was inevitable that scouts would be drawn to a talented 13-year-old shining in school representative games and holding his own in a competitive men's league. That the keenest interest came from Manchester United, giants of the English game, my dad's boyhood club and the team I had supported as a child, was beyond any of our wildest dreams. Once they made their interest known, there was no competition. Gary was invited over for a successful trial before signing schoolboy forms at the age of 14. It was hard not to get carried away. All around United stood reminders of the talent they had produced from within – Bobby Charlton, Nobby Stiles, George Best. Norman Whiteside was in the year ahead of Gary and on a fast track to the first team, with the likes of Mark Hughes and Clayton Blackmore coming through around the same time.

His apprenticeship began encouragingly. I would travel as often as I could to watch him play youth games in the Lancashire and then Central League, alongside David Platt and Mark Robins. He impressed, so much so that he earned himself an England Youth call-up in 1983 for a tournament in Yugoslavia which featured a host of top nations, including the hosts, Russia, Austria and Sweden.

It helped that he had such a solid coaching set-up behind him at United, including a man I knew very well. After our time together at Halifax Town, Eric Harrison's playing career had taken him to Hartlepool, Southport and Barrow over two spells. He subsequently moved into youth coaching, beginning with Everton before Ron Atkinson recruited him to his staff at Old Trafford. When he joined the club, Gary was already there as a teenager.

Eric was brilliant. I had often thought during our playing days together that he might make a decent manager in the Football League but I never suspected he could forge such an illustrious career as a coach of young players. He had lost none of the grit and determination he demonstrated during my mentorship under him at The Shay. I don't think he instructed his young charges to headbutt changing room cupboards but I know he remained tough and uncompromising, refusing to ever accept less than 100 per cent. What came hand in hand with this, though, was an unflinching loyalty to those who gave their all.

Eric's crowning glory would be the emergence of a crop of young players in the early 1990s, including the 'Class of 92', who would form the basis of Sir Alex Ferguson's multi-trophy-winning United side, arguably the greatest to ever grace the Premier League – David Beckham, Nicky Butt, Ryan Giggs, Paul Scholes and the Neville brothers, Gary and Phil. All of them have spoken glowingly of Eric's influence on their glittering careers, of a tough taskmaster but a caring mentor. As a sign of their unflinching respect and affection for my old friend, they – along with many others from across the game – would travel to Halifax to mourn Eric's passing in 2019.

I tried not to speak to Eric about Gary during my son's youth career. I didn't want to interfere. Being at Manchester United meant my old mentor was extremely qualified to coach players how he saw fit. I didn't want to be one of the pushy dads you often see around football, sticking their nose in where it is not welcome, even if I may have been more qualified than most. I got the sense that Eric wanted more from him – to work harder, be tougher. Gary wasn't like me as a player; he relied more on guile than grit, like his uncle, Frank. In my opinion, he lacked a bit of pace, that extra zip that propels a forward player to become a contender at the very top.

There was no doubting my son's resilience, though. Near the end of the 1985/86 season, he was told he would not be kept on at United and was free to find another club. Roy McFarland at Derby immediately made his interest known and arranged a trial for him in reserve-team game against West Bromwich Albion. With me watching on from the stands, Gary Robson, the brother of Manchester United legend Bryan, needlessly went through the back of my son in the centre circle, seriously injuring his knee. Every fibre in my body wanted to charge down the stand and on to the grass to get at the man who had hurt my son. It was devastating to watch on powerlessly from the touchline, to see him in such agony as he was carried from the pitch before being taken to hospital, where they decided an operation was required to fix the damage. As is often the case, the recovery process from one injury leads to others. A subsequent spell at Huddersfield came and went with little game time. It was only when a physio at Darlington diagnosed him with glandular fever that Gary was able to get himself fully fit and begin his career in earnest in the Football League.

Over the years, football morphed from a calling to a hobby for me, providing an enjoyable distraction from the day-to-day demands of the business. I played as long as my body could hold up, competing with all the intensity I could muster. But as my 40s neared, I began to feel all the miles run and blows taken during those near-500 professional games. Joints creaked, muscles ached and my treasured stamina finally began to desert me. I could still don the pads and wicket-keeping gloves in the summer for a more sedate game of cricket for Elland, Northowram or Warley, where Alex South and Rod Green were team-mates, but my days of regularly charging up and down the right wing on winter mudbaths, flinging myself into tackles against much younger wingers, were nearing an end.

I would continue to play in testimonials and charity games, helping raise money for former clubs, team-mates and all manner of worthy causes. I helped arrange a game between Dave Worthington's All Stars and a Shelf Old Boys XI to be played on our old pitch at Shelf Park. Bob, Frank and I all played for the former, along with numerous former Halifax players, while my childhood pals Kenny Reilly, Davey Lewis and 'Nipper' Stuart Harrison featured for the latter. In another game, we raised the money for Brenda's Halifax Catholic Amateur Operatic Society to go on tour to Aachen in Germany by staging a game in Elland featuring the Worthington clan (including a 16-year-old Gary), former England international Mike Summerbee and then Manchester United manager Ron Atkinson. Leeds striker Arthur Graham scored a hat-trick as the Worthington side went down 5-3.

During the 1984/85 season, I was offered the chance to do some part-time scouting for Bradford City. George Mulhall had left as manager but I had remained in contact with others at the club from my days playing reserve-team football with 'Mega', Jacko and Stu. All three were first-team players by then, with Peter the club captain. I knew some of the other scouts, too. Billy Legg was a huge friend of our family, having been a team-mate and regular partner in crime of our Frank's at Huddersfield. So close was he to the family that when his daughter was born they called her Julie, because they so liked the name of my sister. Billy's playing career had been ended suddenly by a car crash, which had required him to have a tracheotomy, but he enjoyed a long secondary career assessing other players for the likes of City, alongside coaching in the community for Halifax and Blackburn Rovers.

It was a nice fit for me, a toe dipped back into pleasant water. The sporadic scouting schedule fit around my own, never took me too far from home and gave me regular free access to games. I was able to put my knowledge and experience to good use and if I could identify a potential transfer target or two for the club it was a bonus. I only wish this could act as a positive prelude to the 20-year scouting career that would define the second half of my footballing life. Instead, it must serve as the harbinger of tragedy.

That should have been a magnificently memorable season for everyone associated with Bradford – players, staff, supporters, the whole city. In the penultimate game of the campaign, a victory at Bolton had clinched the Third Division title, the club's first trophy in 56 years. Having averaged attendances of around 6,500 over the rest of the games, the triumph ensured a bumper crowd of 11,000 for the final-day fixture against Lincoln. My fellow scouts and I were all in attendance, excited to witness Jacko lift the trophy before the game and on a promise from the manager, Trevor Cherry, and his assistant, Terry Yorath, that the party would continue for us after the game and into the night. We were all given seats in the main stand, where I found myself sat behind an old friend – Jim McGuigan, the manager who had signed me for Grimsby, who was there on a scouting assignment of his own. There were smiles, handshakes and hugs and, for 40 minutes on the pitch, a gentle, low-intensity game akin to a friendly.

It was just before half-time that we first noticed the smoke beginning to gather under the roof of the stand. I remember Jim turning to me. 'I dinnae like the look of that Worthy,' he said to me in his deep Scottish accent. 'I'm a wee bit older than you; I'm off for me cup of tea now.' And off he trotted, up into the belly of the stand. There was no real concern at that stage. The wind dispersed the smoke initially and I think most people assumed that, whatever the source, it would be dealt with. This was, after all, a day of celebration, not one for worry. I heard one voice near to me declare: 'Ah, it's just some silly beggar lighting a smoke bomb.'

The mood changed in seconds. The smoke became thicker and darker, spreading across the body of the stand from its left corner. People began to flee, moving in all directions, some into the stand, others towards the front and the safety of the pitch. I made the decision to move to my right, away from the now visible flames. As I did so, I met a tall wooden fence, spiked along the top, there to prevent supporters in the standing area getting to the more expensive seating. To this day, I am not sure how I got over it. I can only think I must have stood on the seats and thrown myself over. From there, I sprinted towards the back of the stand, desperately seeking an exit. It was full of people scrambling and screaming, many of them invisible to me because of the smoke. By now, it had dropped to near floor level, leaving just a yard or so of clear air into which you could see.

I dropped and began to crawl on my knees. Nearby, through the cacophony of noise, I could hear a man yelling: 'Help me! Help me!' I moved in what I thought was his direction, feeling for him with my hands, but I couldn't find him. The smoke was overpowering. I was struggling to breathe. I had to get out. People seemed to be moving in the same direction, so I followed, eventually emerging out into daylight, gasping for clean air. I was at the back of the main stand, which was now engulfed in flames.

My only thought was to find a safe spot, so I walked around the corner to where the scouts would usually meet ahead of a game, hoping some of my colleagues would think to do the same. There I met Billy, frantically pacing back and forth, tears streaming down his face. I could barely get any sense from him initially. 'Billy!' I shouted. 'What's wrong?' He pointed back to Valley Parade. 'It's my daughter,' he stammered. 'She was in there with me. I don't know where she is.' Twelve-year-old Julie had been his guest for the game, the first she had ever attended. Just before half-time, before the real panic kicked in, he had gone to fetch them both a tea, leaving her alone in her seat. In the surge to escape the stand, he had been swept out, unable to get back to help his daughter. He had returned to our meeting spot, hoping she would be there. He was in an utter panic. I tried to calm him. 'Billy, she's a smart kid, she'll have found her way out,' I told him. 'I bet she's safe and made her way back to your car. Let's walk up there and find her.'

We walked a couple of streets over to Manningham Lane, me leading a mumbling Billy, to where he had parked but Julie was nowhere to be seen. He was now inconsolable. Also struggling to hold it together, I dragged us back to the stadium, to the rear of the smaller stand behind the goal, away from the fire. Obviously, the police were shepherding people away but I pled my case to them and they eventually relented, allowing us to enter in a safer spot and make our way to the pitch. There we found hundreds, possibly thousands of people, many still in a panic, some holding loved ones, others staring blank-eyed, all trying to come to terms with the horror in front of them. We worked our way frantically through the crowds, searching. Suddenly, a group parted and there, sat on a wall, in tears but safe, was Julie. I have never felt relief like it. Billy and Julie hugged and the three of us stood on the pitch and cried together.

I remember little of getting home. I know that I found a phone box and called home to tell Brenda and the kids that I was safe.

They had been watching events unfold on the news. I think I got the bus back to Halifax. Back at home, looking at myself in the mirror, I was almost unrecognisable. My hair was blackened, the new cream jacket I had worn for the day now dark with soot. I showered and changed but did not want to remain in the house, running over the horrific events in my mind. I needed a distraction. A drink. We went to Elland Cricket Club nearby, where we found lots of friendly faces, many of whom knew where I had been that day and were overjoyed to discover I was safe. I have rarely felt as loved. Many bought me a drink, mostly whisky. Something stiff to help me forget.

There was an understandable emotional outpour in the aftermath of the Bradford fire. Fifty-six supporters were killed, with hundreds more injured. Billy Legg's wife, Sandra, helped treat many in her role as a nurse at Airedale hospital. There was also an inevitable search for blame, which targeted the club and the failure to modernise their outdated stadium from wooden, litter-strewn stands so vulnerable to something as seemingly innocuous as a dropped cigarette. The disaster would eventually act as a catalyst for much-needed change but the game still had a long way to go to emerge from the dark ages. On the same day as the fire, a 15-year-old Leeds fan was killed when a wall fell on him during fighting between rival fans at Birmingham City's St Andrew's ground. Less than three weeks later, 39 fans died when another wall toppled during clashes between Liverpool and Juventus fans at Heysel Stadium in Brussels. Hillsborough was still to come.

There was an irony to my presence at Valley Parade that day. For so long, I had thought football to be the defining aspect of my person, an all-encompassing master. Witnessing the devastation of the fire and its aftermath, the pain and suffering of those who waved goodbye to excited family members that morning only for them to never return, was revelatory and humbling. In Billy's relief at finding his daughter, the handshakes and drinks bought by friends delighted to see me safe and the emotional reaction of my wife and children as I walked through the door, covered in soot but very much alive, I recognised that there are far more important things in life.

In the years that followed my departure from Cambridge, I felt as though I was having things taken from me. In hindsight, I was gaining all that I needed – some perspective, reaffirmation of the resilience and determination so important to my sense of self-worth and the ability to proudly witness my children overcome adversity to become the well-rounded, decent, driven people they are today. From that point, if football again came calling, I would welcome it as an equal, ready to tackle its challenges on my own terms.

Nine

Shay Man

(1994–2003)

*Saturday, 8 May 1999. The final day of the Football League season.
There is a nervous tension within Exeter City's St James Park ground,
not amongst the home supporters but the small pocket of away fans who
have made the long journey down from West Yorkshire.*

*Their team, Halifax Town, The Shaymen, are about to discover
their fate at the end of a long rollercoaster of a campaign. Over the course
of the last nine months, the club have been going up, staying down, sold
their star striker and sacked their manager. Now, here in Devon, is the
final reckoning – will it be season over or a play-off campaign and a
shot at third-tier football?*

*As kick-off nears, Halifax's caretaker manager, the hometown boy,
former teenage striker and the man promoted from within to save the
season with seven games to go, awkwardly hobbles along the touchline
on a pair of crutches, a grimace on his face. As he makes his slow, painful
journey to his seat, a fan in the away end turns to anther beside him:
'What's happened to Worthy?'*

IT'S COMICAL that one of the worst injuries I suffered during
my time in football came not on a pitch, via a wild tackle from a
midfield nutcase, but from a stupid slip as I excitedly disembarked
the team coach ahead of that final game in 1999. There was little
time for a proper hospital trip, the job at hand too pressing, so I

took painkillers, propped myself up on some crutches and made do as best I could. I would later discover that I had seriously damaged my knee. I'm not sure which was worse – the agony of the injury and subsequent operation to have the cartilage shaved or the embarrassment of the fall itself?

In many ways, the incident encapsulates my second experience with Halifax Town. I stumbled back into my hometown club and put myself on the line, only for it to cause me some pain.

The story of my second spell at Town begins five years prior to that painful but purposeful journey along the touchline in Devon. In late 1994, I was kept busy with my thriving business and ever-growing family. I had seen two of my children marry, with the youngest, Danielle, on course to do so herself before the decade was through. I had also become a granddad, six times over. Gary and his wife Sally had Daisy first in July 1991. They would have the twins, Abbie and Molly, in June 1994 but not before Keely and her husband, Bob, welcomed their two children, Joe (April 1992) and Max (August 1993). Jorja was born to Dani and Ric in September 1994. Ellis would follow in August 1997.

Keely had found her calling, having switched from medical photography to become a scenes-of-crime officer with Halifax police. Dani helped out with the business accounts but would eventually train and move into an illustrious teaching career. After nearly 200 Football League appearances, including productive goalscoring spells with Darlington, Wrexham and Wigan, Gary found himself briefly out of the game. I was delighted that he would soon find himself drawn back in by an offer from Town, assuming the mantle I had been passed by my father to become the third generation of Worthington Shay men.

I have always made it known, to anyone with interest, that I would do anything for Halifax Town. With a historical connection to the club, a son in the first team and a bit of money in my pocket, the club clearly felt this was the time to capitalise on that promise. They offered me the opportunity to make a small investment and join the board. I was delighted to accept, viewing it as a way to get back involved in football. If my days in the changing room were over, the boardroom would have to do.

I dipped my toe back in with a unique and ambitious fundraising drive – one that capitalised on the contacts and reach in the game still held by my family and others. Towards the back end of the 1994/1995 season, BBC television's Duncan Herbert and I were able to convince a host of high-profile football stars to sign and pose in the club's shirt, the idea being that they had 'signed' for Halifax to form a 'Town Dream Team'. The list included a host of internationals, past and present, British and foreign: Paul Gascoigne, Gary Lineker, Stuart Pearce, Des Walker, David Platt, Jimmy Greaves, Alan Hansen, Gary Speed, Mario Basler, Eric Cantona and, of course, our Frank. We even got Bayern Munich boss Otto Rehhagel to 'manage' the side. An expert panel, headed by Halifax-born former World Cup referee Arthur Ellis, was recruited to judge on the outcome of a fictitious game between our XI and a Manchester City side selected by their then boss, Alan Ball. They ruled it to be a 2-2 draw. I still think we were robbed! Before a friendly with Barnsley in the lead-up to the 1995/96 season, the shirts were auctioned, bringing in a vital £3,000 for the club. From that moment, without formality or fanfare, I became the club's part-time commercial manager.

Juggling it with the business proved a major challenge. During the day, I would be directing delivery drivers to their next job, overseeing refuelling of vans, processing payments and other paperwork. At night, I stuck on my club hat and hit the phone to find matchball sponsors or sell tickets for sportsmen's dinners and golf days – any means we could find to bring in an extra quid or two. Eric Harrison was always a willing source of raffle prizes for the dinners, providing a wardrobe's worth of Manchester United shirts signed by Alex Ferguson's Premier League-conquering sides.

Slowly, almost organically, my importance at Town increased and my responsibilities grew. I became a more visible presence, in the directors' box or by the dugout on matchdays. I appeared occasionally in the *Halifax Evening Courier* to speak about my work at the club, provide a familiar, friendly frontman for infrastructure plans or simply to pose for a photo with a couple of first-teamers when a deal was agreed with German company Uhlsport to supply our kit. I travelled to games to perform the occasional scouting job, to watch opponents or try to find players who could improve the first team. At some point, I agreed to help out the second XI with an occasional bit of coaching. Before I knew it, I was being listed on squad photos with the title 'reserve team manager'. Anything to help Halifax Town.

It was exhausting. Days were long and often frustrating, the dual demands on my time and attention leading to a constant worry that I was servicing one part to the detriment of the other. Nights were restless and filled with fear at the possibility of the business coming off the rails or the club going under. Most people work nine to five but I found myself tied to responsibilities from seven in the morning until ten at night for the best part of five challenging years. I still have diaries and planners with my weekly hours for the club recorded in them – regularly I was doing 50 or more, making a mockery of my part-time status.

I had returned to Town in the aftermath of their relegation to non-league in 1993 and, along with my colleagues at the club and supporters, endured the pain and pressures that came with it. At the end of the 1994/95 season – their second in the Conference – it looked like the club might fold, with debts off around £150,000, but thanks to the efforts of many we were able to keep the wolf from the door. In the two seasons that followed, decline bit. A 15th-place finish was followed by the narrowest escape from relegation to the sixth tier of English football, by a single point. Gates at The Shay fell and apathy within the town grew. Had I had greater sense, perhaps been a tad more self-preserving, I would have questioned the sanity of enduring such a strung-out life spent in service of a seemingly hopeless case. I felt a sense of duty to the club, though, a drive to put the team above myself, as I had as a player. Anything to help Halifax Town.

I remained intoxicated by the sights, sounds and smells of the game. Journeys to The Shay on matchday retained their thrill – the waft of onions from burger vans, the glow from the floodlights and the murmur of excitement from an optimistic crowd as it grew ahead of kick-off. All around the club were nostalgic reminders of my teenage playing days – the steps of the stand I would sweep with Malcolm Russell, the pylons we would race each other up to win a quid, the changing room cupboards assaulted by Eric Harrison on a fortnightly basis.

On the occasions that things did go right for us in those initial five busy years, I found it as exhilarating as ever. In 1996, Gary was on the scoresheet as Town beat Bradford 2-1 to seal the West Riding Senior Cup at The Shay. Two years later, with my old mate George Mulhall in charge and striker Geoff Horsfield banging in goal after goal, Town returned to the Football League, winning the Conference in style, 19 points ahead of second-placed Cheltenham Town. I still have a cutting from *The Courier* with a photo marking the moment we won the title, courtesy of a 2-0 win at Kidderminster Harriers. It focusses on George, leading the charge from the bench at full time to celebrate on the pitch with 1,500 travelling Town fans. On the far left of the shot, about to launch from his crouched position is the club's former teenage forward and current commercial manager/reserve team boss/ever-willing servant, arms outstretched, a huge, triumphant grin plastered across his face. It was a special day that vindicated all the long, stressful time at the grindstone. Such experiences helped confirm to me an often unacknowledged but unwavering truth about myself – that, while my head was in the business, my heart was and always would be in football.

When the club asked me if I would take over as caretaker manager in April 1999, I had little hesitation in accepting. Heart over head, anything for Halifax Town. At that time, they'd managed to get themselves into a mess. George had departed as manager to take on a director of football role just a few days before the start of the 1998/99 season, leading to Kieran O'Regan taking over the first team. Kieran had been a Town player and captain for a number of years and had been assisting George in coaching the side since 1997. On the pitch, things began brilliantly for him. He took 36 points from his first 20 league games to lead us to the top of the Third Division. Off it, though, there was some disharmony. In the summer, the chairman, Jim Brown, had brought in Peter Butler from West Brom to be a player-coach. Peter was a Halifax lad and undoubtedly a good player, a tenacious midfielder who had played Premier League football for West Ham in the early 90s. However, he was also the chairman's brother-in-law, which ruffled feathers. It was a factor in George's change of role and Kieran and Peter struggled to build much of a rapport afterwards.

From a position of strength in the table at the end of November, our form faltered from December and into the new year, with a run of just four wins from 19 games. The loss of star striker Geoff

Horsfield to Fulham for £300,000 contributed. On Monday, 5 April, we played out a dour 0-0 home draw with Rochdale – a result that left us 11th in the table, three points off the play-offs. The next day, I was asked to meet with one of the directors, David Greenwood, at The Shay. 'The chairman is going to sack Kieran,' he told me to my surprise. 'Who are they getting to take over as manager?' I asked. 'Well,' he replied. 'You know you've always said you'd do anything for Halifax Town ...'

I know that, initially, Kieran thought I'd been part of some secret plan to have him removed. I can see why, such was the mistrust that had permeated through parts of the club, especially with regard to Peter Butler and his relationship to the chairman. Later, when the heat had died down, I was able to explain that I had played no role in his sacking and had no long-standing designs on his job or, indeed, any managerial role. I didn't have the time or energy, such were my responsibilities to the business and my commercial and coaching job at Town. I think he trusted me enough to believe what I told him. It quickly became clear whose side the fans were on. Kieran's removal focussed ire against those who had swung the axe. In taking the job, it was inevitable I would be tarred with some of the blame but I couldn't think of that – I had a season to try and save.

For seven games – nine or ten at most if we made the play-offs – I felt I could manage the job, absorb the stress and lose a few more hours sleep. To help me when the demands of the day job got too much, I was able to lean on Peter in ways my predecessor had been reluctant to do. He was invaluable in taking training sessions with the Town first team to ready them for upcoming fixtures. I transformed myself into one of the old-school managers of my playing days, the type who would appear before kick-off to talk tactics and offer a rousing team talk. I leant into my natural enthusiasm and positivity, hoping that the players related to me like a Lawrie McMenemy rather than an Arthur Rowley.

I wanted attacking, cavalier football, with an 'if they score four, we'll score five' mentality. It possibly didn't help that the *Yorkshire Sport* paper printed an article saying I was aiming for football as 'sexy as Claudia Schiffer', accompanied by a photo of the German supermodel, but I sensed a more upbeat voice could reawaken some optimism. I had no time to implement a brand-new approach but the squad was clearly capable and just needed a different voice that could harness that again.

In my first game, we did, indeed, concede four to Cambridge United. Unfortunately, we forgot to score the five I'd promised. It was a chastening experience. Three days later, we travelled to Mansfield Town for a crucial game against one of our play-off rivals. Keen to inject some strength into the attack and provide a stern physical and mental test for The Stags' inexperienced centre-back, Craig Allardyce – son of my future boss Sam – I moved Kevin Hulme to centre-forward. Kev largely played in midfield but he was someone I knew would push the laws to the limit and give his opponent a torrid time. It worked a treat. Kev led the home defence a merry dance and we won 1-0 thanks to a goal from full-back Andy Thackeray.

It was the launchpad we required. Belief surged back into the side. They began to run that extra yard, throw themselves into tackles, press and push. They became a team in my own image. The next three games brought seven points, with wins over Brighton and Scunthorpe either side of a draw at Chester. It left us seventh in the table, two points ahead of Mansfield Town and Peterborough United and four better off than Swansea City, who had two games in hand. The play-off dream was back on.

No Town fan will ever forget the penultimate game of that season. It was played at The Shay, the final home fixture of the campaign, against a Scarborough team sitting rock bottom of the table and without a win in five. Defeat would have relegated them that day. With our renewed play-off hopes and self-belief, everything pointed to a home victory. Football does not adhere to such predictability. Perhaps overawed by the pressure against an opponent with nothing to lose, the players froze in the opening ten minutes. By the time we came to and began to play, we were 2-0 down and facing a mountain to climb in front of increasingly frustrated and fractious home fans. Justin Jackson pulled one back midway through the first half to restore some hope and, for an hour, we battered at the door, only to be kept at bay by wayward finishing, desperate saves from keeper Tony Parks, last-gasp defensive blocks or sheer bad luck. It was very quiet in the dressing room afterwards. I tried to gee them up with assurances that our race wasn't yet run but I think deep down we all knew it would take a miracle for us to make the top seven.

As I hobbled to the bench at Exeter on crutches, my knee throbbing and heart pounding, I must have looked a sorry sight from the away end. Despite the outward frailty, I retained some inner steel that we could overturn the odds, even though our fate was now out of our hands. A Swansea win over Hull at Vetch Field would negate whatever result we obtained at St James Park. I had spoken all week in the press about not wanting to know what was going on in the other game, eager just to focus on our job and leave the rest in the lap of the gods. A lot of managers say that and, I'm sure, mean it but it is a difficult thing to do in reality. Like the fans, you find yourself drawn towards any scrap of information to give you hope. In the end, it didn't matter what went on at Swansea. A

90th-minute goal sealed our 2-1 loss and, with it, ended the season. Ironically, Peter Butler had a brilliant game.

It was a crushing conclusion. There had always been an implicit aspect to my promise to Halifax. I didn't want to simply do anything for Town. I aspired to achieve something meaningful. This had been my opportunity – the chance to carve my name into an important part of the club's history by helping them back into the third tier of English football. It would have been my own small thank you to them for taking a chance on me and launching my professional football journey more than three decades prior. I ended my brief stint as caretaker manager with the gratitude of the club but, like any sportsman worth his salt, I am my own harshest critic. I felt I had failed them.

Once the dust had settled and summer began, I was able to reflect on the experience and its lessons. Much like the club, I had spread the resources available to me too thin. I had pushed myself too hard for too long with too little and it had cost me. It was time to ease the workload and, with it, the stress I had endured. The business had served its purpose, providing not just an income when it was most needed but also a project into which I could focus my energy, but any consistent enjoyment from its running had long since gone. With the custom, reputation, skilled workforce, buildings and vehicles, it had a decent value and offered an enticing prospect for someone with the will and ambition to take it on. In August 1999, I agreed to sell to Darvills, another domestic transport and removals company in Bradford. It would take time to see through the deal but a significant burden was lifted.

I now had the time and energy to commit myself to football. It may not have ended how I wished but my brief return to the frontline at the end of the previous season had given me an appetite for more. I did not see my future in management but knew the club could make good use of my abilities. Thankfully, the club felt the same. Eager to build on the previous two seasons and shed the somewhat chaotic off-the-field reputation the club had acquired, the board set about instilling a greater professionalism, aided by some investment. As part of this, it was announced that the club would establish a new, ambitious scouting department. I was appointed full time to be its lead.

The role was right in my wheelhouse, tapping not only into the contacts and knowledge I had acquired as a player but also the eye for detail and organisational abilities acquired through running my business. As well as attending games myself to assess opponents and identify players, I was tasked with setting up a countrywide network to reach far and wide for talent. Some of the team was made up of former Town players from the 1960s – Dave Verity, Lammie Robertson, who covered the north-west and Wales, Hampshire-based Dave Lennard and Toby Paterson, who covered Scotland. Others were people I'd played with and whose judgment I trusted, such as Ronnie Gale from Southend and my old mate, Stuart Brace, the former operating in the south-east and, latter, the south-west.

Below them, I aspired to put in place a group assigned to finding talented under-16 players from the north. I was especially keen to tap into the pool of young players released from the academies of bigger local clubs – Leeds, Bradford, Huddersfield and the two Sheffield sides. I was confident that any young players we signed would have their development well looked after by a coach making encouraging early strides into a post-playing career and whom I trusted inherently – one Gary Worthington. Sadly, only parts of my grand plan ever came to fruition, halted by a lack of money.

Personally, there were benefits to reap. I took to scouting immediately, stimulated by the variety of the role. One day I'd be watching Shrewsbury Town to see what issues they might cause us from corners, the next I would be off to Doncaster Rovers or Sheffield Wednesday to spy on potential recruits in a reserve game with my successor as manager, Mark Lillis. He always made sure I drove so he could have a pint. Cheers Mark! Occasionally, I'd stand on the touchline of muddy fields in Wakefield or Huddersfield, watching local semi-pro sides to see if anyone stood out. In between, I'd be reading reports on players sent in from our new network of observers across the country or liaising with them on their next assignment. It wasn't dissimilar to managing the drivers for my former business but was infinitely more fulfilling.

Without much previous scouting under my belt, I had to be instinctive in those early days, trusting that my years of playing experience and large body of games would correctly inform my judgment. I had played in the third tier for much of my career, so I knew its demands and the skillset required to thrive. A decent first touch was key. They didn't need to be able to kill a ball stone dead but we could ill afford a midfielder whose every second touch was a tackle. Pace would always draw the eye. A certain degree of technical deficiency can be masked if a player can cover ground in significantly less time than an opponent.

Personally, I would look for players with qualities similar to my own – stamina and determination to run throughout the whole game and the fearlessness and commitment to put your body on the line. I found that players revealed themselves to me in little moments, usually in scenarios I knew all too well from playing days – a striker who repeatedly makes the right run in behind his defender, even if a team-mate fails to spot and supply him, or a full-back who neglects to look over his shoulder to make himself aware of an attacker lurking in behind. I'd find myself urging: 'Look over your shoulder, look over your shoulder … too late!' Mentally, a line went through his name on the list.

I wish I could reel off a list of superstar names that we unearthed during that period; players who propelled Halifax up the divisions before moving on for big money to top clubs. There were some successes. Young defender Matt Clarke, who we picked up after his release from Wolves, was a solid addition and went on to play a lot of games for Darlington and Bradford. Former Manchester United youth forward Ian Fitzpatrick was a useful signing and scored goals for the club. Defender Paul Harsley was a big hit at both ends of the pitch after joining from Scunthorpe, scoring 12 goals to be our top scorer in 2001/02, while striker Craig Midgley proved a loyal and committed servant to the club.

There were plenty of players I would have loved to sign, ones I knew would improve the team but who were unavailable to us for obvious reasons. In September 2002, I twice went to watch Leeds reserves and drew up reports on striker Michael Bridges, who was still only 24 but returning from one of the many injuries that would blight his promising career. I was glowing in my praise after seeing him against Sheffield Wednesday: 'Absolutely brilliant in first half. Sheer quality on the ball bringing all midfielders into play and setting up strike partner Jamie McMaster on a few occasions. Always likely to score.' Also around that time, I spied a 16-year-old winger in Leeds' reserves who had great potential. 'Rapidly improving,' I wrote on second viewing of him against Everton reserves in October. 'He has pace, touch and confidence to try his tricks with the ball when facing up his defender.' So rapid was young James Milner's improvement, he would be in Leeds' first team by November – the first step on what has been a truly stellar top-flight career.

We got a bit closer on other deals. I received word about the availability of a young Spanish attacker by the name of Manolo García playing in Tenerife's youth team. I was assured he had excellent technique, so we invited him over for a trial. I've since been to the football club in Tenerife and it is a beautiful place, the ground and training facilities situated on a hillside looking down on to a sea reflecting back a blazing sun. Manolo arrived in Halifax on the first day of a freezing cold December, where he was promptly wrapped in as many layers of kit we could find and sent out to train. He played his trial game at Chesterfield and I can still see him now, breathing out huge clouds of frosty breath, his long sleeves pulled over his balled-up fists, knees knocking. When he came in after the game, he could barely speak, as his teeth were chattering so much. It was clear it wasn't going to work. The next week, he was back on a plane to sunny Spain to continue his career in a more agreeable climate.

At the more experienced end, I made fruitful trips to watch reserve-team games at Wigan and Brighton to check on Neil Redfearn and Chris Wilder, respectively. I knew they had the quality but I wanted to see for myself if they still had the fitness and desire to compete. As you'd expect, they displayed no shortage of either. Both would play a big role for the club in the coming years, both on and off the pitch. Redders filled in twice as caretaker manager, following the departures of Paul Bracewell and his permanent successor, Alan Little. Chris would cut his managerial teeth at The Shay, taking over in 2002 and managing more than 300 games before departing in 2008 for a career that took him all the way to the Premier League.

As the managerial merry-go-round at the club indicates, all was not well in the early 2000s. The memories of our promotion back into the Football League quickly faded as we struggled to compete. There was a stay of execution in 2000/01 when we finished two points above bottom side Barnet but there was no escape the next year as we finished 24th and returned once more to non-league. If money for scouting and signings was tight in the Third Division, it was non-existent in the Conference.

Relegation was the final nail in my ambitious scouting project. Soon, the money would not be there to subsidise the club at all. When they reneged on paying expenses to the scouts and me, it was the final straw. I left in 2002. In the years since, the club have lurched from crisis to false dawn and back again. When I do go back to the now redeveloped Shay to watch them play in the National League, it is technically not even the same club, with the original Town having gone into administration in 2008 before re-forming as FC Halifax Town. They still owe me, and many others, money to this day. I won't chase them for it, though. Anything for Halifax Town.

There have been other, greater emotional costs incurred by my commitment to the Shaymen. As I strove to honour my obligations to two professional masters, my second marriage faltered. Brenda and I steadily grew apart. Matters were complicated when I met Maggie, the gorgeous, funny, interesting receptionist of the printers that supplied Town's matchday programmes. I would visit them fortnightly to collect and pay for printouts as part of my role as commercial manager, during which time we struck up a flirtatious friendship. As my role at the club changed, our regular interactions stopped until a chance meeting outside Ripponden School – as I picked up my grandchildren and she one of her children – led to us reconnecting. We chatted, laughed and joked and, despite us both being married, swapped numbers before eventually meeting up.

We quickly realised there was something special between us that was worth pursuing. I found a calmness in Maggie that I needed in my life. As upsetting and difficult as it was, we both owed it to our partners to tell them, leading ultimately to two divorces. It did not happen overnight but the fact that Brenda and her subsequent husband, also called David, are regular guests at Worthington parties and celebrations is a testament to the bond we share and the friendship we have been able to salvage from our failed marriage. She entered my life at a difficult time and made it better. She has been a wonderful second mum to Gary, Keely and Dani and will always be a much-loved part of the family. Maggie and I have been together ever since. However, little did I realise when I reconnected so fortuitously with her outside that humble, little junior school what adventures the next 20 years had in store.

Ten

The Wanderer

(2003–2007)

The Stade Vélodrome is no place for faint-hearted visitors. For much of the week, it rests innocuously in Marseille, just a few kilometres from the southern coast of France. On matchdays, filled to bursting with flare-carrying, scarf-waving, snarling supporters, it transforms into a simmering bowl of fireworks and ferocity.

On this particular Sunday evening, 16 October 2005, the home fans, famed for their inhospitality, are especially roused and raucous. Auxerre are in town and already trailing to Mamadou Niang's second-minute goal.

In the midst of the maelstrom sits a neutral, one of only a few. He is there not to back or bait but to watch and judge the players involved. At various points, he gets out his notebook and pencil and jots his observations. 'Barthez – kicking fine, nothing to do ... Nasri – quick feet, good awareness ... Cana – breaks stuff up, works well.'

The real gem is Franck Ribery, the quick, dangerous forward with an appetite for work and superb vision. Next to his name in the book is a glowing four-line tribute.

After watching him dance past another two challenges before firing a shot just wide to the sound of further 'oohs' and 'aahs', the neutral prepares to put pencil to paper once more. First, though, he offers a wry smile and a shake of the head, one single thought in his mind – how did a simple lad from Shelf end up here?

I OFTEN think back incredulously to the 20 years I spent scouting for Premier League clubs across the globe. Even with the evidence still in my possession, in the shape of my notebooks, I find it hard sometimes to believe that I did, indeed, get paid to tour Europe, to sit in those grand stadiums and watch those great players. Franck Ribery in the Stade Vélodrome merely scratches the surface. There was Kaká and Andriy Shevchenko in the San Siro, Zinedine Zidane and both Ronaldos in the Bernabéu and Lionel Messi, Xavi and more in the Camp Nou. It is even more remarkable when I consider that just months before my great scouting adventure began, at the age of 57, I was earning a living painting and decorating in Calderdale.

With the business sold and Halifax near penniless, I was at something of a rare loose end and in need of a wage. Thankfully, I had maintained a good relationship with Town chairman Jim Brown, who gave me work with his property development company for a time. I also mentored and drove the bus for a local school, until the council discovered I had a conviction for speeding and put a stop to the latter. I supplemented this with expenses from scouting, largely for Boston United, whose boss, Neil Thompson, I knew from the Yorkshire football scene. It wasn't a demanding job – mainly identifying opposition strengths and weaknesses. However, it led me to Wrexham's Racecourse Ground for a game and a chance meeting that would completely alter the course of my life.

Jack Chapman was Bolton's chief scout, a highly respected figure in football circles, not least of all for the pivotal role he had played in helping manager Sam Allardyce lead Wanderers into the Premier League. I knew him a little from the circuit. I didn't know Sam at that point but certainly knew of him. A larger-than-life character, he had played in the same Bolton team as our Frank. The only time our paths had crossed was in the 1972/73 season when the Trotters had played Grimsby. He was a big, bruising centre-half as a player. As a manager, he was similarly uncompromising but smart, innovative and clearly on the way up. On Jack's recommendation, Bolton had recruited a number of supposedly fading European-based stars to boost Sam's side – Bruno N'Gotty, Bernard Mendy, Youri Djorkaeff, Jay-Jay Okocha – all written off by others but, in his mind, ripe for rejuvenation.

Having both left the Wrexham game a little early to beat the traffic, Jack and I struck up conversation as we walked back to our cars. I filled him in on events at Halifax and the help I was giving Thommo at Boston. As we were about to head our separate ways, he made a proposal: 'Why don't you pop over to our place on Monday. We've got a game behind closed doors to help a lad we've signed from Spain fit into position. I'd be keen to see what you think.'

It didn't feel like an interview but, in hindsight, it was of a sort. As I was sitting in the stands at the Reebok Stadium, every kick and shout from the game in front of me echoing around the largely empty stands, I was taken back to my previous trial in the town for this historic club. Wanderers had rejected me as an aspiring 16-year-old striker, setting me off on the path that had now brought me back. I was determined that they thought better of me now, as a scout nearing his 60s.

As Jack had set out, the focus was Bolton's new signing – a stocky lad at centre-back with a healthy tan and mop of curly hair. I knew he had played at the very top level in Spain, for Real Madrid, before joining Bolton on loan. At just over 6ft, he was decent enough in the air and his technique and touch were sound. What really stood out was his exquisite passing. He would take one look up from the edge of his own box and fire inch-perfect passes that landed bang on the foot of the wide men. To the right; ping! To the left; ping! I was jotting such observations down when suddenly he was fed a pass near his own box that put him under pressure from an onrushing centre-forward. I watched on as he took one glance up before he performed a little drag-back to turn, beat his man and then fired another pass out wide. Ping! Moments later, he pulled out another fancy trick to escape pressure near his own area. Were I a fan, I'd have been on my feet cheering. As a scout, I shook my head and jotted down a few more notes.

After the game, Jack came over to ask me what I thought. 'The lad can certainly play,' I told him, buying myself a little time as I considered whether to speak my full mind. 'But ...' I continued. I saw Jack's eyes narrow a touch. 'I think he's too much of a risk at centre-half in the Premier League.' He mulled this over for a moment. 'Go on,' he urged. 'Well, if he tries those fancy turns and tricks on the edge of his own box, gets the ball nicked off him and the opposition score, the gaffer will do his nut. If you want my advice, he'd be better off playing one in front, in defensive midfield. He's a big lad, he'll still win headers and tackles, he'll be able to spray those superb passes about but he'll have people behind him to cover if he tries a trick and loses it.' Jack nodded, mulling it over. 'Hang around for a bit, will you?' he asked. 'I've just got to go see Sam.' After about an hour, he returned with a smile on his face. 'Well,' he began. 'When can you start for us?'

I tried to mask my excitement, calmly telling him that I could begin as soon as they needed, which Jack suggested could be as early as that very evening if I fancied a little detour on my way home to watch Bury reserves. Not even the prospect of a cold, wet evening at glamorous Gigg Lane could halt the internal cartwheels I was performing. Just short of 42 years after my teenage trial, I'd finally convinced Bolton of my worth. I was going to be scouting, with Wanderers, in the Premier League. Flippin' heck!

Years later, I asked Sam if what I had said to Jack on that Monday visit had been the reason they took me on. 'Fucking hell, Worthy, I can't remember that,' he replied in typical jokey fashion. 'But what I liked about you from the very start was that you had an honest opinion and you weren't afraid to share it. That's what Jack and I wanted from a scout.' I'm fortunate that I was brought up to be straight with people but it's not a facet all share, especially in a competitive and occasionally sycophantic world like football. In my opinion, blunt honesty is a quality every manager should demand from those they send out to assess opponents and players and a challenge every scout should back themselves to meet. If you are going to be judged on your opinions, you should ensure they are true to you – put down what you see, not what you think the gaffer wants to see.

I wasn't telling Sam anything he didn't know. As a defender himself, he was knowledgeable enough to recognise the risk posed by an overplaying centre-half in the toughest league in the world. I'm proud, though, that my instincts were born out in the seasons that followed. Iván Campo, the mop-haired Spaniard I was asked to observe that Monday morning at the Reebok, was a superb addition to Bolton's midfield, playing 194 games, during which he mixed his playmaking guile with defensive grit to superb effect. Such was his impact, Sam would repeat the trick the following year with the signing of Fernando Hierro, another Spaniard from Real Madrid who had played much of his career at centre-back. He proved a better, less risky fit at the back for Bolton but occasionally slotted into midfield when Campo was absent, usually through suspension.

When people picture scouts, it tends to be a solo flat cap-wearing sage, watching on secretly from muddy touchlines, a lone maker or breaker of stardom, forever seeking diamonds in the rough. Rarely is it so romantic. At the upper levels of the game, you are seldom the solitary observer and engineer of a transfer; instead, you play your part in a wider team, one pair of eyes amongst many. My career at Bolton began with opposition assessments – an unsexy but staple and necessary part of the job. At its most basic, this involves establishing the formation a team plays, what variants they adopt and why. For example, a team may start 4-4-2 but if they're losing with 20 minutes to go, what is their go-to attacking switch to try and force a goal? One has to be aware and appreciative of the state a game is in and what any changes might be in response to an opponent's tactics or an injury?

Other factors to take into consideration would be what kind of distribution a goalkeeper adopts, does a defence push up and play a high line and how do they pressure the ball across the pitch? Another nut and bolt is set pieces. Who takes a team's corners from right and left? Where does he tend to aim – short, deep, the six-yard box or penalty spot? And which of his team-mates are most dangerous in such scenarios? Do they have a big striker who lurks at the near post for flick-ons or a strapping centre-back who looks to muscle aside his marker to meet the delivery? On top of that, you have licence to identify specific players and any notable strengths that could pose a threat or weaknesses to exploit.

Near the end of the 2002/03 season, I was sent to observe Middlesbrough ahead of their meeting with Bolton on the final day. The norm at the club at that time was to begin opposition assessment at least a month in advance, taking in numerous games – at least three, usually more – to get as accurate a reflection of their qualities as possible. I would not be the only one watching them during this period. A broad canvas of opinion would be sought from a variety of scouts. I quickly zoned in on Boro's left-back,

Franck Queudrue; not for his ability – he was a decent player – but for his attitude. He often reacted aggressively to tackles, drawn in way too easily to petty, unnecessary conflicts. I made a note next to his name in my pad: 'Wind him up, he'll get sent off.' Weeks later, our final game with Middlesbrough came around – a crucial fixture with victory required to keep us in the Premier League. In the second half, with Wanderers holding a far from secure 2-1 lead against a determined Boro, Campo's dive from a Queudrue foul sent the full-back into a rage for which he was booked. Soon after, he sought revenge on Campo, flinging himself wildly into a late challenge for which he was sent off, just as I'd suggested could happen. Clever lad, Dave. It proved a significant moment in my Bolton career, boosting my standing in the eyes of Jack and Sam. That my intuition played a big part in helping the club stave off relegation only enhanced it.

My Bolton career was really supercharged by my decision to leave the UK and move to France, although work wasn't the primary motivation. I had always wanted to see more of Europe and felt the time had come. My kids were grown up and settled, raising families of their own, my work still only part time, thus not tying me rigidly to a place. In February 2003, Maggie and I took a trip to France to seek out a suitable spot for a holiday home. Near the west coast of the country, near to La Rochelle, we discovered the commune of Bernay-Saint-Martin and, within it, the tiny hamlet of Marnay. There was nothing to it – essentially a farm with a tiny row of two-bedroom cottages. It was classically French. At the rear of the buildings ran yellow fields for miles, a sea of sunflowers. Beyond them were green hills, set perfectly beneath cloudless blue skies. I fell in love with the place and the peaceful seclusion it provided, pining for it upon my return to the UK. A few months later, I was the delighted owner of one of the cottages. The pieces were in place for my European adventure. All bar one.

Maggie was excited by the prospect of a new life with me in France but the needs of her current one in the UK were greater. She had young children – Grace and Laura – and old, frail parents, both in need of her care. We resolved that she would remain in Ripponden and I would travel out to France alone. Each month, she would fly out and stay with me for six days – a period of quality time together. Through the dilemma, we discovered the most important quality in our relationship – our understanding of each other and the ability to compromise to keep it strong. It was hard being apart but it had its positives, both in the short and long term. Having undergone my second divorce relatively recently, the isolated tranquility of my new home enabled me to fully process events and clear my head. It also gave me an even greater appreciation for Maggie, my love growing stronger through her absence and my appreciation of our time together enhanced by its rarity. In ways I had not anticipated, it also lit a fire under my scouting career.

I had suggested to Jack before I left that my move need not be the end of my work for Bolton. Far from it. France's Ligue 1 was a good competition. It lacked the class of the Premier League but possessed some high-profile, talented teams – Lyon, Bordeaux, Lens, Auxerre, Marseille. Riches from the Middle East had yet to be pumped into Paris Saint-Germain and Monaco but they were still useful sides. The league had become something of a gateway for South American footballers, notably from Brazil and Argentina, to gain a foothold in Europe. African players from the country's former colonies, such as Senegal and the Ivory Coast, also gravitated there, attracted partly by the shared language. It was a rich market with bargains to be had, especially for a club like Bolton, so reliant on turning their comparatively meagre resources into something far bigger to compete with wealthier rivals. Jack and Sam were clever enough to see the opportunity I presented.

Bolton didn't have an established European scouting set-up back then. Nowadays, every Premier League club worth their salt have a network of eyes and ears on the continent, feeding reports and statistical analysis into vast databases. It is rare that a player with ability sneaks under the radar, regardless of his location. In 2003, the money and global recognition brought about by the rebranding of England's top flight just over a decade earlier had broadened the reach of English clubs but not across the board. Wanderers had people dotted around the continent – notably a Danish lad, who covered Scandinavia – but until I landed in France they were often reliant on media reports and pitches from player agents.

The lack of a formal set-up worked in my favour. I could set the terms, craft an approach in the way I saw fit, as I had endeavoured to do at Halifax. As someone driven and determined, who treasures independence, it was the perfect role, working under a seasoned and smart chief scout in Jack. It had echoes of my move to Barrow in my late teens. I was older and wiser but once again pushing myself out of a comfort zone, laying down a challenge to which I had no choice but to rise.

I began with a couple of games a week. The club paid a small wage and my expenses, which proved crucial when the miles began to clock up. In time, I would traverse what felt like every major (and many a minor) road in France, travelling hundreds of miles to Metz, Nancy and Strasbourg, near the German border, or the south coast's three Ms – Montpellier, Marseille and Monaco. It wasn't comfortable in my little 1.9l Fiat Punto, especially when crossing mountainous regions on the near seven-hour slog to Lyon. Often,

I would stick a sleeping bag in the back and park up in a lay-by for some kip to break up the journey home. Thankfully, my business trips to Scotland in the van had readied me for such rough, ready and often freezing cold nights.

In the early days, I stuck largely to shorter trips – two hours north to watch a Nantes game in the Stade de la Beaujoire or the same south to take in a Bordeaux fixture at the club's bowl-like and largely uncovered Stade Chaban-Delmas. Toulouse, about four hours away, was my very first destination, to see their opening fixture of the 2003/04 season against Strasbourg. I was almost caught out by the queues at the peages, with an added complication of having to lean over my right-hand-drive car to pay, but thankfully made it just in time. It was a decent enough game, ending 1-1, not that results are ever a scout's business. The chief reason I remember it, though, was a Toulouse attacker by the name of Achille Emana Edzimbi.

Emana immediately stood out. He was head and shoulders above everyone else on the pitch. A world beater. He was a decent height, stocky and quick. Every time he received the ball, it was out of his feet and he was off, weaving his way past challenge after challenge. The Strasbourg defence did not know how to handle him, the opposing full-back a nervous wreck by full time. I consulted the notes I'd made before kick-off to find he was just 21 years old. It may take him a little time to settle in England but his fearlessness would put him in good stead, I decided. I came away convinced he could do a job for Bolton, the prospect of unearthing a diamond on my very first assignment rattling excitedly around my head for the whole four-hour journey home. I was straight on the phone when I got in. 'Jack, I think I've found one already,' I blurted down the line. 'Okay, Worthy,' he replied, coolness personified. 'Calm down. I'll call Sam and pass it on. You look through the upcoming fixtures and make it a priority to go and see him again. Make sure you see him in an away game.'

Soon after, I was at Lyon – then the league's best side – to see Toulouse play. I arrived at the Stade de Gerland in plenty of time, eager to see what thrills Emana would provide. Early in the game, the ball came to him but, instead of darting at his man with purpose, he lazily offloaded possession and offered no run for a return ball. Disappointing. The next time, he tried a half-hearted dribble to beat a full-back but was easily tackled and made no attempt to regain the ball. Very disappointing. As the game wore on, it became clear he wasn't really trying, isolating himself out on the right. Could he be injured, I wondered? Or are his team-mates not giving him the ball when he needs? I was making excuses for him. My fears were perhaps closer to the truth – that he was what, in my playing days, we would call a 'homer'. This was a player who would put it in for home games in front of his own supporters but hide in away games when free from significant criticism from the stands. I left downhearted but determined not to give up on him entirely.

Over the course of the next few months, I would return to watch Toulouse a number of times, cautious but hopeful that Emana would produce something to justify my initial excitement. If anything, he got worse. Not only did he look like he was not trying at times, he was genuinely poor. Passes went astray, his control repeatedly let him down and attempts at dribbles ended with him over-running the ball or being easily dispossessed. My brief love affair with the player was over. I phoned Jack. 'I took your advice and watched that lad a few more times,' I told him. 'You were right. I got carried away.' I was again reminded of an incident from my youth, when I had excitedly attempted to rally my Halifax team-mates after pulling a goal back to make it 5-1 against Northampton. Then, it had been Eric and Southy calming their naive colleague. Forty-odd years later, it was Jack. In my enthusiasm, I had learned a golden rule of scouting – you never judge a player on one performance. In future, I would keep my powder dry until I had seen the player on a number of occasions.

Despite the flaws I observed in his game, Emana had a decent career. He played more than 200 games for Toulouse before joining Spanish club Real Betis, where he impressed in La Liga and, following the club's relegation, La Liga 2. He also won 42 caps for Cameroon. It is unlikely he would have worked out at Bolton. Sam's sides, especially those put together to tackle the Premier League, were an effective composite of craft and graft.

Having won promotion, the gaffer slowly integrated players he knew could provide something special, principally, but not exclusively, in an attacking sense – a defence-splitting pass, a dribble to open up a side, a shot from seemingly nothing, executed to perfection. Bolton were not going to dominate games in the Premier League; chances would be limited, so, when they came, Sam needed players with the calmness to pick the right option a high percentage of the time. The cost-effective route to such qualities was to seek out experienced, talented pros written off by bigger clubs because of age or a perception of waning ability. Essentially broken toys from whom Sam hoped to extract a few more years of quality play. However, it could not just be any superstar with something still to give. They had to have the right attitude, fit into the strategy and be willing to exert as well as excel. As with any transfer policy, some succeeded, some did not. Players like Mario Jardel, Javi Moreno, Ibrahima Ba and Vincent Candela all failed to fully fire. Two of the best were already at the club when I arrived – Jay-Jay Okocha and Youri Djorkaeff.

Youri had excelled for a number of top clubs across Europe, as well as playing a key role in France's 1998 World Cup win, before joining us. Then into his mid-30s, he'd lost a yard of pace but not his touch or ability to execute a pass or shot. In 78 Premier League games, he scored 20 times and provided six assists. Jay-Jay was a treat to watch, an enthusiastic showman with the touch and vision to back it up. At times, it was like he had the ball on a string, such was his mastery over it. Sam instructed him to be disciplined in his own half but gave him licence to run riot once he crossed halfway and he duly delivered. Like Youri, Jay-Jay had played for PSG, France's biggest club, but there was little ego to either of them. They truly bought into Bolton, perhaps best illustrated by the dance Jay-Jay and Sam performed together during the lap of honour at the end of the 2003/04 season, in which we finished eighth in the league. There were other big hits, too. Campo and Hierro I've already mentioned. Both joined Wanderers having played for Real Madrid, the biggest club there is, and brought not only supreme technical skill but brilliant reading of a game. From within the UK, former Leeds, Everton and Newcastle midfielder Gary Speed was recruited late in his career to great effect, both as a player and, later, as a coach.

Part of Sam's tactical nous was recognising that he had to surround his aging superstars with energetic younger players willing to run themselves into the ground. Honest, unselfish lads, not necessarily the most talented but with stamina to burn and an innate understanding of the demands of English football. Players like I had once been. Ricardo Gardner was a tireless mainstay of the side at left-back. On the opposite side was Nicky Hunt, who was limited at Premier League level but a real fighter. Henrik Pedersen and then Kevin Davies, with their strength and work off the ball, provided an unrelenting, physical focal point for our attack. Arguably, the best of them came from within the club. Kevin Nolan was a colossus, a big, strong workaholic who would charge from one end of the pitch to the other for 90 minutes every week. He couldn't do what Jay-Jay could with the ball but he provided his colleague with the platform he needed. It is to Kev's huge credit that he played as many games for Bolton as he did – close to 350 – and that he became emblematic of what was the club's most successful Premier League period. He was always eager to learn and improve and, so, it is no surprise to see him now forging a successful coaching career. I'm delighted for him.

As with any functioning football recruitment department, the manager's requirements set the agenda for my assignments. Any scout worth their salt can watch a game of football and point out the most talented players. An effective scout picks out the ones that best complement the club and their needs. I wasn't scouting for Manchester United, Arsenal or Liverpool, whose demands would be different, most likely with a greater focus on the elite tier of talent capable of being the difference in crucial games. My primary job was to seek out able operators with a high workrate and robust character. They had to be physically adept and focussed. The rest – vision, dribbling, flair – came secondary. There was no room for a Barry Tait, the prolific but often lazy goalscorer from my Halifax playing days. Give me a Kevin Davies every day of the week.

At that time, we had a big interest in a midfielder called Florent Balmont, who I first spotted playing for Toulouse on loan from Lyon. I saw him play eight times over the course of 2003/04 and loved him. He was only a small lad, 5ft 6in, but as strong as an ox, with a shaven head to show he meant business. He always showed for the ball, demanding it from his centre-back before turning to drive the team on with a range of precise passing. What I liked most about him was the work he got through during a game. He never stopped running, harrying and tackling, constantly aware of danger and where he needed to be to snuff it out.

I was convinced he could play in any of our three midfield positions but, for whatever reason, a move never materialised. Maybe Sam felt we had sufficient similar players in midfield already or possibly Balmont and his representatives believed he could aim higher than little Bolton. As a scout, you are rarely privy to the conversations that take place beyond your report. He signed for Nice in 2004 and continued to impress before moving on to Lille, for whom he played more than 300 games. One that got away.

Scouts have to quickly learn to let things go. Ultimately, you are powerless amidst the myriad of factors at play in any single football transfer. It is your job to provide insight upon which others – a manager, sporting director or chairman – can act if they see fit. This is not to say you don't feel frustration when a big recommendation of yours is rejected. In that first year, I attended a number of youth tournaments on Jack's suggestion and was regularly struck by one young player in particular – a budding Lyon striker by the name of Karim Benzema. The world has seen enough of him now to know his talent, a combination of strength, skill and goalscoring prowess unmatched by many. Even at such a young age and without a first-team game yet to his name, you could see his potential.

I filed glowing reports and spoke enthusiastically to Jack about him. I received word, possibly from an agent, that a deal may be possible for €1.1m, approximately £750,000. It quickly became clear, though, that Wanderers chairman Phil Gartside was unwilling or unable to part with such a fee for an untested 16-year-old, regardless of his promise. A bigger, richer club could have taken such a calculated risk. Indeed, Arsenal often did at that time on young talent from France. There's every chance they did try for Benzema but found him unwilling to leave Lyon. And if he wouldn't do so for Arsenal, what chance Bolton?

I would watch Benzema often in the coming years and provide a series of glowing reports, praising his touch, awareness and vision. In a game against Toulouse in August 2007, I spoke of him at 19 as 'oozing with confidence, playing some great one-touch balls to create problems ... loves to shoot and his movement good off the last defender's shoulder'. He did eventually leave his hometown club, joining Real Madrid in 2009 for £30m before going on to become the Spanish giants' second-highest ever goalscorer and winning bundles of trophies, including five Champions Leagues. Hindsight is a wonderful thing.

Football folklore is awash with tales of the deals that failed to cross the line, signings that would have made the difference if only they'd happened. But there's never a guarantee that an alternative version of history pans out like the real one. Bolton didn't get Benzema but, as a scout, I can take solace in the fact that I filed honest, accurate reports. I was proven right. I did my job.

My second season at Bolton, 2004/05, brought with it formal recognition – a better wage from the club to go with my expenses. I remained freelance, as I would throughout my scouting career, but the security and implied trust that came with contracted employment was a huge boost to both my bank balance and confidence. The wage did come with one caveat from Sam: 'Worthy, for fuck's sake go and get yourself a proper car.' I think he was worried that I'd end up breaking down on a mountain somewhere en route to watch an average full-back for the third time and never be heard from again. So, I got rid of the staunch little Punto and upgraded to a Renault Megane – an estate that gave me a lot more room for my impromptu roadside sleepovers and was left-hand drive to make the peages easier to navigate.

Two games a week became three, four or more. I constantly refreshed my knowledge of Ligue 1, setting a schedule that took in the top clubs, along with players given glowing reports in *L'Équipe* and other newspapers. I began to cross the borders into Belgium, Germany, Switzerland, Italy and Spain. I was constantly on the move on a non-stop tour of top-flight football grounds, a one-man European scouting machine. I would still keep six days a month largely free for Maggie's visits, although I have to admit she did become my plus one at quite a few grounds. I think her interest was very different to mine, piqued by the aesthetic qualities of the young, fit lads warming up on the touchline.

I still have large binders containing printouts of many of the typed-up scouting reports I supplied during my career, including the seasons I spent at Bolton. They are a treasure trove of information and opinion, sealed in time; a Who's Who of European-based players I felt were worth pursuing in the mid-2000s, as well as an awful lot more who weren't. The style I adopted for general assessments was to have the two teams formations at the top of a page, with a breakdown of each player beneath. I provided comments on each – a few sentences for some, a single line for others. Very rarely would I leave it blank. I discerned a level for each player, from Premier League down to fourth tier of English football (with the odd, very rare 'world class'), and gave them a grade from A to D. 'A' was a recommendation to sign them, 'B' an indication to watch them again ASAP, 'C' suggested they be monitored and 'D' instructed the club forget about them. This dual ranking ensured each player was assessed in isolation and without any preconception. I could identify the level to which they were capable of performing but not in a manner that compromised my all-important view of their display on the day.

For example, every football fan, let alone scout, knew just how good a player Arsenal's Thierry Henry was at that time. He would have walked into Bolton's side and instantly been its best player.

But when I saw him in two international matches for France, against the Republic of Ireland in October 2004, he was poor. The flexibility of the marking system ensured I could mark him as a Premier League player but grade him 'D', suggesting we forget about him on the strength of the display. 'Disgraceful first half,' I wrote in my notes. 'Never tried a leg, had a super 15 mins straight after half-time then went back into his shell because both centre-halves handled him well in different ways.'

I would often be tasked with providing individual reports on players in whom we had a specific interest. For these, I would go into greater detail on a range of traits. There would be nine categories for technical ability, differing slightly for each player depending on their position, with three for tactical awareness, five for athletic prowess and eight for character. Scores ranged from one to ten, meaning players received an overall score out of 250. There are plenty of names contained within my file that would eventually become familiar to Premier League fans, albeit not at Bolton. I enthused about a then 24-year-old midfielder, Yossi Benayoun, over the course of three visits to see him play for Racing Santander in Spain in 2004. On each viewing, I gave him 197 out of 250 and urged the club to sign him, declaring in capitals that he 'WOULD BE A GOOD BUY FOR ANY TEAM!!'

In the end, that team was West Ham, in July 2005. He would go on to play for Liverpool, Chelsea and Arsenal. Marouane Chamakh crops up often. The Bordeaux striker regularly impressed me with his workrate and bravery – two qualities I felt would complement Bolton's style. In September 2004, after seeing him play against Metz, I gave him 187 and wrote: 'I can't see him being prolific, more of a targetman who will chip in with a dozen a season.' He would hit that figure in Ligue 1 but underwhelmed during a seven-year stay in England, predominantly with Arsenal and Crystal Palace.

Eric and Alice Worthington with baby Dave

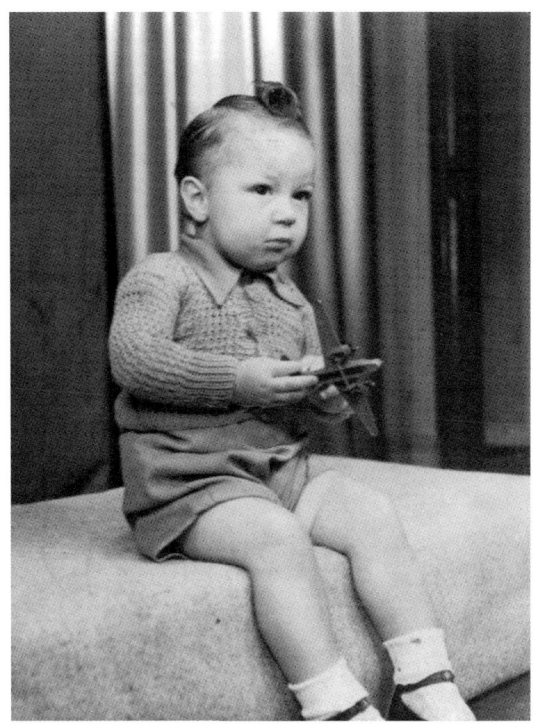

Playing with my war plane and sporting a fine 'brandy snap' curl in my hair

Football in the street in full kit – Left to right: Dave Lewis, John Cutts, Frank, Ken Riley, me and Bob

Captaining Shelf Juniors Under-18s to success aged just 12. To my right is Stuart 'Nipper' Harrison

Reading up on the beautiful game with my dad and brothers. Frank is on the left with Bob leaning over the settee

Always out in front – winning the 800m at Hipperholme School sports day

Lining up for Lightcliffe (bottom row, second from left) between my chief protectors – Jackie Barrett (left) and Brian Hendy (right)

Signing for Halifax Town with Harry Hooper

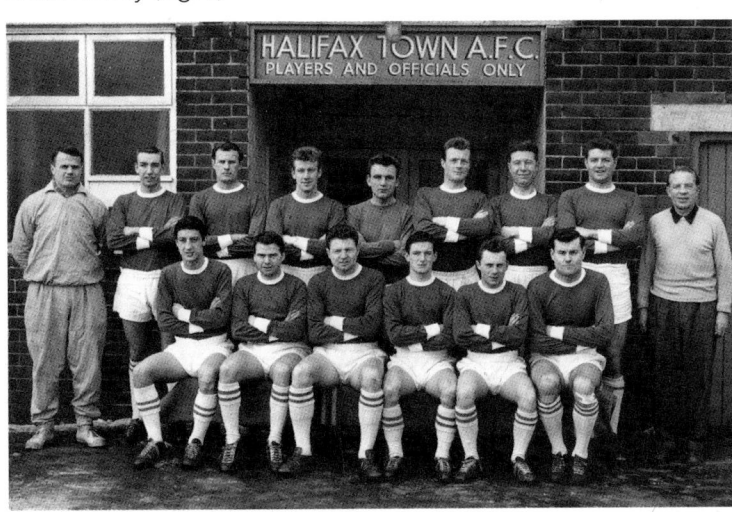

Halifax Town 1963/64 – I sit front row, far left. Behind me, from far left to right are Don McEvoy, Malcolm Russell, Alex South and Eric Harrison

In action for Town as a teenage forward

Barrow 1965/66, captained by Dave Worthington (front, middle)

The Worthington brothers training together at Shelf Hall Park

I look to have given everything at the end of training at Peakes Lane, Grimsby. In the background: Ray Lancaster (crouching), John Wilkinson (sneaking a look at camera) and Jimmy Thompson (with his back to us)

Slotting in a tidy goal at Blundell Park in my early Grimsby days

Honing Gary's left foot during training in the back garden

The Town lads pay a visit to the Grimsby Evening Telegraph – left to right: Alan Campbell, Clive Wigginton, Harry Wainman, Mick Hickman, Jack Lewis, me, Dave Boylen

Proudly showing off the Division Four trophy in Grimsby Town Hall (and sporting some tie!)

Having fun in Spain. Dave Boylen and I helping Clive Wigginton into the pool

The Dynamos squad for my American adventure

Dave Worthington, Halifax Town director/commercial manager/caretaker manager/scout

I was really surprised when Mr Blatter asked if he could have his picture taken with me in 2008!

The greatest 'five-a-side team' of my life – Left to right: Bob, Julie, Frank, mum and me

Maggie and I on our wedding day, in July 2010

Me with my beautiful step-daughters Grace and Laura at my 80th birthday party in 2025

Keeley, Gary and Danielle, filling me with pride for the way they have grown up to be very, very hard-working and wonderful human beings

Hatem Ben Arfa was a great prospect. Even at 18, he shone, thanks to his energy and ability to run with the ball, when I saw him for Lyon in a Ligue 1 game with Sochaux in 2004. 'Watch out Thierry, he will be after your shirt!' I added in my report. I really liked forward Ryan Babel when I saw him play for Ajax against Auxerre in the UEFA Cup in February 2004, marking out his change of pace, quick feet and maturity for an 18-year-old, although I was concerned by his inability to win a header (this was for Bolton, remember). Some familiar names get shorter shrift in my reports. Of 32-year-old former Liverpool forward Vladimir Smicer, off the back of an ineffective, disinterested display for Bordeaux against Nantes in 2005, I wrote: 'Would not play him in Chorley's team.'

Defender Karim Haggui is less well-known in England but someone I rated very highly. A Moroccan defender, I watched him a number of times for Strasbourg and was always struck by his bravery, leadership and eagerness to work for the team. In 2006, with Strasbourg destined for relegation, I urged Bolton to move quickly to sign him but he instead went to Bayer Leverkusen and enjoyed a decent subsequent career in Germany.

Every few months, I would send a list of the best players I had seen from each position to Jack, including where I felt they might fit in at Bolton and any information I might have gleaned from clubs or agents about their availability and likely fee. At the end of 2004/05, my list included a list of young keepers to possibly become understudy to Jääskeläinen, including Metz's Ludovic Butelle and Yohann Pelé of Le Mans. In other positions, the likes of Patrice Evra (then at Monaco), Philippe Mexes (Auxerre), Gerald Cid (Bordeaux), Jeremy Mathieu (Sochaux), Kim Källström (Rennes), Didier Drogba (Marseille) and Djibril Cisse (Auxerre) appeared on my lists. Lyon midfielder Mahamadou Diarra was a regular fixture. He oozed class, a huge talent who was beyond Bolton's reaches but demanded inclusion on any list. It was no surprise to me that he ended up at Real Madrid.

Back in Bolton, Jack and Sam were reaping the rewards of my endeavours. My ever-growing database of reports gave the gaffer not only a vital resource of possible recruits but a useful tool with which to deal with agents. Sam would be beset with calls from player representatives during the day, all of them claiming to speak for the next Henry or Zidane.

Professionalism dictated that these be followed up, to judge for ourselves on their quality – a time-consuming and often wasteful process. With my reports, he had a trustworthy library he could consult when the calls came. If I'd suggested he wasn't Premier League calibre, Sam would call back the agent and make it clear he wasn't interested. My work became his shield.

If I spotted a player and felt he was worth pursuing, Jack, Sam or both would join me at a game to see for themselves. The gaffer was as hands on as he was able, always eager, if possible, to observe players that fit our criteria and passed the initial hurdles of assessment. Throughout the process, he had one primary question for his scouts: 'Is he better than what we've got?' It was drilled into me to view every potential recruit through this prism. I could spot a big, strong, box-to-box midfielder with a tough tackle and ability to impact the game at both ends but I would then have to seriously consider: 'Is he better than Kevin Nolan?' If my conclusion was no, then you could be certain Sam would reject him as a signing.

One midfielder who did pass the test was Abdoulaye Faye, so much so that I risked my job over him. I first took notice of Abdoulaye playing for Istres, on loan from Lens, during the 2004/05 season. I was struck by his size and power. He was strong on the ball, could run and you could see he was tough mentally. He was maybe not the best passer, but decent enough. In one game towards the end of the campaign, against Toulouse, Istres were under the cosh but he never shirked his responsibilities or allowed his head to drop. Late in the first half, he threw himself into a 50-50 tackle and cut this poor bloke in half. He got booked for it but I was impressed by his fearlessness. When he came back out after half-time, I noticed he was limping, possibly injured from the tackle, but he soldiered on. Another positive. In my notes, I made it crystal clear – this lad can do a job for us in the Premier League. We should sign him.

Matters were complicated by Istres' following game at Saint-Étienne, in the season's penultimate round of games. I loved going to the tight, enclosed Stade Geoffroy-Guichard. It was often feisty but never nasty in the way Marseille often was. For some reason, back in my Grimsby playing days I had owned one of their green and-white-striped shirts. So, if I was to claim to have a French team, Les Verts would be the one. Unfortunately for Abdoulaye, he managed to get himself sent off in the game meaning he would miss the final match through suspension. There would be no more opportunities before the summer for Sam to head out and see him.

When I returned to the UK in the off-season, I brought up Faye with the gaffer, urging him to make the signing. Sam was sceptical, having not seen him in person, but I was adamant. After pleading my case, Sam came to my office. 'I'm going to ask you a question, Worthy,' he began. 'You're telling me he's a Premier League player. Would you lose your job over him if he turns out not to be?' He left me to stew on the question. I liked Faye a lot and I backed my judgment – but risk my career on him? I had a family to support. I thought for a moment, went to Sam's office and put my money where my mouth was. 'Yes,' I told him.

Abdoulaye joined us in July 2005, initially on loan before it was made permanent that December. On his debut, as an injury-enforced substitute parachuted into the middle of our defence, he kept Alan Shearer, the Premier League's record goalscorer quiet, as part of a dominant physical display in a 2-0 win. He would play 72 games for us over two years, eventually settling into a superb centre-back partnership with another player I had scouted in France playing for Marseille and recommended, Ivorian defender Abdoulaye Meite. Faye was everything I said he would be – strong, energetic, fearless. Sam loved him. So much so that when he left Bolton for Newcastle, he made the player one of his first signings. I'll always be grateful to him for keeping me in my job with his performances!

There was a downside to Bolton signing a significant number of players of African origin. Every two years, come January, you would lose the most talented to the Africa Cup of Nations. In 2006, four of our important players departed midway through the season – Abdoulaye Faye, his fellow Senegalese, El-Hadji Diouf, Nigerian Jay-Jay and Tunisian Rahdi Jaidi. Prior to the turn of the year, we had been flying high, pushing for a Champions League place. We still competed in January but lacked that bit extra to turn draws into wins, dropping vital points. With Senegal and Nigeria facing each other in the third-place match in that Afcon, our players returned tired. Our results in March and April suffered and we ended up finishing a respectable but ultimately below-par eighth. We also saw our European adventure come to an end in February, with defeat in Marseille. Maggie was in France at the time and we both went to the second leg at the Stade Velodrome, although I possibly wasn't the best company after the linesman missed a clear offside in the build-up to the home side's winner.

It may not have been good for the club, but that year's Afcon was better for me personally, as it provided an unforgettable work trip to a new continent. Sam was keen for me to attend the tournament in Egypt for two reasons – to see what talent might be out there to potentially add to our squad and also to keep an eye on the quartet already on our books and ensure they remained professional. So that we had eyes on as many games as possible, the club sent another scout, Bobby Saxton, to split the workload with myself. Having had a long playing and coaching career, Bobby was a good judge of players but with his own approach to the role. I would tend to make notes on most players during a game but he would keep it short and to the point. His reports would have lots of blank spaces next to names but when he did make an encouraging note, you knew it was worth acting on. I was certainly grateful to see him at a packed and frantic Schiphol airport for the journey out to Cairo. Our intention was to get a nap on the flight but, instead, we found two empty seats near the back of the plane and spent the whole five hours talking football and sharing stories about Sam and our Frank.

We were based in Cairo, where the majority of the games were played, but would often be darting around the north of the country to watch teams play on bare and bobbly surfaces in dilapidated venues in Alexandria, Ismailia and Port Said. The general standard of players at Afcon tournaments at that time was poor, with some nations' players not even of a level I would have considered for Halifax. For a game between Zambia and Guinea in the group stages I have written prominently in capitals across one page of my notebook: 'NOT MANY HERE FOR THE PREMIER LEAGUE.'

There were enough high-profile names and talent on show, though, to make the trip a worthwhile one for scouting purposes.

Some I rated on the day, some not. I saw the hosts play Morocco early on and they had a good side, mainly based at home but with the odd exception, like Tottenham striker Mido ('Can't get a kick,' I wrote. 'Lazy, scruffy, goes down. Poor game'). Ivory Coast I saw a few times, firstly against Libya in the group stages. They were strong, with the Touré brothers, Kolo ('Decent but not troubled. Fine on ball. Did job when needed') and Yaya ('On ball constantly, decent in air. Slow to get back. Casual-looking at times but picked out some great passes. Terrific going forward, lazy getting back') and Chelsea striker Didier Drogba ('Not involved much but picks up goal from rebound off keeper, poor effort throughout'). Arguably the biggest star on show was Barcelona and Cameroon striker Samuel Eto'o, who underwhelmed massively when I watched him against Ivory Coast in the quarter-finals: 'Coward and dropped off straight into the hole to avoid strong challenges from two big lads at back'. On my trips to check up on our lads, I was pleased to find them playing their normal game: 'Abdoulaye Faye – stopped danger, passing simple, snapped No.7 in two in first challenge.'

It wasn't all work. There was scope to experience the culture of Egypt and do some sightseeing on our off days during breaks in the tournament, although Bob couldn't have been less interested. His wife, June, had come out to join him and see some of the country for herself. One day, we dragged him out to Giza to see the pyramids. The 30-minute journey there was an experience in itself. I'd never seen traffic like it nor drivers so careless and risky on a road. As we neared Giza, the sun baking us in the taxi, we passed a dried-up riverbed, in which was laid a dead camel, its legs poking straight up in the air – a fine sight just after breakfast. At the pyramid complex itself, we secured ourselves a tour on what I assumed would be carriages for all three of us. But we were informed that they were for two people only. Not to worry, though, the driver had a colleague behind with a spare horse for me. So off went Bob and June in their carriage, followed closely behind by me on horseback, a traditional headdress on to protect myself from the dust and sun – Worthington of Arabia. By the time we reached the pyramids themselves, Bob had had his fill. He spied a little café with a newsstand nearby and declared: 'You two head off in there, I'm staying here.' We left him sitting contentedly with a coffee and a copy of the *Daily Mirror*, one of the Seven Wonders of the World looming completely ignored behind him. June and I spent our hours exploring the pyramids, marvelling at their structure from the outside before going in to see all the amazing passageways and tombs. We also visited the Tutankhamun Museum on the site. It was a wonderful, unforgettable experience. When we emerged, blinking out into the sun, our minds blown, we sauntered back to the café. There was Bob, still reading his paper.

I was fortunate to be sent to a number of international tournaments during my time at Bolton. Stationed in France, I was a regular at the Toulon Tournament, an event in the Provence-Alpes-Côte d'Azur for under-23 international sides. Many scouts would only show up for the semi-finals and final but I was able to attend the group stages and check out young players with potential from the lesser nations. In 2005, I went to Germany to follow the Confederations Cup, during which I kept an eye on our Greek winger Stelios Giannakopoulos, who we had signed from Olympiakos in 2003. Stelios was a good player, stocky, strong and hard-working with an ability to ghost into the box, unnoticed by defenders. At the same tournament, I scouted Hidetoshi Nakata, the Japanese midfielder who had forged an impressive career in Italy but fallen out of favour at Fiorentina. I was impressed. He had class he could bring to our midfield – another slightly broken toy for Sam to fix. We signed him on loan that August and he did a decent job for us the following season.

While I was in Egypt, Jack was calling it a day back in Bolton. His retirement brought to a close a stellar career and a hugely productive partnership with Sam – one that had helped propel them into the top half of the Premier League. The club explored other options and then, a few months later, much to my surprise and delight, offered me the chance to fill Jack's extremely large shoes. I accepted immediately. Being chief scout meant returning to the UK but no less travelling. I remained constantly on the go, driving over to Bolton from our home in Ripponden five days a week and all over the country to watch games on an evening and at weekends. Often, I would be heading to Leeds/Bradford or Manchester airport early in the morning to fly to Europe to watch players, broadening my remit beyond France to Germany, Italy, the Netherlands, Spain and more.

The role brought with it more organisational responsibility. I was now the head of a network of around 10 to 15 scouts, tasked with overseeing their schedule and liaising with them on reports. I went from answering that all-important question of Sam's – is he better than what we have? – to asking it of my charges. I recruited members to the team, including Dave Verity, who had scouted for me at Halifax and whose opinion I respected. Dave went on to work for Manchester United and Chelsea before calling it a day but, when we meet up now, he often reminds me of the trips I sent him on, especially a three-week jolly in Canada to cover a tournament. You're welcome, Dave!

As a regular member of the recruitment team, especially one based abroad, I rarely saw other staff members and players outside of tri-annual scout meetings and occasional trips to see the first team to refresh my knowledge of their level. With my new role and office at the training ground in Euxton, I got to better know my colleagues, the likes of assistant Sammy Lee and coaches Ricky Spragia, Gary Speed, Neil McDonald and Jimmy Phillips. The role inevitably dictates a much closer relationship with the manager. I became not only quality control between the scouts and Sam but also his confidant on recruitment matters. We would often head out to games together to watch the players that had shone their way through the first phases of assessment.

Sam clearly trusted my judgment when it came to footballers but less so in other areas. On my return to the UK, he got his first look at the car he had insisted I go out and buy to replace the Punto. I was quite proud of my Renault Megane. It had served me well during my long journeys around France, as both a vehicle and makeshift hotel room. As we walked together back to the training ground car park after a day at the coalface, he spotted it and his face twisted in disgust. 'I thought I told you to get a comfortable, reliable, quality car, Worthy!' he declared. Soon after, armed with my chief scout's wage, I went out and bought a lovely, big, brand-new Mercedes.

As a scout, it is rare that you become embroiled in the machinations of a transfer. Usually, your part has been played long before it reaches the stage of a player meeting the manager and other club officials to discuss tactics, fees and contracts. A chief scout is closer to the action, responsible for compiling all reports into a dossier that also includes any information the club may have gleaned on a player's availability. During my time at Bolton, we had a long-standing interest in Icelandic defender Grétar Steinsson. Over the seasons, we built a large file on him, with numerous reports, many of which I supplied. I was impressed by his work ethic, energy, pace and mobility. I was certain he would improve us at right-back, although others, including Sam, were less sure in their own reports. As our interest in him grew, the front page of his dossier became ever more populated with scrawled updates. 'Asked Guðni Bergsson about background, he wants to come to Bolton – been his club from afar, prefers them to any other in Premier League,' read one. 'Club would probably ask €2-2.5m,' stated another. On a Post-it note, I have added, for the attention of Sam: 'Gaffer, this lad played centre-half for Young Boys before Alkmaar. Also left-back. Could solve any problems across the back four.' In July 2007, Steinsson eventually made the move to Bolton, many years after he had first appeared on our radar.

Arguably, the most high-profile transfer in which I was involved at Bolton was the signing of Nicolas Anelka in August 2006. It began with a phone call I received from an agent who knew Nic from his childhood in the Trappes region of Paris. He informed me that his friend was unhappy with his current club – Fenerbahçe in Turkey – and was keen to return to England. In what had been a rollercoaster career, the striker had played his best football in the Premier League, initially at Arsène Wenger's Arsenal and then Manchester City, under Kevin Keegan. In between, he had struggled at Real Madrid, PSG and during a loan spell at Liverpool. He had done fine in Turkey but their Super Lig felt like the fringe of European football, from which he was keen to escape. My initial response to the agent was the obvious one: 'I'm not sure Bolton will be able to afford what Fenerbahçe or the player are after.' He told me not to worry, that he was certain there was a deal to be done. The other elephant in the room related to Nic's reputation. Nicknamed 'Le Sulk' during the back end of his time at Arsenal, the perception that he was moody, difficult and only out for himself had dogged his career. Again, the agent eased my concerns. He had been badly advised in his younger days by those that represented him but they were no longer involved. He was in a serious, positive relationship now, with a Belgian choreographer named Barbara. He had found religion, converting to Islam in 2004. He was changed – a calmer, more settled and focussed individual.

If true and he still possessed the ability seen inconsistently but impressively throughout his career, he would be a huge asset for Bolton. At his best, he was a devastatingly quick and direct forward with superb touch, movement and finishing. An elite footballer. At 27, he was theoretically in his peak years. When I informed Sam, he was understandably sceptical, having heard from plenty of his peers how problematic the Frenchman could be, but told me to get out to Turkey and see for myself if his ability and attitude were up to scratch. Watching in the flesh, his quality was unquestionable and his effort levels high. He could, of course, have been applying himself in order to secure a move but I suspected it came from an honest place. I reported back positively to Sam and a date was set for us to meet with Nic and the agent in the penthouse room of a hotel at Charles de Gaulle Airport.

There, we would pitch the move. Sam was out in Germany for the summer, working on the World Cup as a pundit for ITV, so we both took a short flight over to Paris. Nic barely said a word during what was a lengthy meeting, listening closely as Sam laid out his thoughts on where he would fit into Wanderers' attack. He made it very clear that we were not Manchester City or Liverpool, our style of play would dictate less of the ball and more work. Nic was polite and respectful throughout, sitting patiently through a video we had put together highlighting the places he could live, in Manchester and Cheshire. He left with the promise to inform us of his decision the next day. As we were sitting eating together that evening, Sam was unsure whether we'd done enough but I was confident. 'Gaffer, he was hanging on your every word,' I told him. 'I think he liked what you were saying.' Shortly after my return to the UK, I got a call from Sam. 'Worthy, he's signing, he's coming to Bolton.'

I can't vouch for other scouts but I always had mixed emotions when a player I had provided reports on signed for the club. It was great to see them acting on your insight but once he is in the building that quickly becomes a nervous worry that he won't live up to the billing, especially in the Premier League when the fees spent on signings are so vast. If a club have done their proper due diligence, you won't have been the only scout with eyes on the player but his performances are still a reflection of your judgment. This was even more pronounced with Nic. I had brought the player to Sam and been far more hands on than I had in previous transfers. He had cost £7m, a club record amount for Bolton. If he flopped, the failure would leave a bit of a mark on me. I needn't have been concerned. Nic was superb for us from the off, playing as one third of an effective, interchangeable front three with Kevin Davies and El-Hadji Diouf. Kev was ostensibly the big targetman in the middle but he was capable of pulling wide, having played on the wing previously. Nic and Dioufy were both strong, smart and technically adept enough to play anywhere in a front three. It made them a nightmare to mark. Nic hit double figures for goals in each of his two seasons at Wanderers, scoring 23 in 61 appearances in total. In contrast to his reputation, he was a model professional – quiet, humble and dedicated.

Football is a fickle sport. I was conditioned to its whims via a playing career spent during a time when long contracts did not exist and you had to continually earn the right to play the following season. Clubs could be ruthless if you picked up a bad injury. Contracts are longer and more weighted in favour of players these days but job security in other areas of the modern game remain fragile. When the end came for me at Bolton, I was sad but not entirely surprised. I knew I was vulnerable as soon as Sam resigned as manager towards the end of the 2006/07 season. He felt he had taken the club as far as he could – back into the Premier League and Europe on a comparative shoestring of a budget compared to his rivals. In time, the decline of the club in his absence would prove his point.

That Sam's successor was his assistant, Sammy Lee, gave me hope that I might continue in my role. I was certainly encouraged to believe as much by the warm way in which Sammy treated Maggie and me during a trip to Marrakesh in the summer of 2007 for Nic's wedding celebrations. For two or three weeks after, back in Bolton, it was business as usual but then, out of the blue, Sammy called me to his office and told me he was letting me go. His reasons were clichéd but understandable – with Sam gone and a new season approaching, he wanted a fresh start with his own men in place, including a new chief scout.

It was disappointing to lose a job I loved but I had to take it on the chin. Maggie greeted the news better than I. She found the period I spent as chief scout challenging. We were living under the same roof again but the demands of the job meant we spent less quality time together than when I was abroad and she travelling to see me for six days. Losing my job rankled with me but, for her, the conclusion of my time at Bolton brought relief.

When I reflect now on the time I spent with Wanderers, I do so with a smile. They were five magnificent years, with a club full of good people, relentlessly on the up. The Trotters were my gateway into top-level scouting and a supportive backer as I cut my teeth in the role. In Jack and Sam, I found kindred colleagues who became firm friends. I like to think I gave back to the club in equal measure through my dedication, diligence, miles travelled and multitude of reports provided to help them build and hone a first team capable of taking on the best. I chuckle when I think of Arsène Wenger's visible irritation at seeing his all-conquering Arsenal given another bloody nose by plucky little Bolton during that period. Few managers got under the Frenchman's skin quite like our gaffer. Sam's sides are now ingrained within the club's folklore, the names within them remembered with reverence – Jussi Jääskeläinen, Ricardo Gardner, Tel Ben Haim, Iván Campo, Kevin Nolan, Abdoulaye Faye, Youri Djorkaeff, Jay-Jay Okocha, Kevin Davies, Nicolas Anelka and more. They were an embodiment of the spirit of their manager – relentlessly hard-working, with a bit of swagger and a refusal to kowtow to anyone. It was a group I was proud to have played a part in helping assemble.

In the years since, Sam and I have spoken often about our time together at Bolton. It is humbling to hear him speak so positively about the job I performed, how my move to France was good for me but great for the club. He has expressed regret for how little I was paid, especially in the first few years, for the miles I travelled without proper compensation and the long, cold nights spent sleeping in my car on a French mountain road. 'For the job you did for us,' he once told me, 'we should have paid you a lot more.'

There would be no such concerns at my next club.

11

A Year in the Roman Empire

(2007–2008)

It is a warm June evening in Switzerland and Basel's St Jakob-Park is beginning to stir into life. In 90 minutes time, Portugal will take on Germany in a heavyweight Euro 2008 quarter-final clash. At either end of the ground, fans file in with face paint applied and flags to unfurl.

Above them, in one of the plush executive suites, a group of football's most senior dignitaries are gathered. They are FIFA's top brass, leaders from all seven continents of the globe, powerbrokers of the modern game. At the heart of the group stands Sepp Blatter, the governing body's president and chief decision-maker on the planet's most popular sport.

A few yards to his right, away from suited VIPs, stands a man who is not meant to be there, a lowly scout inconveniently early for a meeting of his own. He is here as the guest of Roman Abramovich, the Chelsea owner – his boss. Somehow, it has fallen on the scout to clear the room ahead of the Russian oligarch's arrival. He watches for his moment, waits for a break in conversation before moving in – a beeline straight for Blatter.

His heart is pumping, nerves jangling. He is moments away from meeting the most influential man in world football. First, though, he must tell the second most powerful to sling his hook.

ROMAN ABRAMOVICH'S arrival at Chelsea changed football in England and beyond. There had been clubs with wealthy, profligate owners before – Jack Walker, for example, bankrolled Blackburn's rise to title winners in 1994/95 – but nothing on the scale witnessed at Stamford Bridge from 2003. The Russian's riches transformed the club into an elite trophy-winning machine. No expense was spared in improving the infrastructure of the club and recruiting the best of world football. In came players like Claude Makélélé, Hernán Crespo, Didier Drogba, Arjen Robben, Michael Ballack, Andriy Shevchenko and many, many more. José Mourinho, the 'Special One', was appointed manager to much fanfare and success. At Bolton, we watched on enviously at the money being spent on players, many of whom I had scouted and recommended to Jack and Sam but who were way out of our budget. I could only dream of having Abramovich's riches underpinning my work.

In the summer of 2007, I was back in France, now living in the south of the country, out of work but with an iron in the fire. Sam had taken over as Newcastle boss that May and had suggested I reunite with him there as a foreign scout once I'd resolved the financial aspects of my departure from Bolton. However, before anything could be signed, I received another call, from Chelsea chief scout Frank Arnesen. I had met Frank once during a scouting trip to Ajax. Ironically, it was Sam that introduced us. I can only assume I left a small impression on him, certainly enough for him to call me now, knowing I was out of work. 'Are you thinking of joining Sam at Newcastle?' he asked me – a leading question. 'Because I was hoping you might come to Chelsea.'

He painted an extremely positive picture of the club. When he then told me what I would be earning, I couldn't help but be excited. It was more than I had earned as chief scout at Bolton.

'Fuuuuucking hell,' declared Sam when I informed him of the numbers. I was thinking the same but it took my old gaffer to voice it in typically to-the-point fashion. 'Listen Worthy, you have to do it for yourself and your family,' he told me, adding prophetically: 'We'll meet up again somewhere else.' And so, on 20 July, I travelled to Chelsea's Cobham training ground to meet Frank, observe the club's first team train and sign a deal to become their scout.

In keeping with the respective sizes of the clubs, the scale and scope of Chelsea's scouting operation far exceeded that at Bolton. The Blues had a 30-strong group scouring the globe for talent, more than twice the number in position at Wanderers. They had people on all the major footballing continents, principally Europe and South America. There were some prominent names. Juan Sol, who had played for Valencia and Real Madrid, covered Spain. Former West Germany international and Scotland Under-21 coach Rainer Bonhof scoured his home country for the club. Back in the UK, the north-west was covered by former Everton player Barry Horne. There were the newer kids on the block, like Lee Congerton, who had coached at Liverpool before Frank recruited him to be UK head scout, seeking out promising young players alongside academy manager Neil Bath. Overseeing it all was former Denmark international Frank, ably assisted by his No.2 – ex-Netherlands international Hans Gillhaus. It was finely tuned, well embedded and very professional.

I became the second Worthington in their ranks. Our Gary was already in place, having joined as a coach from Leeds before becoming a senior scout. I would see him around the place now and again, at scouts' meetings and the occasional game on the continent, but we were largely kept apart, he working mainly out of the UK and me on a constant expedition around western Europe.

Frank and I devised a plan whereby I would work in conjunction with Guy Hillion, the club's man in the north of France, and Carlo Jacomuzzi, who covered Italy and Switzerland. Based as I was in the south, I could cover the games they were unable to attend because of schedule or travel restrictions. It meant a lot more trips to Marseille, Monaco and Montpellier. It also brought new adventures, crossing the Alps by car to visit Juventus' Stadio delle Alpi or the magnificent San Siro to watch the two Milan clubs, AC and Inter. There was also the occasional Swiss sojourn, to see FC Basel, Young Boys of Bern and Grasshopper Club Zürich. It dictated ever more miles for the Mercedes, in tricky conditions and on occasionally treacherous terrain, and that was before I even got to Italy and faced the cut-throat madness of the locals' driving!

The ethos at Chelsea was always to seek out the very best, a gold-plated version of Sam's 'are they better than what we have?' mantra. They already possessed a stellar squad, arguably the best in England, if not Europe. They had Petr Čech in goal, John Terry, Ashley Cole, Paulo Ferreira and Ricardo Carvalho in defence, Frank Lampard, Joe Cole, Michael Essien and Ballack in midfield and Drogba and Shevchenko up front. Then there were Alex, Juliano Belletti, Shaun Wright-Phillips, Makélélé and Salomon Kalou – all internationals, all world class. In the summer, they had added a familiar face from my Bolton days, Tal Ben Haim, and French winger Florent Malouda, who I had scouted numerous times at Lyon and rated highly. From watching them train on that initial visit to Cobham, I knew they had the capacity to challenge on all fronts in the coming season.

Money was no issue. Hundreds of millions had already been spent. They had recently broken the British transfer record to sign Shevchenko and it was clear they would have no qualms about doing so again for the right player. Such a situation is what you dream of as a scout – no financial barrier, every player an option. In theory, it frees you to judge with impunity. However, the reality is not so liberating. While the pool is bigger, the number of players who are actually better than those already in your squad is tiny. How many attacking midfielders were as effective in front of goal as Frank Lampard at that time? How many centre-backs as dominant and consistent as John Terry? You would do well to find a left-back with as good an all-round game as Ashley Cole or a striker who could lead the line with the same pace and power as Didier Drogba.

That Chelsea had such resources and were seeking the cream of the crop afforded them a more discerning approach. Time could be taken. This was another reason for the big scouting department – they wanted players to be assessed as thoroughly as possible, by multiple scouts over many, many games. An individual could be watched on at least eight or nine occasions, with reports from a variety of voices. A dossier would be built and filled with reports. With such huge sums on the table, there was no room for error.

Of course, players remain human, frail and fallible. You can still be caught out by the unobservable or unexpected. Having scouts who have played the game and are, thus, experienced and empathetic to the manner in which life can impact a player's performance helps mitigate this but not completely eradicate it. I remember during my own playing days the impact that a night's sleep lost to a crying baby had on me. All it needs is a few of these and your stamina for a game can be heavily impaired.

Branislav Ivanovic is a good test case. Midway through my time at Chelsea, the club signed the highly rated full-back from Lokomotiv Moscow for around £10m, beating off strong competition from Europe's elite to do so. He was given the No.2 shirt – an indication that much was expected. However, he arrived rusty from the Russian off-season and couldn't get a look-in for an admittedly flourishing first team. At 24, he was still young and his confidence suffered, making him an even less viable option for the manager. A vicious cycle. He would not make his debut until a month into the following season. Ivanovic would go on to be a superb signing – a big, strong, mobile full-back, tough in the tackle but with something to offer in attack. But no scout could have spotted the troubles he would endure early on.

Interestingly, the very first scouts' meeting I attended at Chelsea was heavily centred around a search that would lead to Ivanovic's signing. The reason I remember it so well is that it also constituted my one meaningful interaction as a Chelsea scout with Mourinho. We had met once before, when I was on a mission for Bolton at the Parc des Princes and found myself sitting next to him and his coach, André Villas-Boas, who I knew a little. We chatted during the game and, at half-time, José headed off to hospitality to get a drink. A few minutes later, André's phone rang. 'Hello. Yep, yeah, okay, I'll tell him,' I heard him say before hanging up and turning to me. 'That was José. He says to tell you Bolton are drawing 1-1.' It wasn't a big thing but illustrated the man's thoughtfulness. At the scouts' meeting at Cobham, José came in to address all the gathered scouts, explaining that the first team would possibly need a new right full-back in the coming season and to focus our efforts on this specific area. I felt I needed more detail and raised my hand to speak. The focus of the room turned in my direction. 'Excuse me,' I began. 'But what sort of right-back are you wanting? Is it a proper defender, someone who does his job at the back first and foremost and looks to get forward when the opportunity arises? Or are you wanting someone who wears a No.2 and starts at right-back but is essentially a right-winger, rarely getting back to defend?' I knew that, in my day, the full-back role meant stopping a winger and working with the centre-backs, keeping the defensive line straight for offsides. I was willing to get up and down and had the energy to do so but knew my primary objective was to defend.

The modern game had started to see the introduction of wing-backs – players who were essentially wingers and whose objective was to attack, often leaving big holes in behind. José told me he wanted a defender. Someone who would do his duty at the back and get forward when asked. The eyes of the room shifted away from me. It was nerve-racking to put my hand up and address the boss in a room full of renowned former players and esteemed scouts, especially as one of the new boys, but I was proud of myself for doing so.

In September 2007, not long after that meeting, José left Chelsea amid a media frenzy. His working relationship with Abramovich had become strained and the club felt this had contributed to our indifferent early season results. I was sad to see José leave. On the few occasions I met him, I found him to be a thoroughly decent man. Somewhat surprisingly, former Israel boss Avram Grant, who had come in as director of football in the summer, took over as manager. He would get the squad punching its weight, leading them to a second-placed finish in the league off the back of a 21-game unbeaten run over the back half of the season. He also led the club to two finals – the League Cup and Champions League – although we would end the campaign trophyless. This was a high crime in the Abramovich era.

Scouts are largely detached from in-season drama at a club. Results on the field and managerial changes impact on your work but do not fundamentally alter the mission. You are part of a team within a team, focussed not on what your club does on the pitch but what the players of other teams do on fields elsewhere. While, at Stamford Bridge, Čech made saves, Terry flew into tackles and Lampard scored goals, I was hot-footing it around Europe at the request of the chief scout, liaising with Carlo and Guy over which games to attend and which players to watch.

It was the same non-stop working tour of the continent as I had experienced at Bolton but with some key differences. I began to factor in more international games featuring the world's highest-ranking sides. On 13 October 2007, I travelled to Brussels to watch a Belgium team containing a number of future Premier League players draw 0-0 with Finland in a Euro 2008 qualifier. I came away impressed by the technique and link-up play of future Tottenham player Mousa Dembélé. Four days later, I was in Paris to see an all-star France beat Lithuania and was tasked with keeping a watchful eye on two Chelsea players – Claude Makélélé and Florent Malouda – as well as the vast array of talent around them. Once again, Benzema caught the eye, earning an 'A' from me for his display. I added in my notes to the club: 'This boy will go to Real Madrid, Barcelona or Milan if we do not get in quick.'

I attended more fixtures in European club competitions, especially in the Champions League. They showcased many of the usual suspects – Roma and the two Milan sides in Italy, Barcelona and Real Madrid in Spain. These were showpiece games, played under floodlights in crackling atmospheres. The best against the best, laying bare a player's ability under pressure. The top players – those sought by Chelsea – would shine. I regularly praised AC Milan's Brazilian forward Kaká, declaring in my assessment of his display against Benfica in September 2007 that 'his touch, pace and strength, vision, inventiveness and awareness would be wonderful at Chelsea'. And everywhere else, too!

It was often best to watch teams against English opposition if possible, to try and effectively gauge a player's suitability for the Premier League. I could see Marseille brush aside average Ligue 1 opponents most weeks but that risked giving a warped impression of the ability of some of their players. Put them up against Liverpool in a Champions League group stage game, though, and you would see what Samir Nasri really had to offer. For the record, my reports on the future Arsenal and Manchester City midfielder speak of a very able but inconsistent talent, good on the ball, with quick feet, but occasionally lacking in his decision-making.

The initial list of players I supplied to Frank in August 2007 reflected the higher bracket in which I was now operating – Kaká, Samuel Eto'o of Barcelona, Ajax's Wesley Sneijder and Porto's Ricardo Quaresma, who would join the Blues on loan in 2009. That list is also replete with young, promising players I felt had the highest ceiling. Some would go to the very top, while others failed to meet their potential. They include goalkeepers Manuel Neuer (21 years old and then at Schalke) and Hugo Lloris (20 and at Nice), defenders Ezequiel Garay (20, Racing Santander) and Andrea Ranocchia (19, Arezzo), midfielders Moustapha Bayal Sal, Blaise Matuidi and Dimitri Payet (all 21 and playing for Saint-Étienne) and forwards Benzema and David N'Gog (18, Paris Saint-Germain).

Over the course of the season, other young talents caught my eye. I was especially impressed by Bordeaux's 18-year-old winger Gabriel Obertan, giving him an 'A' for his display against Austria Vienna in a UEFA Cup tie in November. 'He wanted every ball to feet,' I wrote. 'He showed tremendous touches, good awareness in creating space; he has class, balance and pace. Needs more strength but will be a class act soon.' Scouts from Manchester United clearly agreed with me, as the player joined them in the summer of 2009. He would produce a few flashes of the brilliance I had seen but ultimately disappointed at Old Trafford and during a subsequent spell at Newcastle.

As part of my Swiss duties, I went to Basel, tasked with observing forward Xherdan Shaqiri, then a largely unknown

16-year-old beginning to make an impression in the second team. Small, stocky and skilful, I could see why I'd been sent to check on him but I came away unimpressed. I felt he had a touch of laziness and arrogance that impacted on his application for the team. Such behaviours can be knocked out of a young player with time and experience but it is impossible to predict. Growing up in Shelf, I played alongside kids with more ability than me and, then, more likely to go pro. It would only be later – when surrounded by the distractions of an adult world – that my greater dedication came to the fore. It is the reason I have never felt comfortable scouting youth players. I prefer to judge an individual when they are older and you can be more confident of observing something closer to the finished product, as a player and person.

An illustrative example of this came later in my career, when I was sent to Denmark to watch a game featuring a 16-year-old Martin Ødegaard. He had clear talent but my overriding critique was that he was an arrogant little sod. He strutted around the pitch, trying too many clever little flicks and tricks (in scouting you often hear people refer to a 'flicks and tricks man' to describe a player with good ability but dubious team effort). When they didn't come off, he sulked rather than trying to win the ball back. I found out afterwards that he had already agreed a deal to sign for Real Madrid. Maybe he thought he'd already made it? For whatever reason, it didn't work out for him in Spain but that failure was the making of him. Now older and wiser at Arsenal, I consider him one of the best – if not *the* best – midfielders in the Premier League. The cocky kid I witnessed in Denmark has become a true team player, a captain, almost understated in his brilliance. Shaqiri's ability earned him a few big moves, too – Bayern Munich, Inter Milan and Liverpool are fine additions to any player's CV. However, unlike Ødegaard, he never changed my initial opinion of him.

Another young player I watched during this period was Eden Hazard, also 16 and excelling for Lille's second team. It was clear to me, even then, that he was destined for the top. We had been instructed at a scouts' meeting towards the end of 2007 that the club wanted an attacking midfielder who could hold the ball but was also creative. It was a bit too soon to expect a raw, teenage Hazard to perform such a job in the Premier League but a few years later he would do just that and more for the club. I wonder if the reports I filed as far back as 2007 were still floating around when the Blues finally made their move to recruit the Belgian midfielder in 2012?

In the meantime, while they waited for Hazard to mature, the club signed Deco from Barcelona in the summer of 2008.

I was also able to check in on my old friend Achille Emana Edzimbi. I left Toulouse versus Lyon on 11 August 2007 having given him a 'D' and stating he was no better than the third tier in English football. 'I cannot understand why he is still playing at this level,' was my damning assessment.

One player I was able to recommend to the club with little extra scouting was Nicolas Anelka, who was mending his reputation at my former club. With Drogba and Kalou away at the Africa Cup of Nations and Shevchenko injured and out of form, Anelka became an enticing option. I attended France's Euro 2008 qualifier with Scotland in September 2007 to witness him put on a superb display in an otherwise drab French performance. Nic worked the frontline virtually on his own. 'Sublime touch always,' I wrote. 'Graceful and athletic, linked brilliantly, stretched defenders.' I gave his display an 'A'. That I was able to vouch for him as a person as well as laud his ability helped to convince the club he was the right man. For Nic, it was his chance to return to an elite club challenging at the very top. He wasn't an instant success but his four seasons, during which he scored 59 goals, made his £15m fee look a snip.

I understood Nic's choice. With all due respect to my previous club, Chelsea's name carried extra clout, something I experienced myself as a scout. Previously, upon arriving at grounds in France, Italy and Spain, I would often have to slowly repeat the name 'Bolton' to a confused-looking staff member through a ticket office window. 'Ah sì, Boool-ton,' they would say after running their finger down the list in front of them. I would then be handed a piece of paper with an apologetic shrug. As a Chelsea scout, I only needed to mention the club's name once before being ushered in with a smile and impressed nod. It always felt like the seats were better, too.

Barcelona took it to a whole new level. Literally. The area for scouts at the Camp Nou is high in the stand, requiring lift access. Once there, you are treated to a standard of luxury unlike anywhere else. You are first treated to a huge room with coloured lights everywhere, TV screens showing famous old footage and more recent highlights, live music and food and drink readily available. You are then ushered to a private box to view the game. You almost forget that you have a job to do.

There was one notable downside to being a scout for a club of Chelsea's size and financial might – unscrupulous agents. As a player, I needed not worry about their often draining presence. They simply weren't a common part of football back then. But over the years since, the industry has grown in prominence. The arrival of the Premier League and the ever-increasing amounts of money it generated saw an influx of canny operators and opportunists looking to skim a bit of cream off the top of six-figure player wages and transfer fees that had inflated into the tens of millions. I was fortunate that they would largely bypass me in my early scouting days at Bolton but as soon as Wanderers became a fixture in the top half of the league table and entered European competition, they would circle.

I liked to arrive early at games, to begin my research and preparation. It wouldn't be long before I felt a tap on my shoulder followed by the familiar sales pitch. 'Hi, I'm X's agent, here's my card, he's a great player, he could do a wonderful job in the Premier League, blah, blah, blah.' Others would come and sit with me during the game, distracting me throughout with a glowing summary of their client's performance. Any initial politeness I could muster would soon run dry.

While at Bolton, I met an agent who was especially pushy about his player, a Burkina Faso international striker called Moumouni Dagano, who was then playing for En Avant Guingamp in France. 'You must see him, you must,' he told me. 'He can easily play in the Premier League, easily play for Bolton; he will be the next Drogba, I promise you.' I arranged to go and watch him play and quickly realised he had been oversold. The next time we spoke, I made my opinion clear. 'But he is a Burkina Faso international,' he protested. Looking at the player's career since Guingamp, I am content with my decision.

It can be frustrating and exhausting dealing with the nonsense from some agents but it has become a necessary byproduct of working in football recruitment. In amongst the disingenuous operators are honest, decent professionals, working hard for their clients. It is through a scout's relationship with them that the foundation for many a deal is laid. It would be naive to think that conversations do not take place between the representatives of a player and a club interested in buying them before an approach is made to his current employer. The player's interest in a move and the buyer's ability to afford his wage demands need to be ascertained, otherwise it is a waste of time and energy for all involved.

I've become friends with a number of agents over the years. Bibian Weggelaar is one. I would meet often with her and her colleague, Joaquín Macanás, at their offices in Barcelona to discuss players. They were good, trustworthy people. Even now, Bibian likes to remind me of the time she tried to push one of her players to me as a potential signing. He was a Brazilian who had spent five years impressing at Sevilla but was eager to step up. 'He is unbelievable,' she told me. 'A brilliant full-back. He has played 150 games in Spain, he has played for the Brazil national side. He can be the best in the world.' I had seen the player a number of times before and was very impressed but I was adamant he was not a right-back, a position I knew a little about. For me, he was a right-winger, with his only urge being to go forward and to get in crosses and shots. As a wing-back in a five-man defence, he could work in the Premier League but in a back four, he would leave his team too exposed. The player moved in 2008 to Barcelona, where he won six La Liga titles, four Copa del Reys, three Champions Leagues and a trio of Club World Cups. He is widely regarded as one of the best full-backs to play the game. His name? Dani Alves.

It might seem stubborn but I still hold to my opinion. He found the right team at the right time – one with a manager, in Pep Guardiola, and a tactical approach and dominance that allowed him to thrive. Would he have worked as a flying, attack-minded full-back in a Mourinho Chelsea side? In the years to come, I would return often to Bibian's offices to be met by walls adorned with images of Alves, television screens playing footage of his greatest hits and memorabilia adorned with his signature. In the middle would be Bibian, a smirk on her face. In 2013, she invited me to the screening of a film about the Brazilian, where she introduced me to him. If he was aware of what I had said years earlier, he was good enough not to mention it.

Mike Morris is another agent with whom I became friendly. A different character to Bibian, Mike used to be a car tyre fitter in Manchester, through which he got to know and socialise with a number of footballers, including Sam, our Frank and Peter Reid when they were Wanderers players. It was the association he needed to gain access to football agency – a world in which he thrived. He ended up in Monaco and played a big role in helping Arsène Wenger sign many of the French superstars that formed his all-conquering Arsenal teams of the early 2000s. His position in France also meant he was very useful to me in finding out details on Ligue 1 players of interest to Bolton and then Chelsea. It was seeing the life Mike made for himself that truly brought home to me the amount of money that had entered the game. He was kind enough one time to allow Maggie and I stay in his apartment for a few days while he was away, telling us to help ourselves to some of the many bottles of expensive champagne he kept receiving as gifts for securing deals. There was a moment of panic when we forgot the code to exit the underground car park but once someone had rescued us and we made our way upstairs, we could only marvel at the place. It was beautiful, the 13th floor of an apartment block on a hairpin bend of the Circuit de Monaco – the track for the Formula One Grand Prix in the Principality. Maggie and I sat out on his balcony, a bottle of champagne each, taking in a panoramic view of Port Hercule and its many moored super yachts. A different world.

The opulence of my trip to Monaco was merely the hors d'oeuvre for a memorable meal with one of the game's real financial powerbrokers. My only meaningful interaction with Roman Abramovich, the Chelsea owner, my boss, came at the Euro 2008 quarter-final game between Germany and Portugal, for which I was invited to dine with him in the private box he had secured for the game. Having invested such vast sums into the club, he was clearly keen to hear first-hand about the players on whom some of his riches may soon be invested. I had been stationed in Switzerland during the tournament, watching games in Geneva, Bern and Zürich.

Portugal were my primary focus, which was understandable considering the number of their players Chelsea had signed in recent seasons. Two members of that Euro 2008 squad, Paulo Ferreira and Ricardo Carvalho, were already on the club's books and three more would join during the 2008/09 season – José Bosingwa and Deco that summer and Quaresma in January. On the evidence of the group stage games, I felt right-back Bosingwa to be a pacey asset going forward but woeful as a defender, bordering on the irresponsible. Deco was occasionally sloppy in possession and lacked some pace but his speed of thought and skill on the ball got him by. Of Quaresma, who only started the final group game, I wrote: 'This lad has unbelievable quality and control, oozing confidence and ability … needs someone to get hold of him now and sort him as a team player; he has everything.'

Of further interest to me as a scout was the fact that Portugal's manager, Luiz Felipe Scolari, had agreed to succeed Avram Grant as Blues boss for the 2008/09 season. Seeing their games gave me some insight into how the new gaffer liked his sides to play and what players might suit his approach.

At the ground, I was met by one of Abramovich's security guards, who led me up to the private box, where I presumed I would meet the top man. Instead, I found myself in a room full of dignitaries, there for a meeting that had overrun. And that is how it came to pass that I, Dave Worthington from Shelf, former Halifax and Grimsby full-back, came to be face to face with FIFA president Sepp Blatter, telling him he had to leave so that I could have my dinner. He could not have been more polite and agreeable, even when I stopped him to ask if we could have our photo taken together.

After such excitement, I had to recompose myself again for the arrival of Abramovich and his other guests, including some of his family and friends. I found him to be extremely charming. His wealth was clear from the immaculate way he dressed and the fact the room was dotted with bodyguards but he seemed very down to earth. It was also clear he was a huge football fan. He spoke with real joy and excitement about the game – matches he had seen, players he loved. He was not only passionate but extremely serious about Chelsea. He was hands on and wanted Frank Arnesen to keep him in the loop on everything that was going on regarding players and recruitment. Who were the scouts recommending? What players were we interested in? Was there anybody he hadn't heard of? As one of his club's European scouts, he spied an opportunity to give me a bit of a grilling.

Midway through the meal, he turned to me and said: 'So, Frank tells me we are having a good look at Gomis.' Over the course of the season, I'd been to watch the French striker Bafétimbi Gomis play for Saint-Étienne a number of times, including just recently. He had scored 16 goals in 35 games in Ligue 1 but I had come away unimpressed on each occasion. Immobile and lacking control, I often felt he wasn't making enough effort. Not only did I state he wasn't a Chelsea level player, I indicated that, in my opinion, he wasn't even good enough for the Premier League. 'No, I don't like him,' I told Abramovich. 'He's not very good. Not for us.' There was a moment of silence. The owner stared back at me with a very confused expression on his face. 'But Frank tells me he is an excellent player,' he said. 'He scores lots of goals and is worth a lot of money.' Suddenly, I felt a little rush of panic. This is the top man at the club, my employer, and I'm breaking ranks to slate a player Frank has backed. I've always held firm to the belief that you speak your mind but I was suddenly fearful that I was dropping Frank in the soup. Or worse, talking myself out of a job! Abramovich turned away to engage in another conversation as I pushed food around my plate, trying to work out where I'd gone wrong. Then it dawned on me; he wasn't talking about Gomis, he was referring to a different player, Mario Gómez. Of course he was. Gómez was a young German international striker who had scored nearly a goal a game for Stuttgart the season before and was on the radar of every top club in Europe; the player who was warming up for that night's game a hundred or so yards away from us at that very moment. You idiot, Dave. I attracted my boss' attention again. 'I think we're at crossed purposes here, Mr Abramovich,' I said. 'You're talking about a player from Germany and I'm talking about one from France. You mean Mario Gómez.' He smiled. 'Yes, yes, Mario Gómez,' he replied, although he was possibly thinking, 'What sort of a scout have I got here?!' I have to admit, for purely selfish reasons, I was quite pleased a few years later to see Gomis join Swansea in the Premier League and do okay but not great. I had left Chelsea by then but I'd like to think Abramovich remembered our conversation and thought: 'At least Dave got that one right.'

I was very happy at Chelsea, not just because of the money. It was a brilliant club to work for, with supremely talented people. As a recruitment team, we enjoyed our opportunities to socialise, going out for meals after meetings. During them, plenty would be drunk and, afterwards, Juan Sol would get up to sing beautifully. For the Champions League Final in Moscow at the end of the season, the club flew us all out to watch our dramatic game with Manchester United. We had a brief amount of time to head into the city and see Red Square and the Kremlin before heading to the ground to get soaked through and watch United win the contest on penalties. Needless to say, because of my fondness for the Red Devils, I was less upset about the outcome than a lot of my colleagues. I think I did well not to let my happiness show.

I suppose there was an aptness to the way my time at the club ended. Chelsea had the wealthiest backer but even he was not immune to market forces. The 2008 global financial crash took its toll on most, including Abramovich. A restructuring of the club's recruitment team had been planned but the poor economic climate hastened it, with 15 scouts losing their jobs in November 2008. I was one of them. Money was predominantly the reason I joined Chelsea and it also brought my brief time at the club to a close.

12

Spain, Trains and Automobiles

(2008–2015)

Scouting report for Sunderland AFC
Date: Sunday, 8 January 2012
Game: Espanyol 1-1 Barcelona
Report by: Dave Worthington

Barcelona player comments (same for every player):

Any of these players on their day would improve our team but we would not be able to meet their wage demands. Some were never really tested by the opposition and two or three, including Messi, were having a quiet night but there is little point in writing or recommending this squad of top players.

IN MANY ways, Chelsea was the pinnacle of my scouting career. I would work for other big, historic teams but none of them with the same financial might or draw. It had been a dizzying, gilded and privileged 12 months, unlike any I would experience again. It was not my intention to do so, at least not consciously, but my response to leaving the Blues would be a return to more humble and familiar professional environments. Over seven subsequent years, I found employment with four clubs outside of the elite, with stature and budgets that meant the targeting of a broader but less brilliant pool of players, clubs whose primary aim was to remain in the Premier

League rather than win it, clubs with pluck and passion rather than endless cash and clout.

Either side of working for Sunderland for two seasons from 2011 to 2013, I would spend a couple of campaigns with both Blackburn Rovers (June 2009–June 2011) and West Ham United (July 2013–July 2015), both coming about because of the presence there of my old Wanderers gaffer, Sam Allardyce. It was like slipping back into a pair of comfortable shoes. I knew Sam's methods, knew the type and standard of player he wanted and the work he would demand from his scouting staff.

Hull City, my first post-Chelsea employer, who I joined for a seven-month spell in November of 2008, were practically 'Bolton Lite'. Manager Phil Brown had been Sam's assistant for six years at the Trotters before becoming boss at Derby County and then the Tigers. He had brought in an able ex-colleague of mine from the recruitment team, Bob Shaw, to be his chief scout. Together, they had built a team that earned promotion to the Premier League via the play-offs and was now ready to kick on and give the top flight a bloody nose. Very Bolton.

I firstly had to reset my player radar. No longer would I be able to realistically recommend Europe's elite players to my constrained new employers, as I had at free-spending Chelsea. I would continue to provide reports on the best of the best – professionalism demanded it – but I would not do so with the same zeal. Instead, my focus would be on the best of the rest – players who did not produce with the same unerring consistency as their elite peers but still had the capacity to impact games in England's top flight. For teams with limited budgets, identifying a willing and available player like Jay-Jay Okocha could be the key to realising their ambition.

With such clubs, the athletic and character traits of a player come more to the fore. I could forgive an occasional lapse in ball control or passing accuracy if I felt they had the stamina and drive to keep going for 90 minutes. Only hitting a team-mate with one out of six or seven crosses is not a sin if that one creates a good goalscoring chance or they then work their socks off to regain the lost ball. Are they competitive? Are they a team player? Do they work, do they fight? If Hull or West Ham were to defy the odds and stay in the Premier League straight after promotion, they would need a firm 'yes' to all of these questions. If Blackburn and Sunderland wanted to arrest their slide into the bottom half of the table, such players could prove invaluable.

Identifying strong mental traits in a player is often tougher than spotting the technical skills so clearly on show in a game. A player's behaviour in and around a match provides key indicators. Observing the warm-up was an important part of my routine in this regard. In my early days scouting at Bolton, I watched one substitute, who had been left out of the starting XI from the week before, actively disrupting a pre-game drill with his surly behaviour. For me, such a lack of professionalism prompts an immediate black mark. The in-game signs are more subtle – an unwillingness to track back or, like the old team-mate of mine at Southend, a habit of shifting the ball to an equally under-pressure team-mate to avoid looking culpable for a mistake.

When I scouted games featuring Italian side Palermo during my time at Hull, agents would approach me to preach the virtues of then 20-year-old Danish centre-half Simon Kjær. He certainly looked the part – 6ft 3in and blonde with a quick turn of pace for a defender and decent with the ball at his feet. However, he would regularly do things in a game that made me question his mental suitability for the very top. He did not commit wholeheartedly to every aerial challenge and would occasionally pull out of a 50/50 tackle. To me, such habits suggest a player is not tough enough. I was scouting for the Premier League, the best division in Europe, if not the world, and which featured the most able strikers, sharp and ruthless. In such company, a defender who pulls his tackles or is half a yard late to a ball is toast. I would see plenty of him during my career, playing for Lille, Sevilla and AC Milan, all fine clubs. He would play an impressive 132 times for Denmark, so he clearly had ability. But I would not have been comfortable with him in my team, facing up to Didier Drogba, Fernando Torres or Wayne Rooney.

Sam's old mantra returned to my work with a renewed import, 'Are they better than what we've got?' rattling around my head as I watched every potential new recruit. Each season involved a continual process of refreshing my take on our players to use as a barometer for those I was watching. I'd sit at Montpellier wondering if a central midfielder I'd noticed was better than Blackburn's David Dunn? At Espanyol, I would ponder if an able full-back had enough about him to take Phil Bardsley's spot at Sunderland.

At some of the clubs, the bar to gain a positive answer to the question was lower. When I joined them, Hull and West Ham had both just come up from the second tier, with squads comprising players befitting of that level but not necessarily the one above. Even in the late 2000s and early 2010s, the gulf between the two leagues was vast. On a pure technical level, many of the players I scouted were superior but that's only part of the battle. The incumbents had demonstrated their appetite for the fight and suitability for some of the unique challenges an English league season offers. They had thrived in a successful team. Would a recruit from another country, regardless of their superior touch or vision, bring the same qualities? As with so many aspects of football, the key was balance. It was a relief that many of these considerations fell with substantial weight on the shoulders of a manager rather than a scout. It was crucial, though, that I do my job efficiently – using my knowledge and experience to give as much insight on a player as possible – to enable the gaffer to do his. While the work itself had a familiar feel, the environment in which I was performing it did not.

In March 2009, I left France and moved to Spain, initially to Malaga, where I rented a home previously occupied by my daughter, Keely, and then to Castelldefels, a small town 12 miles to the south-west of Barcelona. The latter was recommended to me by Barça-based Bibian Weggelaar, who had witnessed first-hand the rapid rise of La Liga as a competition. The Spanish top flight boasted a raft of high quality sides – Barça and Real Madrid, of course, but just behind them were Atlético Madrid, Sevilla, Villarreal, Valencia and Athletic Bilbao. The ever-growing riches of the Premier League's elite acted as a magnet for much of the world's talent but Spain's two big guns had an unparalleled romanticism and allure, as demonstrated by Cristiano Ronaldo's move from Manchester United to Real Madrid in the summer of 2009 for a then world record £80m.

My new base enabled me to visit Real's Bernabéu on a regular basis, to see Ronaldo, Kaká and Benzema, now finally at a club fitting of his ability and making very good on all that early promise. This was the back end of the 'Galacticos' era and Real's visits to smaller clubs drew vast crowds eager to catch a glimpse of their travelling band of superstars. I recall one particular scouting trip to Eibar for West Ham when Real were in town. Eibar is a tiny place, situated in a valley between mountains, with the team's Ipurua Municipal Stadium situated at the top of a steep hillside, requiring escalators to assist fans in the upward hike. Hoping to explore a little and soak up the pre-game atmosphere, I took a short walk prior to kick-off and ended up in a small coffee bar. Over the next half an hour, I watched on as the narrow street outside and beyond filled with people, thousands of them lining the pavement in anticipation of the away team coach. I was compelled to join them and inadvertently became part of the frenzy provoked by Real's arrival. This was the away side but they were greeted like all-conquering heroes. Kick-off in the game was delayed because of the time it took for the coach to work its way through the crowds and up to the ground.

Barcelona and their swish scouting area was just down the road. The club were at the peak of their powers under the management of Pep Guardiola, propelled to trophy after trophy by a spine of elite homegrown talent – Carles Puyol, Gerard Piqué, Sergio Busquets, Andrés Iniesta, Xavi and, of course, Lionel Messi. Scouting that side often became a string of increasingly emphatic superlatives, underpinned by the knowledge that there was zero chance of any of my employers at that time convincing Eric Abidal to join them, let alone Messi.

There were reasons for keeping a keen eye on Barça, beyond my own enjoyment and the ease of getting there. So stellar were the standards of their La Masia youth academy, so high the calibre of the young players emerging from it, there would occasionally be top quality cast-offs for clubs like West Ham or Blackburn to snap up. They might not be immediately available but banking early reports allowed a club to play a longer game on their potential release. I would regularly attend matches at the Mini Estadi to watch Barcelona B.

It was during such visits that my attention was caught by the blistering pace, technique and ball-carrying ability of Adama Traore. His final ball needed work but, at 19, it was clear to see, even then, why a string of clubs have taken a chance on trying to coax the best from him in his post-Barça career.

Ruben Rochina was another I filed reports on, although its unlikely Blackburn paid much heed to them when they signed him the January after I left the club in 2011. I thought him a nice, neat player but not a worker or fighter and you need those qualities in abundance in a squad if you are going to last a 38-game Premier League season unscathed. In a team filled with grafters, he could have done a job but in a side lacking such qualities he becomes an ill-afforded luxury.

I once again threw myself into a relentless schedule of games in Spain, with the occasional trip into neighbouring countries. If I wasn't driving to Madrid or Malaga, I was on a train to Seville or a plane to France or Portugal. It was a constant journey of discovery, mixing professional duty with personal enrichment – an exhausting, exhilarating, frustrating, fulfilling tour of European football, society and culture.

France was familiar. I was able to dust off and refresh reports on players I thought to be talented but beneath Chelsea's level. With Hull in search of an upgrade on Andy Dawson at left-back, a return to Toulouse prompted me to highlight Jérémy Mathieu – a good all-round defender I felt would make a sound investment for a mid-table Premier League club. He would end up higher, at Barcelona. They also had Étienne Capoue, a powerful, energetic midfielder who I liked and who did eventually make it to England with Tottenham and Watford. I also pushed centre-half Steven Moukoulou's name to City off the back of a trip to the picturesque coastal town of Boulogne to see them take on Lens in January 2009. I praised his sharpness, mobility and confidence on a tricky, icy surface. 'A "B" for now on first viewing,' I wrote. 'But could easily be an "A".' City signed him the following July, after I had left the club, and he played 23 times in their relegation season.

I would revisit the beautiful little spot of Amiens, with its impressive gothic cathedral, to watch Steven Nzonzi, the football team's own imposing focal point. He had enough quality but his heart and desire were the assets I felt would most benefit Blackburn's midfield – correctly, as it turned out. I once again experienced the fireworks and ferocity of Marseille, returning with reports on Gaël Givet (committed but limited – a Championship player) and Morgan Amalfitano (a decent player but, in my opinion, lacking the requisite mental toughness for the Premier League) to add to the growing dossiers of Blackburn and West Ham, respectively.

I still made the occasional trip to Italy, braving the roads to reach Milan's San Siro, to climb its unique and magnificent winding ramps to reach my seat. It was there that I viewed Internazionale's 19-year-old Brazilian midfielder Philippe Coutinho, reporting back that he was a 'class act' but likely out of Blackburn's price range.

Spain brought new experiences. In the north, I would enjoy trips to San Sebastián to watch Real Sociedad and the beautiful coastal towns in Galicia, to see Deportivo La Coruña and Celta Vigo. The latter had attacking players who would later come to England with varying degrees of success – Michu, Joselu and Iago Aspas. In the south, it was a joy to visit Andalusia to see Cordoba, Granada and Málaga, with their Arabic architecture, flamenco dancers in every café and solid football sides. In Cádiz, I would sample the sherry, walk on the huge beachfront, advance my school history knowledge of Francis Drake's attack on the Spanish armada in the waters off the city and run the rule over their 19-year-old Colombian centre-back, Jeison Murillo.

I was battered by a freezing cold wind in Osasuna's El Sadar Stadium, so much so that I made the rare decision not to make notes and, instead, bury my frozen hands inside my coat. I basked in sunshine at Villarreal, a truly remarkable club who have defied their tiny, humble location in the province of Castellon. I never bored of the striking sudden emergence of the club's all-yellow stadium after winding through the city's terrace house-lined streets or listening to their fans sing 'Yellow Submarine' – their adopted theme song.

Seville is my favourite – a beautiful city in Andalusia. I loved sitting in its picturesque squares, eating at restaurants, sitting under orange trees in the afternoon sun and then walking its narrow, cobbled streets en route to a game. As a man of routine, my seven or eight visits a season brought with them an increased familiarity with the waiters and bar staff in my favourite spots, many of them only too eager to argue the merits of the city's two clubs – Sevilla and Real Betis. There were other restaurants, in different cities. In Valencia, my old Chelsea scouting colleague Juan Sol owned a pizzeria and I would always make sure to call in when I was in town. He was too kind, insisting the meal was on him. I later found out I was one of many benefiting from his generosity, to his own financial detriment.

I picked my battles in Portugal. There were some fine clubs to visit, with good players and decent crowds, like Benfica and Sporting Lisbon. I enjoyed trips to Belenenses, not for the football but the custard tarts for which the town of Belem was famous. I would contentedly sit and watch what was, in truth, a mediocre football team with three or four of those resting in my stomach. In the north of the country, Braga was a superb trip, for the gobsmacking ground if nothing else. Nicknamed 'A Pedreira' (The Quarry), one end of the stadium is a rock face. It doesn't help their attendance figures but it is a sight to behold.

A high quality of player was guaranteed at Porto. One, Héctor Herrera, caught my eye immediately during a scouting visit for Sunderland. I had previously noticed him at the Toulon Tournament in 2012, where he was awarded best player for his displays for Mexico. The son of former UK prime minister Tony Blair, Nicky, was his agent and made clear to me then that he was destined for a bigger club than my current employer. I would continue to track his progress, reporting back that he was sharp and tricky. For all his talent, I wonder even now if he would have suited Sunderland at that time. He would likely have flourished at either of the Manchester clubs, where he would have been given the time and possession to play, but maybe not in the cut and thrust of a battle near the bottom of the league.

One constant during all of my travels and scouting missions was the desire for a competent striker. Finding a finisher capable of scoring you 10 or 12 goals – especially for a struggling side in the January window – can be the big difference between staying up and going down. Unfortunately, they are also the hardest players to unearth. A striker can be prolific in many of Europe's other top leagues but fail to replicate it in the Premier League, where there are more good teams with better defenders. I set a high bar.

I observed André-Pierre Gignac at Toulouse, and later Marseille, on Hull's behalf but, despite his reasonable record in Ligue 1, I never felt him to be a natural goalscorer or possessing of that extra bit of pace or skill to give him an edge. Roberto Soldado was scoring goals regularly in La Liga in the late 2000s and early 2010s, for Getafe and Valencia, but again I didn't see the requisite mettle to make it in England. For me, his quality was undercut by a lack of work, an unwillingness to run for his team – something he would have had to do plenty of for Blackburn at that time. He did, of course, come to England for an infamously disastrous spell at Tottenham, where he scored just seven times in 52 games before heading back to Spain.

Watching games featuring Tours and Montpellier, I compiled reports on Olivier Giroud, who was a handful with his size and willingness to put himself about but was another I felt didn't have a true top-level goalscorer instinct. Regardless, my then employer Sunderland could not compete with clubs possessing deeper pockets and greater draw for his signature. His subsequent record of a goal every two and a half games for Arsenal and closer to four and a half at Chelsea – two clubs who created a lot more chances per game than the Black Cats – suggests he may not have been the difference-maker they sought. My two years at Sunderland are a good encapsulation of the mad scramble undertaken for a striker to get those prized 10 or 12 goals. Between 2011 and 2013, a succession of No.9s joined the club to varying degrees of moderate success: Connor Wickham, Nicklas Bendtner, Louis Saha, Steven Fletcher, Danny Graham. Throw enough shots at the wall and see what sticks.

There were few players in this period I pushed a club to sign more than Marco Asensio. I first saw him in October 2014 playing on the wing as an 18-year-old for Real Mallorca at Real Zaragoza and was struck by his technique and skill. He was a decent size, even at that young age, and had the pace and trickery to beat his man. He didn't demonstrate a huge desire to work back but I could forgo that to acquire the quality creative supply he could provide for West Ham's forwards – Andy Carroll, Carlton Cole and Diafra Sakho. I was informed by his agent that Mallorca were willing to let him go for a modest €3.9m – around £3.5m – which was comfortably within West Ham's budget and, in my mind, something of a snip for such a talent.

So convinced was I of his brilliance over subsequent viewings, I brought Sam over to watch him in a game against Lugo at the San Moix on 1 November. Unfortunately, it was a terrible match and, while Asensio provided an assist for the first of Mallorca's goals in a 2-1 win, he showed precious little of the abilities I had previously witnessed, failing to get involved enough in the game. Sam was unimpressed. 'The game was poor, he was poor and the red wine is bloody awful,' he told me. That was the end of Asensio potentially becoming a Hammer. He would move to Real Madrid soon after and demonstrate what he is about, playing close to 200 games and winning three La Liga titles and a trio of Champions Leagues.

I suspect it would have proved a challenge to convince Asensio to move to West Ham at that time, especially when faced with a challenge from Real Madrid for his signature.

In general, convincing players of the value of joining clubs for whom I was employed in this period was the most significant challenge. West Ham were arguably the biggest of the four but had only just come back up from a reputation-damaging relegation and a season in the Championship. Blackburn were a former Premier League champion but had failed to capitalise on that victory, suffering their own spell in the second tier at the turn of the century. Sunderland had distant history that counted for little to foreign footballers and Hull didn't even possess that.

Money had been sloshing around England's top flight for some time but this was the period in which increased television revenues and billionaire owners sent transfer fees and wages into the stratosphere. However, the division had also fragmented, with a small group of elite clubs at the top ruling the roost and drawing all the best talent to them. I would be drawn into a familiar dance with agents who were keen to push their client to the Premier League but holding out for an Arsenal, Chelsea, Liverpool or one of the Manchester clubs. When faced with a raft of trophies, global fanbase and regular Champions League football, Sunderland's six titles nearly a century ago didn't cut through.

Foreign players would often want to live in one of the UK's major footballing cities – London, Manchester and Liverpool. I would often resort to selling my club's even vague geographical proximity to the aforementioned places as a plus. West Ham had London to its advantage but a move to Blackburn would allow a player to live in Manchester. With Sunderland, I could preach the merits of Durham or the presence of a healthy French contingent of players at Newcastle to potential Ligue 1 recruits. There was little I could do with Hull, sadly. No matter how much I tried to massage the distance, it was too isolated and unknown out on the east coast.

I was fortunate to be backed by so many good, able people during this period. I had known Bob and Browny for years, which made for a familiar and friendly working environment at Hull. At Blackburn, Martin Glover, a former PE teacher who worked his way up through the ranks to become Rovers' head of recruitment under Sam, was a key ally. He had a keen eye for a player and Sam's trust, much like Jack at Bolton. The three of us would reunite at West Ham, where I would also reconnect with another familiar face. Chris McMenemy, Lawrie's son, had moved into scouting and out to Spain. Sam asked me to set him up with some games and he became a trusted foil for me, allowing us to cover a greater number of games and players.

What would ultimately be a tricky time at Sunderland was made better by the presence of Bryan 'Pop' Robson as chief scout. From the city originally, he played for the club three times over his career as a centre-forward, as well as Newcastle and West Ham twice. He had a fantastic goalscoring record, not far off a goal every two games. Despite this, he was one of the most modest men I have ever had the pleasure of knowing. He was quiet, unassuming, genuine and a fine judge of footballing talent. His methods differed slightly from Sam in that he asked for monthly reports, from which he would decide whether to travel to see individual players, but I felt a similar trust between us.

I felt empowered to make decisions beyond simply what games to see and hotels to book. I liaised with two other scouts – former players Dean White and Mohammed Camara – to better cover games in France. I also helped set up a relationship with Gava, the semi-professional team of the town one over from Castelldefels as a feeder club for the Black Cats. Knowing they had a reputation for producing good young players, I had made the short journey from my home to see Gava play a few times and come away impressed with the humble but efficient set-up. I enlisted the help of my agent friend Bibian to act as a go-between/translator and brought Pop and various other Sunderland officials, including head of youth development Jed McNamee, over to visit. The agreement was made official in October 2015. I can't recall it bearing fruit in a significant way, certainly not in the remainder of my time at the club, but it was a positive, progressive step of the kind ambitious clubs should be making.

I worked under eight managers in my seven years at these four clubs. Some I got to know better than others, some I like more than others. I've always got on well with Browny, as we have a fair bit in common. He's a big character, much like Sam. I was back in England and inside the City of Manchester Stadium when he conducted his infamous on-field team talk at half-time. The first half hadn't gone well for us, with City scoring four times, but I still remember thinking to myself 'what the hell is going on?' when Browny marched on to the pitch at the break and instructed his players to sit in a circle in the penalty area in front of the away fans before reading them the riot act. It will have been humiliating for the players and Browny was slaughtered in the media afterwards. I think he was trying to show them what it meant to be playing for those fans, to try and inspire them, but I'm not sure it had the desired effect.

I didn't have chance to build a bond with any manager at Sunderland, such was the brevity of their stay at the club. I saw Steve Bruce once or twice during my time there and found him to be straightforward and honest. In one early scouts' meeting, I recall him and Eric Black came in raving about a player whose name I can't recall but they had seen during a recent trip to France. 'He was fantastic,' exclaimed the gaffer. 'He's exactly the sort of player I want to bring to Sunderland.' He then turned to me. 'Worthy, you'll have seen plenty of him, what do you think?' I paused a moment. 'Well, I've seen him seven or eight times and, in my opinion, he's not right for the Premier League or Sunderland,' I began. 'I've seen him be very good, too, but I've watched him be average and lazy more often. We need players to work their socks off every game and that isn't him.' There was a moment of silence before I added: 'But you've seen him and liked him, as I have before. This is just my opinion.' That was that. Nothing more was said on the matter but Steve, Eric and Pop must have gone away, looked at my reports and discussed it. We didn't end up signing the player.

I never really got to know Steve's successor as manager, Martin O'Neill. I wasn't able to build up the rapport with him that I had found so advantageous in previous jobs, under different managers. He was above me and made that fact clear. He would last just 54 games before being replaced by Paolo Di Canio, with whom I had even less interaction. He lasted only 13 games over the end of one season and the start of another but by the time he was sacked, I was at West Ham.

Whilst often out of sight and with an ongoing job to do, I was still impacted by managerial changes at a club when they happened. Often, a new man would allow the scouting department to function as it had been, minimising the potentially disruptive upheaval that greets any switch of boss. However, there was always the risk that a new manager had designs on a more complete overhaul, to sweep out what was seen as the failing old and bring in a fresh, untarnished new. I had worked in the game long enough, played during a time when a new contract had to be earned each year, seen colleagues come and go and suffer the same fate myself to know football futures are often built on sand.

This is why a strong, trusting, respectful relationship with a manager is of such benefit to a scout and in my career no other working affiliation fits this description like the one I shared with Sam. That he repeatedly came calling to offer me work and that I was – Chelsea excepting – so quick to accept, demonstrates the mutual high regard we held for each other. He gave me my big break scouting and helped me to grow in the role. Without his wisdom, I wouldn't have been able to forge such a career. I think, in me, he recognised qualities he shares and treasures – determination, dedication, loyalty, an eagerness to improve and knowing when to play as well as work hard.

I think one thing that most people can identify in 'Big Sam' is that, for all the ferocity he demonstrates when it is needed, he is also a lot of fun. His laugh would echo around the corridors of the offices at Bolton's Euxton training complex. It was funny to see the glint appear in his eye and the giggle enter his voice when he recalled his ability to get up Arsène Wenger's nose by regularly beating his all-conquering Arsenal side with lowly little Bolton. The Frenchman may balk at the suggestion but Wenger and Sam have a fair amount in common.

Now, Sam is written off by many as a dinosaur – an old-school relic to be wheeled out to steer off relegation with ugly, long-ball football. It's an ignorant stance, utterly unrepresentative of the man and his work. At Bolton, he was as much an innovator as the man being showered with plaudits at Highbury. Upon arrival, I was struck by the modernisations the club had instigated under our forward-thinking and innovative manager. Mike Forde was at the club as performance director and helped Sam implement statistical analysis to see how players were performing and set targets for the future. I couldn't have done my job as effectively but for the insights and guidance of our video and information technology department, led by Dave Fallows, who joined Wanderers from ProZone, a company that provided detailed in-game tracking data for players. Ours was one of the first clubs to employ its use, along with Derby and Everton. He was a wizard at finding patterns and trends to aid with scouting. He identified France as a common destination for South American players and one from which clubs were recruiting most intelligently, such as Lyon. He helped us recognise the value of signing lads that had left Africa to move to France – a path that often indicated an inner drive and determination to overcome hardship. When a player popped on to our radar, he had information readily available and could provide footage of him in action to give an early indicator of his ability. There is no bigger testament to Dave's ability than to see the way his career has flourished. After Bolton, he acquired a prominent recruitment role at Manchester City, working alongside my son, Gary, before becoming head of scouting and recruitment at Liverpool. But it was Sam who brought him in and gave him his early platform.

Sam wasn't reluctant to delegate but equally not scared to pull you up if you failed in your job. I think he recognised that if he gave me the freedom and responsibility to forge my own path, I would reward him. I took my early lessons – and the occasional rollicking – learned quickly and earned my stripes. He has often said that a quality he most valued in me was that I stuck to my guns and spoke my mind. I make sure to do that now if ever I hear Sam being unjustly criticised. He is a manager who understands the game, the importance of recognising your strengths and weaknesses and playing to them – be that with an evolving side he has led from the second tier to Europe or one he has been parachuted into for a battle against relegation. There are only a handful of people I have continued to call 'gaffer' after my time working under them. Sam is the main one.

I wish some club owners and investors had an ounce of Sam's football intelligence. Scouts rarely interact with the men at the very top – barring invites from Russian oligarchs to dine in their private box – but the decisions they make can have a significant impact on their job, sometimes for the better, but often for the worse. In this period, I saw first-hand the impact of poor choices by owners.

At Blackburn, a new ownership group listened to the wrong people. Sam had turned things around for the better on the pitch after replacing Paul Ince but he would soon find the carpet whipped from beneath his feet. The club had been under the control of the Jack Walker Trust, with John Williams in place as chairman on their behalf, but clearly wished to sell. Enter Venky's, the Indian chicken company, which took control in November 2010. Within a few weeks, Sam was gone, sacked by the new guys and replaced as manager by his assistant coach, Steve Keen. As a scout, easily disposable, and Sam's man to boot, I started to feel that unsettling shift of earth beneath me. These were machinations above my pay grade, though. I had a family to keep, a mortgage to pay and a job to do for the club until someone informed me otherwise. My task remained unaltered. I spoke briefly to Sam but only to pass on my best wishes and to share the usual: 'See you again at the next club, maybe.'

I had little interaction with Steve Keen before and after his elevation to manager. Any demands he may have made on recruitment would come to me via Martin. I didn't especially warm to him on the rare occasions we did meet. Something about the situation felt off to me, an instinct exacerbated by my loyalties to Sam. It soured my experience at the club. I would later discover the considerable role Jerome Anderson had played in the whole affair. A sports agent, he had advised the Venky's on their takeover of the club and continued to be a presence afterwards. Keen was one of his clients.

Sam's sacking was the writing on the wall as regards my time at Blackburn. When Pop enquired if I fancied a switch to Sunderland, I leapt at the chance to work with such a terrific man. It would end up being a leap from frying pan to fire.

Pop was fantastic but he would be my only real constant during a time of flux and ensuing chaos at the Black Cats. Regular managerial changes were detrimental but it was no less stable behind the scenes. American owner Ellis Short took over from Niall Quinn as chairman shortly after I arrived. Later, in March 2013, in a move of much more significance to my role, the club brought in agent Roberto De Fanti to advise on player recruitment. I first met him at a scouts' meeting, during which he waxed lyrical about Italian forward Antonio Cassano, a prodigious talent who had made a name for himself at Roma before joining Real Madrid. I had seen him most recently at Sampdoria and AC Milan, thinking him to be able and confident but tipping into the arrogant. When asked my thoughts, I began by saying that 'if he was made of chocolate, he would eat himself'. From De Fanti's angry reaction, I knew I had overstepped the line. I attempted to rescue the situation by expanding that I felt he would struggle to make an impact in our side in the Premier League, that he simply would not get the time and possession he required. But the damage was done. Afterwards, in the car on the way to Pop's house, where I was staying, I turned to him and declared: 'Well, I don't know about you but that's me getting the sack.' He responded with a laugh but also the flicker of a grimace.

The call from the club came soon after – 'thanks, but we're letting you go'. Pop and the rest of the scouting team would also get the boot shortly after, with another Italian, Valentino Angeloni, installed as chief scout under director of football De Fanti. The pair would last less than a year at the Stadium of Light, during which they brought in a raft of new signings, many of them with Italian connections, none of them Cassano. By that point, I was back working with Sam and Martin in a much saner environment at West Ham.

I was engaged in another battle at this time, one of far more import than the comparatively frivolous game of football. In February 2013, I was diagnosed with prostate cancer. It was a huge shock. There had been no signs, no symptoms at all. I was 68 years old but still fit and active. With Maggie alongside me for support, the doctor calmly and seemingly with no sense of urgency laid out to me all the options for treatment. I began by telling him that I was working out in Spain and that the football season ended in May. I could come back to the UK then and begin a course of radiotherapy or chemotherapy. 'Dave!' said a voice next to me. 'You've got prostate cancer. You're going to need to do better than that.' It was Maggie, fully engaging in the severity of the situation and acting with a sense of purpose in a way I was perhaps too fearful to do.

I was lucky. The doctors had caught the cancer early and, so, I was able to consider all the options and schedule in treatment over the following months. This allowed me to return to Spain and continue to scout in the meantime. It was during the wait that I attended the meeting with De Fanti that ended my time at Sunderland. The illness haunted my thoughts. At games, the memory of its existence would flash into my mind. On long, dull journeys to games, my thoughts would wander to dark places.

On 25 June, I returned to St Luke's Hospital and underwent a successful operation to have the growth removed. In the years since, I have regularly returned for check-ups which, God willing, continue to show I am cancer-free. The doctors and medical staff who cared for me throughout and continue to do so have my eternal gratitude.

There, throughout the whole experience, giving me her unflinching emotional support, as she has during the whole of my European scouting adventure, was Maggie, my rock. In that specific moment, she had the clarity and concern to force me to act. Beyond that, she has demonstrated an empathy and understanding beyond the normal requirements of a partner as I pursued my professional aims.

She may not have been physically present for most of my time abroad but in the periods that she has, we have made the very most of it. There have been plenty of adventures over the years. One escapade provides a lesson in the perils of European road travel. It took place on a Sunday morning, on a drive from Barcelona down to watch Hercules, a team in Alicante. Midway through the journey, near to Tarragona, a police car came in behind us and signalled for Maggie to pull the car over into a lay-by. There, they informed us that we had been speeding and demanded an on-the-spot €80 fine, giving us no choice but to pay.

Shortly afterwards, we stopped at some services for a drink. When we came back to the car, we noticed two suspicious-looking men nearby, who quickly headed off when they noticed us approaching. It should have been a warning sign because, a few miles after restarting the journey, a light appeared on the dashboard to say we had lost tyre pressure. As soon as we had pulled over, another car parked up 25 yards in front of us and two men emerged, one wearing a yellow hi-vis jacket. Under the pretence of trying to help, they had popped the boot of our car and brought us round the back to locate the spare tyre. However, having removed the spare, they then quickly made noises about leaving, returned to their car and shot off, leaving us dazed by the side of the road. It was only then that we discovered Maggie's handbag and my rucksack missing from the front seat.

It had been a slick operation, involving puncturing our tyre, following the car and then conducting their quick-fire robbery. We had naively fallen for the kind Samaritan act. Fortunately, Maggie remembered an old mobile phone we kept in the car, which we used to call her daughter and get the bank cards cancelled, but not before the robbers had taken out a few hundred euros in a nearby town. Having taken us for €80 earlier, the police came to our aid, two officers pulling over to help us fit the new tyre. A week later, they contacted me again to say they had found my bag, dumped in a hedge and still with my scouting notebooks inside, full of player recommendations. I can imagine the Tarragona police put together a hell of a five-a-side team that year.

We have long lost count of the number of flights Maggie has taken to join me for long weekends in Europe. At first, with our finances compromised by our respective divorces, she sailed over the channel by ferry and then catamaran but sea sickness put an end to that. The flights weren't expensive but did sometimes involve travelling to Blackpool to get a plane to Stansted and then on to Poitiers and Limoges. Later, when I was living in Barcelona and with the money from being Bolton's chief scout and employed by Chelsea, she could make her way from Manchester or Liverpool. We accepted it as a necessary byproduct of my work and the care needs of her parents, who would blessedly soldier on into their 90s.

One positive was that I was able to share with her the discoveries I had made on my travels. She could see places like Andalusia, La Rochelle or Seville and enjoy wonderful, life-affirming experiences – the Eiffel Tower at night, Barcelona carnival and Belenenses versus Freamunde in the Portuguese second division. It gave us a thirst for further travel. In June 2012, we went to China on holiday, during which we saw the Terracotta Army, stood in Tiananmen Square and walked the Great Wall. We've also been to Petra in Jordan to see the stunning rock-carved architecture and to Peru to trek up to Machu Picchu, which was a real test for what stamina I still had in the tank.

The bug for travel is something we've passed on to our children. Both Keely and Danielle have lived in Spain during their lives and Gary's work, especially with Manchester City, has taken him all over the globe. Our apartment in Casteldefells, with its communal garden, swimming pool and proximity to the beach, became a base for our grandchildren (along with boyfriends and girlfriends) for a holiday in their teens. We got the odd holiday out of it, too, such as a trip to Australia to visit my granddaughter, Molly and her partner, Jack, who had moved to Adelaide. At its worst, my experience in Europe could feel isolating and lonely but at its best it was a joyous, enriching shared experience.

On 23 July 2010, 12 days after Andrés Iniesta's extra-time goal had given Spain victory over the Netherlands in the World Cup Final in Johannesburg, Maggie and I, with a select group of family and friends in attendance, married. Afterwards, we headed away for a week-long honeymoon in Madeira. It would have been longer but I had to be back in Blackburn on 4 August for a scouts' meeting.

13

Frankly Exceptional
(2015–2016)

Saturday, 21 April 1979. 12:36pm.

The defences are on top. Little of note has yet happened at Burnden Park in the First Division clash between Bolton Wanderers and Ipswich Town. But that is all about to change.

The home side have a throw on the left. Sam Allardyce, the big, burly centre-half, responds to Alan Gowling's run and hurls the ball into the box. Gowling leaps but a second too soon, his header, as he falls, only directing the ball into empty space near the edge of a penalty area packed with visitors in blue and white.

The first to react is Frank Worthington, with a change of direction and controlling header. What happens next is the stuff of magic. Worthington offers the pledge, meeting the dropping ball with his left foot, keeping it up once, twice, steadying himself as four Town men gather to pen him in. Now comes the turn, a flick of the ball over his head and rapid 180-degree spin that flips him through the defence and in on goal. Finally, the big finish, a crisp left-footed volley past diving goalkeeper Paul Cooper. From first touch to last, not one blade of grass touches ball. The prestige.

BARELY A month goes by without me receiving a link to or stumbling across an online clip of our Frank's most famous goal. It is one of those glorious moments that has lodged itself into the consciousness of football fans, even those not born when it occurred. It transcends generations, a goal of such impudent daring and brilliant execution that it appeals to the joy-seeking wonder in every supporter.

It is the perfect encapsulation of what made my youngest brother so special. Not only did he have the ability to perform each intricate skill involved in the move – the deft, controlling header, the ball juggling, the rapid turn and precise volley – he also possessed the sheer audacity to even attempt it in the first place. There are other players with the former in their locker but precious few with the latter. It speaks not only to the carefree, instinctive, joyous way in which he played the game but the similar way in which he lived his life.

He was loved by fans throughout his career, most dearly at Huddersfield Town, Leicester City, Bolton Wanderers and Birmingham City – the clubs he represented during his prime. I think what endeared him – and other similar 'mavericks' of the era, such as George Best, Rodney Marsh and Stan Bowles – to supporters was the manner in which he reconnected them with a youthful, hopeful love for the game. Frank played in the manner of which young boys would dream of one day being capable. He was the fantasy come true, a dashing ambassador for the romance of the game, reminding us of its wonders, joyful unpredictability and constant capacity to amaze.

From the moment I arrived at Leicester in the summer of 2015 to be their scout, people wanted to talk to me about Frank. So indelible was the mark he had left on the club, so long was the list of stories he left in his wake, everyone from the girls in the ticket office to the blokes selling burgers outside on matchday seized their chance to share their memories with the brother of the revered hero. The stories would inevitably lead them down a wistful path of remembrance for a great side. Alongside Frank were Peter Shilton, Lenny Glover and Keith Weller. I would often see another member of that team, Alan Birchenall, during my time there. He was working as a club ambassador and would swing by the training ground when we had our scouts' meetings. Our chats would inevitably lead to gales of laughter over tales of our kid.

It immediately made me feel welcome at what was a friendly, happy and humble club. I was brought in by head of recruitment/assistant manager Steve Walsh following a conversation between him and Sam, during which the latter mentioned my availability. Whilst he had not played the game professionally, Walshy had built a reputation as an astute spotter of talent with a huge capacity and appetite to learn over an impressive scouting career at clubs such as Chelsea and Newcastle. Now in his second spell at Leicester, he was looking to build a team off the field to help the Foxes get ahead of the competition on it.

They had snatched relative success from the jaws of disaster in 2014/15. Having been bottom and seven points from safety with 29 games played, they remarkably won seven of the last nine to stay up by a comfortable six points. It was not enough to keep manager Nigel Pearson in a job, with Italian Claudio Ranieri replacing him in the role just before my arrival.

Walshy was a good communicator, quiet, intelligent and to the point. I've worked with some people in positions of authority who are loud and seemed to cherish an argument over a player – but not Steve. You always knew exactly what he was looking for and that you could challenge him if you had a valid point to make. A good team leader.

The previous season had somewhat masked some of the intelligent signings he had brought to the club – players I watched in training during my first visit and could see had more to offer than they had previously shown. Much like Bolton under Sam, they had a solid base of dependable operators. Wes Morgan was a big, battling centre-half, Marc Albrighton an intelligent, hard-working midfielder and Danny Drinkwater possessed a huge engine and appetite for graft.

I was aware of Jamie Vardy from looking out for Halifax's results from abroad, picking up a paper each week in 2010/11 to see regular mention of a rapid, free-scoring forward destined for bigger things. Walshy had followed him closely and convinced Leicester to part with £1m to sign him from Fleetwood Town, a record amount for a non-league player. Watching training, he immediately stood out for his raw speed and clever finishing, something the team had clearly failed to capitalise on the previous season, during which he'd only scored five times.

They had also signed two players I had previously watched in France – winger Riyad Mahrez and midfielder N'Golo Kanté. Mahrez had emerged at Le Havre, a club with a solid record of finding and nurturing young players. I liked his ability to run with the ball and his sense of purpose but also felt him to be a little inconsistent. He was maybe not ready for a top club but certainly good enough for the Premier League when at his best. Kanté I had watched over a number of years at Caen and, before that, Boulogne. He was a very clever player. In congested midfields he would often disappear from the pack, moving a few yards to his right or left. It may appear he had abdicated responsibility but then, in a flash, the ball would be at his feet, him having foreseen the development of the move ahead of everyone else. He was a non-stop runner, a tackler and a creator – a rarity I was eager to recommend.

Considering what both would go on to produce in the coming season and beyond, it seems ridiculous that no other Premier League club had yet taken a chance on either player. That is sometimes how it goes, though, for a variety of reasons. Talented players do get missed, although this has become far less common in an era of global scouting networks armed with vast databases and information. Scouts can recommend players but, if their employer is not seeking one in that position, the opportunity passes by. Often, a player will underperform in a game attended by a key figure in the recruitment process, as Asensio decisively had when I brought Sam over to see him in Mallorca. It is to Walshy's huge credit that he had the courage to act when others would not, on more than one occasion. Leicester would capitalise on this reluctance in the most emphatic manner.

Scouts pride themselves on their foresight but I certainly did not envisage nine months into the future that the Leicester squad I witnessed in pre-season training would win the title. I've yet to meet anyone who can convince me they thought it even a possibility. The bookies certainly didn't, placing their odds at 5,000-1 before a ball had been kicked. I felt the team was at a similar level to West Ham, the club I had recently departed, and that, with a decent start and a bit of luck, they might avoid another desperate scramble to stay up. From a scouting point of view, I saw it as an opportunity to push some recommendations to the club, improve my standing and potentially cement a longer stay.

Whilst there may have been doubts about Leicester succeeding in that 2015/16 season, there had never been any doubt in my mind that our Frank was going to be a success. Even as a young lad, kicking a ball around with Bob and me, his ability shone – the touch, the balance, the tricks. Later, he would look to replicate the ball-juggling skills of the Brazilians he witnessed on TV, taking to the street with a ball to emulate Didi and Garrincha. It would never take him long to do a passable impression.

He always had bullet-proof confidence. It would often come out as cheekiness in his childhood, which would get him into trouble at school. But he rarely seemed to care. He enjoyed being viewed as the naughty one. Dennis the Menace. He certainly backed himself where football was concerned. At Huddersfield, he would declare to the other apprentices that he would one day play for England. I'm sure it's a boast many a young player foolishly makes. But Frank truly meant it and followed through.

Because they were the two younger brothers, Bob and Frank were closer than I was to either. Being two years older, I'd reached adolescence first and didn't want my two younger brothers cramping my style around the older lads. I was protective of Frank, though. As the eldest, I held seniority and would play bodyguard to who I saw as the more vulnerable sibling when he and Bob fought. It was probably a bit unfair to our Bob but it forged an early bond between my youngest brother and me. There would be many times in the subsequent decades that I would feel that urge to defend Frank, even when he was old enough to look after himself, recoiled at the aid or didn't deserve it, which was often!

My own commitments to football, which would quickly lead me away to Barrow and beyond, meant that I missed the majority of Frank's career, from his early days running rings around the poor, helpless defenders in other local youth teams through to his prime years, running rings around the poor, helpless defenders in other First Division sides. I would be sure to catch up on the latest tales of his exploits, though, whenever I spoke to my parents or siblings. One time, calling back home from Barrow, I got talking on the phone with our Bob, who told me of Frank's earlier return to the house from a game. My youngest brother was 15 by then and had just signed as an apprentice for Huddersfield but was still playing locally on a weekend. Bob relayed how he had asked Frank how he'd got on. 'Oh, we won 23-0,' came the blasé reply. 'I scored 17 of them.' Bob was gobsmacked. 'Seventeen? Bloody hell!' Frank's grinning face appeared around the doorframe. 'Yeah,' he said. 'And I made the other six.'

It wasn't long before I was reading about him in the newspapers, which had quickly cottoned on to his box-office draw, on and off the pitch. I would see reports revelling in his latest bit of brilliance or goalscoring exploits. It helped his cause that he wasn't a bad-looking lad, in my mind the second-most handsome of the Worthington brothers! It was Huddersfield boss Ian Greaves who coined the description of Frank as the 'working man's George Best' – a nod not only to his ability but his looks and enjoyment of the high life. He wasn't much of a boozer – Sam always described the both of us as 'lightweights' – but he certainly enjoyed the attention he received from the ladies, which would only increase alongside his fame.

He leant into the image with his distinctive style – a flowing mullet and David Niven-esque moustache – and his clothes, part inspired by his hero Elvis Presley. You'd be hard pressed not to spot him in his jeans, cowboy boots and tasselled leather jacket in the pub after Huddersfield games, ever the non-conformist. I recall a particular night out when I joined Frank and some of his Town team-mates – Trevor Cherry, Billy Legg, Jimmy McGill and others – for a few drinks. It was near the start of one season because they were all sporting brand-new club suits; grey and formal, with a club badge on the pocket. Frank spent the night shifting about and pulling at it, his disdain for such stuffy, uniform attire clear for all to see. Later, having left the pub, with a few drinks inside him and ever the showman, he ended up trotting along the top of a wall as we walked down the street. When he reached the end, he leapt from it, to the sound of cloth tearing. He had split his new suit trousers along the seam, from near the crotch down to his ankle, leaving one leg flapping. As you can imagine, we all fell about laughing, including Frank. 'Ah well,' he said after composing himself. 'Doesn't matter does it.' And, with that, he grabbed the other leg and ripped it to match, creating himself a pair of grey, cotton cowboy chaps. The following Saturday, with everyone else in their suit, in strides Frank in his leather jacket and boots, once again standing out from the crowd. You'd almost think he planned it.

Far be it from me to bust any myths but I feel I need to state here and now that Frank is a cheat. For years, he cultivated the image and convinced many to call him Elvis but I was, in fact, the original 'King' in the Worthington household. I was a fan from the start, buying his LPs as a teenager and playing them endlessly in my bedroom in Shelf, beginning a lifelong love for his music. When I left Halifax to move to Barrow, I put all my vinyl records in boxes and brought them with me so that I at least had one constant from home. However, when I arrived and unpacked, I discovered two of the Elvis ones missing. Frank swore blind to me that he wasn't responsible but I found it increasingly difficult to believe the innocence of the man with the big hair, swivelling hips and leather jacket. All the clues pointed to just one, cheeky culprit.

I didn't get to see Frank play in the flesh anywhere near as often as I would have liked. There was one game, while I was at Southend, when I took the short journey into London to see him play at West Ham. Comedian Freddie Starr was in attendance and had a bit of banter with the crowd on the way to his seat, just to add a little extra razzmatazz. Not that it needed it with Frank on the pitch. I revelled in the way the crowd shifted in their seats, an expectant murmur filling the air whenever he had the ball at his feet. I've been able to catch snippets of his play over the years, either on *Match of the Day* at the time or via clips later on the internet. His two England goals, against Argentina and Bulgaria, pop up now and again, although not as often as THAT Bolton goal. I'm privileged in knowing that shortly after scoring, Frank would go up to Ipswich centre-back Terry Butcher – one of those who had stood slack-jawed and powerless as he swivelled and fired in – to cheekily suggest that he would probably have enjoyed the moment a lot more if he'd been sitting in the stands rather than trying to mark him. Terry can at least console himself that he wasn't the last defender to be embarrassed by our Frank in a playing career that stretched across more than 20 clubs and into his mid-40s.

One way we Worthington brothers did keep in touch during our playing days was via regular Friday evening phone calls. These gave us the chance to check in on each other but also, more importantly, to glean what inside information the other two may have about the next day's opponents. What were the strikers like? Did they have any dirty players to look out for in midfield? I would always be keen to hear of any particularly quick or tricky left-wingers. Bob and I were largely in the same division, so would have plenty to offer the other, but Frank could chip in on any lads that had dropped down from higher up. 'Oh, you'll have no bother with these lot. Just bring the ball down with your head, do two keepy-ups, swivel through the entire defence and volley it in. Simple.' Cheers, Frank.

Just as I had to view Frank's continuing career from a distance, I also had to watch on from afar as Leicester staged arguably the greatest single season in English football history. It was surreal, unlike any of my previous scouting experiences for a club out in Europe. It began in a familiar enough fashion, bouncing around from game to game, compiling report after report on players, some I'd seen before, others new. I liked Victor Campuzano, a 17-year-old striker playing youth team football at Espanyol. He was big and strong for his age, with extremely good technique. I felt Leicester could have made him into a good player. Another player I recommended was Bernardo Espinosa, a big tough Colombian centre-half for Sporting Gijón. Leicester did act on that one and were close to signing him but a serious knee injury scuppered a potential move in January 2016. He did move to Middlesbrough the next season before spending six years at Girona back in Spain.

I really rated João Palhinha, then a skinny 21-year-old playing in midfield for Moreirense on loan from Sporting Lisbon. In one game in particular, against Tondela in February, he was superb – up and down the pitch, strong, tough-tackling, neat with the ball. I told Leicester to sign him but they clearly didn't think we needed him. To be fair, they did have N'Golo Kanté in central midfield at that time. I was amazed in the seasons that followed that no Premier League team had signed him, so was not at all surprised when Fulham did make a move and just how good he was during his time in England.

The two best players in the world were at the peak of their powers in Spain at that time. It was a pleasure to regularly watch Lionel Messi and Cristiano Ronaldo during this period of my career, to see their supreme, unmatched talent and the way they pushed each other on to ever greater heights.

Messi, along with a number of his Barcelona team-mates, including Luis Suárez and Cesc Fàbregas, lived in Castelldefels, albeit in a slightly more upmarket part of town than I. Occasionally, I would catch a glimpse of his car, with its blacked-out windows, as it flew past. The journey down the road to the Camp Nou was one I made often, a feeling of giddy anticipation testing my professional decorum. The little Argentine rarely let me down. Scouting him was a difficult task. Every report had to be written with the knowledge that the club I was working for, even Chelsea, weren't going to get him. He was on such a higher plane of performance that the normal terms of description or assessment almost didn't apply.

If you take as accepted his technical proficiency, what makes him so great is his understanding of where he needs to be in relation to the ball. I was always taught to pass and run. But Messi would pass and walk. I would watch him lay off the ball and almost saunter, preserving energy as he made his way into empty space on the pitch. Then, suddenly, the ball would be back at his feet, like the whole move was scripted and he was simply arriving at his mark on stage to await his cue. Twenty seconds later, the ball would be in the back of the net. If you were to tell me Messi had the ability to stop time, look around to see where everyone else was positioned and then restart the clock, it wouldn't surprise me.

Ronaldo is a different animal, a physical specimen unlike any other. He has manufactured himself into the player he is with utter determination, application and self-belief. He has trained himself to be more skilful, to run quicker and leap higher than almost any other footballer on the planet. In some of my early reports on him, from appearances for Portugal, I was quite dismissive, my patience worn thin by endless tricks and precious little end product. His brilliance became undeniable, especially during his time at Madrid, but, of the two, I've always felt a greater affinity and appreciation for Messi.

One thing was for certain, neither were going to be coming to Leicester.

My first few months there were spent in near anonymity. Nobody cared about my club. Many struggled to even pronounce its name – 'Sorry, señor, Lycester?' Come February, though, they all knew Leicester City, the plucky Foxes, sticking it to the big boys. The victories over Chelsea, Tottenham, Liverpool and Manchester City had been beamed around the world. Everyone was talking about the prospect of the impossible happening in England. On my trips to Portugal, I would often hire a car at Lisbon airport and became friendly with the guys at the rental place. One was a Benfica supporter, the other followed Sporting Lisbon and I would joke with them about which team's players I was going to watch and take to England. Over the course of that season, they got more and more excited by what was going on in the Premier League. Come the last few months, they would leap from their seats as I entered: 'Ahhh, Leicester! Wow! Top of the league still!' I would then go through it all again with the reception staff when I reached my hotel and at the ground as I collected my ticket. It was brilliant to feel connected to something that made people so excited and happy.

One positive of Leicester's lowly early-season standing was that agents generally left me alone to do my job. Presumably, they weren't so keen to push their clients towards a club they believed might soon be playing in the Championship. However, as the campaign wore on and the possibility of European qualification or more came into view, they would seek me out in the stands to sound out the club and place early feelers regarding their clients. Other scouts were fascinated by the form of our players, having either recommended or rejected them as signings to their own employer. What did you see in Jamie Vardy? Did you know Mahrez was this good? Why were no big clubs in for Kanté? I would simply tell them: 'You're better off asking Walshy.'

I was able to properly see for myself what all the fuss was about when I returned at Christmas for two weeks, during which I attended a few City games to refresh my knowledge and opinion of the squad. Watching on as they won 3-2 at Everton, what struck me was the confidence of a team happy to play firmly on the front foot, epitomised by Vardy. His pace and relentless running scared defenders; he would take just a little touch of the ball into space and he was off. He was intelligent, too, clever enough to conserve his energy and wait for the opportunities from which he knew he could be most effective and smart enough to make the right run when the chance arose.

Mahrez had a similar dynamism but where he was most effective was with the ball at his feet against isolated defenders. He would absolutely murder them one on one. I think many had written off Kanté because of his size, wrongly believing he would be physically outmatched in England. But this overlooks his athleticism, attitude and astuteness. He was nimble, always on his toes and anticipated to turn potential tackles into interceptions. When he did lose the ball, he fought back to retrieve it. In a team game, Kanté is a true team player.

The training ground was bouncing, full of happy, smiling faces from people loving the ongoing achievement to which they were contributing. I didn't meet Claudio Ranieri often but, on the occasions I did, I found him to be a friendly, humble and thoughtful man. At Christmas in the title-winning season, he bought every member of staff at the club a brass handbell inscribed with 'Merry Christmas 2015 – from Claudio Ranieri' as a gift. A lovely touch. I would interact more regularly with Walshy and his fellow assistant manager, Craig Shakespeare. Rightly, Ranieri earned a huge amount of credit for taking City to the title but, in my mind, Walshy and Shakey deserve just as many plaudits for their contribution. They put in a huge amount of work on the training pitch to sculpt that side and were heavily influential in managing substitutions during games. Again, though, it is a team game, both on and off the pitch, and the combination Leicester put together in the dugout had an alchemy to it.

I was back working in Spain when the title was sealed but I watched the joyous celebrations on television and spoke with Walshy afterwards to get a sense of what it was like in the King Power Stadium. In a nice touch, the club ensured all the staff, along with wives and partners, attended the Community Shield game with Manchester United ahead of the following season to show their appreciation and allow us to belatedly celebrate together.

As remarkable as it was, Leicester's title success brought challenges. For all of the money and recognition, it also heaped demands and expectation on a small and perhaps ill-prepared club. Nobody expected the title win. Few would then have foreseen them suffering relegation seven years later. Despite some of the struggles that have followed, I'm delighted that a fine and friendly club were able to enjoy such a unique and joyous experience as that season. I've only ever had positive experiences with people I have met with City connections. In the season after the title win, I bumped into Nigel Pearson, the man Ranieri replaced as Foxes manager, outside of Guimaraes' stadium in Portugal. I went over to introduce myself, explaining for whom I worked. Despite the way his time at City ended, he could not have been kinder about the club. At one point during my initial introduction, he did stop me. 'Hang on, Worthington you said?' I nodded. 'You're not Frank's brother are you? I know a story or two about him!'

Frank had some challenging moments dealing with his own success and fame. A narrative took hold about the kind of person he was, a perception of his character based not on reality but the general view of the group of 1970s playboy mavericks into which he had been pigeonholed. He enjoyed some of the trappings but I don't think the fame ever truly mattered to him. It certainly never made him arrogant. At heart, he was a decent, honest lad. He'd had the same upbringing as me, been handed the same moral code by our parents. He would flaunt it a tad more often but never out of maliciousness. If anything, he maybe just didn't think enough about the repercussions of his actions. On a football pitch, he would think two, three steps ahead of everyone else. But in real life, he lacked some commonsense.

When Bob and I first started picking up a wage as a professional, we would give a portion of it to my mum and dad for food and lodgings – a small but important gesture of respect for everything they'd done for us growing up. Frank received his first wage as a 15-year-old at Huddersfield and immediately went into town and spent it all on clothes. As soon as I found out, I gave Frank a rollicking, reminding him of his responsibilities to our parents. He followed my instruction from then on but I'm not sure he fully took on board the lesson.

A few years later, when I was at Grimsby, I received a call from my mum in tears, upset that the police had been round to speak to Frank again. He had amassed multiple parking fines but was ignoring my parents' pleas to pay them. My mum wanted me to come across to try and get him to listen to sense. That afternoon, I drove over to Halifax and collared him at home. 'Right, come on, get in your car,' I told him. 'We're driving to Leeds and you're going to pay these fines in person at the courthouse.' I genuinely believed this would finally teach him a lesson in doing the right thing. We got to Leeds and located the courthouse, just off the main street, the Headrow, in the city centre. In a flash, Frank accelerated into a side street, came to a stop diagonally over some double yellow lines and jumped out the car. 'Won't be a sec,' he said. 'Frank!' I yelled in disbelief. 'You're here to pay parking fines and you're leaving your car like this right next to the courthouse?!' Sheepishly, he returned to the car and we found a proper car park before he went inside to settle his debts. A few years later, he would be back in court for having turned his Lotus Elan around and gone back up a slip road after a wrong turn on to the motorway. I'd given up trying to impart lessons to him by that point.

When he wasn't paying parking fines or buying clothes, Frank was incredibly generous with his money – a little indication of the kind, considerate man he was at heart. I once met a lad who had been an apprentice at Birmingham when Frank had played there in the early 1980s. He told me my brother would often give his expensive clothes away to the young players at the club, handing over shirts, jeans and coats in the car park after training. It got to the point that the apprentices would gather near his car on his arrival so they could get first dibs on the best items.

On a night out, he would be the first one to the bar, often buying drinks for complete strangers before regaling them with tales. Every summer during my scouting days, I would return to Halifax for a couple of weeks and we would organise a catch-up of our core group of Yorkshire former footballing mates at the Moorings pub in Sowerby Bridge. Along with the three Worthington brothers, there would be Eric Harrison, Alex South, Dave Verity, Billy Legg, Les Chapman, Phil Black and others. None of us moved as fast as we once had but Frank still made sure he got to the bar first. He would return laden with drinks before launching loudly into another story to set us all off in hysterics.

Frank was most in his element with an audience, be it stands full of a cheering supporters or surrounded by friends and family. In the early 2000s, we initiated a Worthington Christmas party – a gathering for what was by then a vast tree of relations, with plenty of food, drink, music and laughter. We're a rowdy bunch in general but Frank made sure he had his moments, often via getting up in front of everyone to sing an Elvis number. I've done the odd turn myself, usually a rendition of 'The Wonder of You'. I obviously had to defend my turf as the original 'King of the Worthington clan'. Later, we began hiring an Elvis impersonator, a lovely bloke called Darren Lee, to take the weight off our shoulders but mainly to spare the ears of the rest of the family!

It was in 2003 that I first noticed something wasn't right with our kid. We were putting our clubs away after a pleasant round of golf at Bradley Hall in Halifax when he called me over to look at something in the boot of his car. It was pictures and other merchandise signed by a whole raft of comedians and celebrities, with whom he'd been working on the after-dinner circuit. 'Great that, Frank,' I told him and thought nothing more about it. Two weeks later, we were back in the same car park after another round and again he called me over. 'What do you think of this, then?' he asked, pointing to the boot. It was the same signed merchandise. I dismissed it as a bit of forgetfulness on his part. No big deal. When we then went through the same scenario once again a fortnight later, I began to worry.

Dementia has become all too common in my generation of players and our predecessors. I have lost numerous former team-mates – good friends – to the disease in recent years. Studies are finally starting to illustrate the heightened risks of developing degenerative brain problems after having played the game but in the early 2000s this was less well-known or publicised. I thought back then it was something that only affected much older people. Frank was in his mid-50s at this point. Moving to Europe and throwing myself into scouting meant I was not in regular contact with him, so I couldn't keep a watchful eye. I could only trust that his wife would do so. It was clear to me, though, when I returned the following summer, that Frank's memory was getting worse, his behaviour more out of character. I took it upon myself to call the doctor. I also contacted the Professional Footballers' Association for advice. He wasn't diagnosed with dementia at that point but I firmly believe this was the early stages of it.

It was a steady decline over the next 17 years. It was only in the last seven or eight that things got really bad, the grip the disease then had on him undeniable. One evening, I received a call from my former Grimsby Town team-mate, Dave Boylen. He had been at a function at our old club, at which Frank had been a speaker. My brother had an hour-long routine full of funny stories, which he could reel off with ease. He'd had plenty of practice in the years following his playing days, with the after-dinner circuit providing him with an income. Dave told me the speech had gone really well, prompting gales of laughter from the audience. However, once Frank had finished he started all over again, telling the same stories, word for word. The laughter from the crowd turned to murmurs of concern. The organiser of the event had to step in and make excuses to spare any embarrassment.

Frank's deterioration was hard to witness for those who loved him most. The colourful, comic, combative character drained away, leaving him grey, thin and frail, a shadow of the fit, handsome, charismatic man who had terrorised defences on the pitch and husbands off it. Bob and I would go round as often as we could, to take him out for walks, but it got harder and harder. He became frightened of the noises of the outside world. When cars drove past us, even on quiet country roads, he would cower, uttering 'no, no, no, no, no' as he did so. Soon, even a breeze of wind through the trees would startle him. It was upsetting to see so stark a contrast to the younger man we had known, so fearless and full of the joys of life.

On 22 March 2021, around 10pm, I got a call at home from a nurse asking me to come to the hospital, as Frank was in a bad way. Bob received a similar call. By the time we got there, he'd already gone. We sat with him a while in silence, remembering the man he had been in his pomp, the little brother we loved so dearly. He died that night but the real Frank had left us long before.

The Covid pandemic prevented us having a funeral initially but, as soon as we were able, we arranged a proper memorial at Halifax minster. We weren't sure how many would attend, it being so soon after the public lockdowns, but plenty did, including a group from Leicester. My old gaffer and Frank's old team-mate Sam spoke about their time together at Bolton, as did Peter Reid. It was important to us that the occasion reflected the real Frank, capturing some of the joy by which he had lived his life. We interspersed it with three Elvis songs, all performed by Darren. One of them was a brilliant and moving rendition of one of the King's earlier gospel songs, 'How Great Thou Art'.

Frank left a huge hole in our family, an absence felt keenly by Bob, Julie and me. For a while, it was hard to think about him but I'm now very grateful for the stories he has left behind, with so many people eager to share them with me. Through these and the videos I regularly stumble across online, my brother is kept alive in my mind. There is one video I possess that I prize above all others. It is from a Worthington party – I forget which year – taken with a mobile phone. It is of Darren singing an Elvis number, in amongst the four Worthington siblings, our arms draped over each others' shoulders. My youngest brother was struggling badly with his illness at the time but as we all sing together – 'and you're always there to lend a hand, in everything I do, that's the wonder, the wonder of you ...' – I can see the joy and recognition in his face. Just a small flash of the old Frank.

14

Stats All, Folks

(2016–2022)

In the stands of the Mini Estadi in Barcelona sit two scouts at work, a couple of empty seats and at least three decades between them.

One is a veteran, 'old school' if you will, a wily exponent of the art of watching, assessing and chronicling the qualities of the very best players. In front of him is a notepad, in which two line-ups are written out in full, an age, height and preferred foot annotated beside each entry. Already, the page is populated with notes from the fixture in front of him, insight and wisdom aided by more than 50 years of playing and watching the game.

As the ball goes out for a corner, he uses the opportunity of the brief break in play to scribble another note. Returning his eyes to the game, his attention is captured by the activity of the younger man two seats down – or rather the lack of it. He slumps in his seat, his attention not on the game but his partner next to him, with whom he laughs and jokes.

Play restarts, the corner is taken and cleared, all closely observed by the veteran. Two seats away, his peer glances up, ticks a box on the screen in front of him and returns to his conversation.

NOBODY WANTS to consider they are becoming obsolete in their career. Witnessing the ways in which scouting began to change in the latter half of the 2010s, with its increasing focus on stats on a sheet over eyes on a player, it began to dawn on me that my time was potentially coming to an end. Even in my early 70s, though, I still felt I had plenty to offer at the highest level and, thankfully, some clubs felt the same.

In the summer of 2016, Everton – hoping to replicate some of the Leicester magic – appointed Walshy as their new director of football, with Martyn Glover joining him as chief scout. A large part of the reason for my long and productive career has been the relationships I have built, including with both Steve and Martin. When the former came calling to take me to the Toffees with him, I was happy to accept. In my eyes, a club have always come second to the people when considering an employer but there was also no denying Everton's size and history. They had maybe not punched their weight in recent years but were still a club for which I was proud to work. That they had hitched their wagon to people I trusted also made me think I might get a good five years of employment out of them. It felt like the right choice.

Ronald Koeman had joined them as manager that summer, swept in on the crest of a wave after leading Southampton to a sixth-place finish and European qualification the previous season. I would only meet him once during my time with the Toffees, poking my head around his office door for a chat after an early scouts' meeting. We didn't discuss players, or even football, instead speaking about our respective joyful experiences of living in Castelldefels, near Barcelona. I resisted the urge to bring up the role he'd played in getting my mate Graham Taylor the sack as England boss.

I could see that the squad had enough quality. They weren't going to stage a title bid – although people had insisted that of Leicester – but a top-half, possibly top-six finish was achievable. They had that mix of grit and guile. Defenders Phil Jagielka, Leighton Baines and Seamus Coleman were solid, canny operators.

Idrissa Gueye and Gareth Barry brought strength and solidity to the midfield, the former reminding me of N'Golo Kanté, although maybe not quite at his level of reading a game. Further forward, Ross Barkley and Kevin Mirallas had creativity and flair in their locker. Everton also had a goalscorer, although not one that had consistently convinced me during scouting assignments. Romelu Lukaku could be magnificent and maddening, often in the same ten-minute spell of a game. He was a big, strong, quick lad, with many good attributes, but he let himself down too often with his attitude and application. In that first year, though, he scored a lot of goals – 25 in the league – a tally that earned him a move to Manchester United and Everton £75m.

In hindsight, there were small signs of the friction that would ultimately undermine Everton's new off-field team. In January 2017, the club signed forward Ademola Lookman from Charlton. I don't think Walshy was sold on the move. They also began to spend significant amounts of money on players who were, arguably, no better than what they had – Yannick Bolasie and Morgan Schneiderlin both costing more than £20m in that first season. Neither would, ultimately, justify the fee.

As usual, I cracked on with the job in Spain and beyond. I sent in reports on a 16-year-old South Korean forward called Lee Kang-in, who I spotted playing for Valencia's B team. He was a tricky, skilful runner with the ball, quick and direct, much like his compatriot Son Heung-min at Tottenham. He would make a name for himself at Real Mallorca before joining PSG in 2023. At the same time and same club, I saw and really liked a young Ferran Torres, who would later go on to Manchester City and Barcelona. I was also directed to check out two players, both named Gómez and both forwards: Maxi at Celta Vigo and Dani for Real Madrid's B team. Their agents insisted on telling me they were world beaters and easily good enough for the Premier League. After watching them, I informed them that, in my opinion, they were not.

Glancing back through my notebooks from this time, certain players names appear often and are enshrined in glowing terms. I admired the strength and pressing of Toulouse right-back Kelvin Amian and the speed and intent of forward Nordi Mukiele at Montpellier. Three central midfielders caught my eye: Lucas Evangelista for his quick feet and vision on loan at Estoril from Udinese; Jefferson Lerma, who was an energetic and unselfish figure at Levante prior to joining Bournemouth in the summer of 2018; and Geoffrey Kondogbia, a powerful, battling competitor in the middle of the park for Valencia. Head and shoulders above all three, though, was Rodrigo Hernández, otherwise known as Rodri. After seeing him for Villarreal against Deportivo La Coruña in January 2018, I wrote: 'Always makes himself available, wants to help everybody, rarely wastes a pass, movement superb.' He has demonstrated all of this and more since joining Manchester City in 2019.

Another player I thought had the potential to be world class was Riqui Puig at Barcelona. Short and slim, with a low centre of gravity and great technical skill, his prime asset was his brain. He wasn't physically rapid but his reading of a game made him a yard quicker than anyone else. Having seen him a few times for Barça's Under-19 and B teams, I gave him repeated 'A' grades for his performances. More than that, I genuinely felt he had the potential to rival Messi. But scouting is not an exact science. So many unknown factors can impact and undermine a player's development. Somewhere along the line, Puig's progress stalled and his future as one of the game's greats was consigned to an optimistic opinion in my scouting notebook.

A recommendation of mine that Everton did act on was forward Sandro. I had seen him play for Barcelona's B side and then for Málaga, developing into a very useful forward – not necessarily in the centre but someone who could operate out wide. At Málaga in 2016/17, he scored at a rate of a goal every two games in La Liga. He might not have been able to replicate that against tougher Premier League defences but a goal every three games was not beyond him. Everton were able to pick him up for £5.2m. Unfortunately, like Puig, he was never able to fulfil his potential, becoming a victim of the misjudgments and resulting disfunction that seized the club from the summer of 2017 onwards.

Emboldened by the progress of the previous season and bolstered by the money from Lukaku's sale, Everton embarked on a signing spree, of which Sandro was a comparatively cheap part. There were some moves that have proved sensible, such as goalkeeper Jordan Pickford and centre-back Michael Keane, but a greater number of others that were not. That summer window was defined by the expensive outlay on three No.10s – Gylfi Sigurðsson, Davy Klaasen and Wayne Rooney. In January, after a poor first half of the season, they would throw good money after bad, bringing in more forwards in Theo Walcott and Cenk Tosun. The former was fine, albeit faded from the young, promising player for Arsenal and England. The latter, I felt, was way below the level required to play in the Premier League.

I rarely felt that failed signings undermined my position as a scout at any club. I was paid to provide a professional opinion but I was only ever one voice amongst many. Vulnerability in the role came from changes within the management and recruitment team and, from October 2017, these were in a continual state of flux at Everton. Perversely, the first major change arguably benefitted my position, as Koeman was sacked and replaced by none other than Sam Allardyce. It raised a bit of a chuckle between us – 'Oh, hello again gaffer, fancy seeing you here!' I only wish I could have enjoyed the reunion for a bit longer.

Sam's reputation had taken a battering by this point, tarnished by his brief time with England and the unjust dismissal as a long-ball, relegation escape specialist that had followed. He arrived at Everton with them hovering around the relegation zone and took them to an eight-place finish – a season-end position they would subsequently kill for. For his efforts, he was sacked, the club informing him they wanted to go in another direction. They certainly did that and it wasn't up!

I think that one hit Sam quite hard. He felt he'd done enough to warrant more time, as did I. I offered my sympathies and we shared the usual 'maybe see you at the next club' but that would be the end of the road for him and me professionally. We still speak fairly regularly, to have a good laugh and reminisce about the clubs, the people – and the cars I used to own.

Having lost a close ally in Sam that summer, it was a serious blow to my position at the club when they also parted company with Walshy. Over our years working together, we had built up a degree of trust. With his successor, Marcel Brands, I had none. I was optimistic I could forge a bond with the club's new chief scout, Grétar Steinsson, over our respective experiences at Bolton and the fact I had recommended that they sign him. It became clear very quickly, though, that I did not fit with the new regime.

The writing was on the wall from an early scouts' meeting chaired by Brands. Having secured Marco Silva as manager, the new director of football was eager to recruit players that could fit the new manager's ideas for a bold, new Everton. Part of that involved tapping into the club just down the road from my apartment, with the signing of Lucas Digne, Andre Gomes and Yerry Mina from

Barcelona. I had long thought Gomes a fine midfield player, from his days playing in his native Portugal for Benfica. He wasn't quick but he had a superb range of passing that diminished his need to get around the pitch at speed. I rated left-back Digne, too. He never stood out in games I saw but had a very good all-round set of attributes.

I didn't rate centre-back Mina. I thought him a big lump, lacking the technical skills and temperament to be a good defender in the Premier League. However, his stock was boosted that summer by the late goal he scored for Colombia against England to take the World Cup quarter-final between the two to extra time. Brands, in particular, seemed very excited. As is my way, I spoke my mind in the meeting, making it clear that I didn't think he would stand up to Premier League strikers. He might get you the odd goal from a set piece but he would likely cost us more at the other end. In hindsight, I could have been more diplomatic than insinuating our new director of football didn't know what he was talking about.

I remained in post during that season but felt increasingly isolated out in Spain. With Walshy and Martyn, I was part of the team, constantly in communication about players I was watching. Their successors paid me less heed, seemingly uninterested in my activities or suggestions. When the end finally came, it left a bitter taste. In May, Grétar came out to Spain and we attended a game in the final round of La Liga fixtures. We went for a meal but he never once spoke of my situation at the club. A few weeks later, another of the club's scouts, Dan Purdy, let it slip that I was going to be let go. It was only after this that Brands phoned me to break the news.

I don't think it was just my association to the former regime that cost me my job at Everton. I had increasingly begun to feel that my age and approach counted against me. Scouting changed as more and more money came into the game, technology advanced and clubs sought out ever more creative and comprehensive means to get ahead of the competition. Statistics came much more to the fore, with vast breakdowns of every possible action a player can undertake pored over to ascertain their value and potential impact. There was now a negative perception, factual or not, of a scout in his 70s with a notebook tucked under his arm.

The concept of 'Moneyball' and its stats-based recruitment principles had entered the public sphere. We older guys in the room, using our bountiful experience to judge talent, were now out of style and firmly out of touch in the opinion of the young detractors sweeping in to replace us. Less weight was given to the qualities our experienced eye could identify – actions that indicate bravery, determination or composure and the tell-tale body language of a potentially surly and selfish player.

There was a change in the profile of the scouts sitting alongside me at games. Fewer and fewer were former players, certainly from my era. In their place came an army of tech-savvy, laptop-wielding individuals in their 20s and 30s. Few of them had any meaningful playing experience, instead coming into the game via university degrees or other data-driven industries. Some were bloggers on the game who had captured the attention of a senior figure at a club with their armchair insights. I stuck out like a sore thumb.

Contrary to the perception at that time, I'm not against the use of stats in scouting. I was part of a team at Bolton under Sam that embraced data-driven analysis to superb effect near the turn of the century. The wealth of information available on a player as a means of assessing his every action on a pitch has increased dramatically, creating a rich resource. However, I feel it can only be used effectively when placed in context and used in conjunction with a knowledgeable observer – someone who has played the game to a decent level and understands its intricacies and demands. Without this, stats risk being meaningless.

Take successful passes as an illustration. Completing a high percentage of 35 passes in a game looks impressive on a screen but can be highly misleading in reality. If most of those passes were by a midfielder over five to ten yards, back and forth to a centre-back, it gives you no indication of a player's ability or attitude, barring, perhaps, that he likes to play it very, very safe. In contrast, a pass success rate of 50 per cent looks poor in isolation but if a high number of those were an attempt to thread through a killer ball to unlock a defence, leading to an equalizer or winning goal and even one of them has come off, it is a badge of honour.

This is just one simple example. There are scores of others across the game. A player could be marked down for a poor cross completion stat but what if he is attempting the right ball time after time but failing? Do you see his intent as a positive and back a good coach at your club to work on his technique? And what weight do you give other possible reasons for the lack of success – an attacking team-mate lacking the awareness or determination to get on the end of a delivery, the positional and defensive brilliance of an opponent or the ineptitude of an official not spotting the illegal blocking of a run? What, too, of a player's work off the ball? Can raw stats flag up the effort someone puts in to track back and hold up an attack if he doesn't touch the ball? How, for example, would they represent the intelligent, slow-paced but purposeful movement of Messi to put himself in the right place at the right time?

This brings us back to Barcelona, to the Mini Estadi, in particular, and the young scout sitting two seats down from me, engaged in conversation with his partner whilst inattentively marking his stats sheet. The situation upset me more than it should.

It was a few months on from my final conversation with Brands and I was still without another full-time job. Never one for giving up, I had continued to attend games for no immediate reward, relying on scouting friends to get me tickets but paying the travel costs myself. I was out on a limb but staying professional, doing the job to the best of my ability on the chance that another club might call. And here was a young upstart, on a jolly at his club's expense, not observing enough of the game and conducting a literal box-ticking exercise. It played to some of my worst fears about the state of modern scouting. As we were packing up after full time, I took the opportunity to clock his accreditation. I didn't recognise the name but I knew his employer – Everton Football Club.

These were challenging times professionally but more positive upon a personal front. After all the years based in different countries and the many, many flights taken to spend long weekends together, Maggie moved out to Spain in early 2020. Finally, we had some permanence in our marriage, a shared home in which we could enjoy the sunshine, eat fine food and walk on the beach together. However, if my football career has conditioned me to anything, it is the unpredictability of life. Fate has its own plans.

The first case of Covid-19 in Spain was recorded in late January. By the end of March, a national state of alarm was triggered in response to its spread. Maggie had already returned home by this point, keen to be with her daughters – one of whom, Grace, was pregnant – and out of concern for the fact we did not have a doctor in Spain. I had never registered for one, having always returned home for treatment on serious health issues. I still wanted to attend games, which were still on at that time, on the off-chance a job arrived. So, I remained in Barcelona, much to the frustration of the family. As the kids told Maggie when she informed them of my decision: 'Just leave him there, the stubborn bugger!'

Soon I had no choice. Lockdown arrived and life became a surreal shadow of itself. The usually busy streets of Castelldefels emptied, the sounds of nature filled the air in the absence of car engines and the hustle and bustle of people. Football ceased, leaving me to potter around the apartment in search of distraction. Unsure of what the future held, I delved into the past, digging out old photos from my youth and a multitude of newspaper cuttings from my playing days. I took to the balcony and spent hours in the sunshine sticking them into scrapbooks and reminiscing, promising myself that one day I would record all my stories in a book.

I took every opportunity I could to get out for exercise, in the two two-hour windows allowed during lockdown. My long walks would take me far from my home, down for a newspaper at the local shop and then on to the beach, which stretches for five miles, before sauntering back. Sometimes, I would go close to the large gated homes at the top of the hill that housed Messi, Suárez and Fàbregas. One afternoon, back at the apartment, I bumped into a neighbour, a policeman called Sebas, who beckoned me over with a serious look on his face. 'David, where do you go for your walks?' he asked. As I explained my route, he began shaking his head before adding: 'Don't do it.' When I asked why, he explained that lockdown rules prohibited anyone from walking more than a kilometre and a half from their house. Some of his colleagues had recognised me out and about and had told Sebas to warn me to prevent me getting a fine or possibly locked up. From then on, I did multiple small laps of the streets around the apartment.

The Spanish football season recommenced in June. I returned to stadiums to keep my eye in but no job offers came. With a heavy heart, I accepted that my time in Spain was up. The adventure was over. I returned to the UK, to Ripponden near Halifax, to be with

Maggie and within easy travelling distance of the rest of my family. I think in doing so, I accepted that my Premier League scouting career was also likely at an end. I didn't get the send-off I would have wished for after almost 60 years of near-unbroken service to the game but it is rare that people do in football. Thinking back, not just over those six decades, but also the youthful years that preceded them, elicits a lot of emotions – lots of joy, some sadness, a bit of frustration but a greater feeling of fulfilment.

I think, more than anything, I'm proud, not necessarily for what I achieved – although you can't sniff at a 1971/72 Fourth Division winner's medal – or for how long my career in the game lasted, but for how I went about it. I've made mistakes (who hasn't) but I've largely stayed true to myself, to the person my parents set me on course to become, a person I then forged through determination, hard work, resilience, honesty and, I hope, decency. I've been called Worthy my entire life. I'll leave it up to others to decide if I truly deserve the title.

The final trip I undertook before leaving Spain was a 20-minute train journey into the heart of Barcelona. From there, I walked down to the port area, to a building I have visited many times before. Near the seafront, within the narrow streets of the Ribera district, stands the Basilica Santa Maria del Mar, the 'Saint Mary of the Sea', also known by its nickname 'The Fisherman's Church'. It maybe lacks the scale and magnificence of the city's famous Sagrada Família but has its own unique beauty. On my first visit there, I was told the story of how it came to be. Over 54 years in the 14th century, the huge, heavy rocks used in its construction were transported via boat from a nearby quarry to its site by local fishermen and dockworkers. It was they and other common folk – driven only by a devotion to the cause – who then dragged the stones inland and built the church from the ground up.

As I stood inside, almost 650 years on from its completion, staring up at its tall pillars and beautiful stained-glass windows, the tale of its origin still fresh, I was moved. I thought of the sacrifice, the blood, sweat and tears shed, the dedication, resolve and unity of a humble people, performing an act out of nothing more than faith and devotion. There was something about the tale that struck a chord with me then and has stuck with me ever since. I'm not sure why.

Epilogue

Moving On

THE HARDEST part about retirement for me is how still it often feels. I have spent a life on the move, charging around the streets of Shelf as a child, up and down the right wing at Blundell Park as a player and hot-footing it around Europe during my scouting career. I find it very hard now, even with so many miles on the clock, to stay put.

Granted, some of the inactivity is enforced, an unavoidable side effect of age. All the years of putting my body through the wringer – the pre-season runs, in-season tackles and later-life camp-outs in the car – have started to catch up with me. My knees often tighten, I've had issues with my hip, shin and osteoarthritis in my neck. I have a lengthy regime of morning exercises to loosen me up for the day.

There are positives to the stasis, too. It's nice to finally have a settled spot with Maggie, a home we can finally share together. It also affords me more time with an ever-growing family. Gary, Keely and Dani know where I am if they need me and occasionally pay visits with their respective partners, Kerry, Mark and Johnnie.

My status has now been upgraded to great-grandfather. The most regular visitors to the house are our infant granddaughters on Maggie's side. Isla, still too young to walk, shuffles around the carpet with a grin on her face. Clemmie, the eldest at four, is a bundle of energy, charging round the living room, selling me perfect dummies to get by me and into the kitchen for a biscuit. She loves kicking a ball about. On more than one occasion, and much to her grandma's amusement, I have tried to teach her the proper technique for shooting – the same lesson my dad imparted to me and I handed down to Gary. We even play on same pitch where Bob and Frank represented Ryburn United in their youth. You never know, with the proper teaching we could have another England international in the family!

In general, though, I rail against the inactivity, seeking out every small opportunity to remain mobile. I walk the picturesque, hilly country roads of Ripponden and beyond as often as my body will allow and regardless of the weather. Once you've stood in shorts and felt the icy, sleet-filled wind blast into Blundell Park from the North Sea, a bit of Yorkshire wind and rain is practically tropical. Mainly, my walks are a brisk few miles. I take pride in clocking up 25,000 steps a day on my watch, although in the last year or two it has been closer to 15,000. If I'm feeling particularly adventurous, I'll travel the nine miles to Shelf – with a little assistance from the bus – to nurse a pint in a window seat at the Duke of York, staring out at the triangular car park and the tiny house beyond, where it all began. Sometimes, 'Nipper' Harrison joins me and we reminisce together about our youth.

I still have the odd meet-up with the Yorkshire football crew but our numbers have dwindled. It's often now just Bob, Dave Verity and me – with the occasional visit from Manchester mates Les Chapman and Phil Black – telling old stories and raising a pint to the memory of Eric, Southy, Billy, our Frank and more.

I miss the real action, the unique thrills that come from being on the frontline of football's talent hunt. I occasionally long to be navigating my way around a bustling Paris using only a battered map and my wits, crossing the snow-covered Alps to take my life into my own hands on Italian roads or embarking on ten-hour journeys across Spain to sit under a canopy of orange trees in a Seville square. Each time, a new game, full of players and potential, would be waiting for me at the end.

It hits hardest when I watch matches on television. I've been in the thick of fiery, French fixtures at Marseille and Saint-Étienne, watched Milan derbies through flare smoke at the San Siro and held my breath along with 90,000 others as Messi ghosted into space to gather the ball just outside a penalty area at the Camp Nou. Such experiences are drained of their potency when viewed on a screen from the comfort of your own armchair. The Champions League anthem has a triggering effect, transporting me back into those electric atmospheres under floodlights when the best players would go toe to toe and I would be there to run the rule.

I did briefly try to carry on my scouting career back in England. A chance meeting with Rochdale manager Robbie Stockdale at a Grimsby game in January 2022 led to some work for the then League Two club. It was a big step down from what I'd been used to but one I never considered myself above. It was clear very quickly, though, that Dale simply did not have the funds to act on any of my recommendations, most of which were talented young loan options from the reserves of clubs higher up the football pyramid. I pushed Blackburn midfielder Adam Wharton and Brighton forward Evan Ferguson to no avail and repeatedly praised the able, honest and confident displays of Altrincham defender Toby Mullarkey.

Dale would eventually find the money to sign Mullarkey in January 2023 but, by then, the club were too deep in the mire, heading for relegation out of the Football League under Robbie's replacement, Jim Bentley, a decent man on a hiding to nothing. I wasn't around to see their fate sealed. I had grown weary of the frustration, the freezing cold nights and late-night car journeys home on roadwork-affected motorways. With minimal fuss, I called it quits.

I still get my fix thanks to regular trips to The Shay and Blundell Park to watch my two favourite Towns. I always get recognised at Grimsby, from fans of a certain vintage who wistfully recall that glorious little period under Lawrie when I was a permanent fixture up and down the right wing. When I have a weekend spare, I occasionally accept an invite from Gary to join him for a game at Manchester City. There, I get to spend 90 minutes giving my player insights to a man who has spent the last 15 years as a leading recruitment figure for arguably the world's most successful football operation. I'm sure he appreciates it!

The two of us are also part of a scouts group that meet up every year for a Christmas party at San Carlos Italian restaurant in Manchester. Ian Broomfield, formerly of Leeds and Tottenham, acts as organiser. Steve Hitchen, who was also at Tottenham, as well as Liverpool, is a regular, as is Alan Watson at Manchester City, along with two former Premier League goalkeepers turned recruiters, Tony Coton and Bryan Gunn. Viv Anderson, Mick Brown, Ian Butterworth, Brian Cary, Glyn Chamberlain, Mick Doherty, Alan Harper, Jamie Hoyland, Rob Newman – it's a healthy crew of current and former talent spotters. Peter Reid usually pops in for a drink.

There's a lot of fun, laughter and mickey-taking. Unsurprisingly, one topic dominates the conversation.

I have tried to get away from football, to find something else to occupy my time – a crossword, the cricket, sitting in the garden organising scrapbooks. But the beautiful game soon draws me back in. It's like a drug. I can be sitting in the living room on an evening with Maggie, watching some crime drama on TV and I will feel

hand reaching out for the tablet, to flick on that night's cup
, just to check the score. An hour later, my wife will be in bed
d I'll still be sitting there, engrossed in extra time. Now that I've
80 years of age, I should simply be enjoying a happy retirement
I know that if a club rang tomorrow to see if I fancied heading
t to a couple of games to watch some players, I probably would.

In the meantime, I have discovered a different and positive use
my experiences in the game. In late 2024, I made the familiar
urney to Blundell Park, not to watch a match but to meet with
group of very special supporters. It was for a weekly event,
ganised by the Mariners Trust in part to help supporters suffering
ith dementia. Many of them are of an age to have followed the
ub during the early 1970s, when Lawrie led us to that famous
tle win. As a surviving member of that side and its captain, the
ganisers felt I could do some good by sharing some of my old
ories to stimulate the fans' recollection, to use my memories to
elp bolster theirs.

I've witnessed at close quarters the pain and suffering dementia
n cause. It has robbed our family of Frank and me of many
iends. A great deal has been written about the links between
otball and the disease. Barely a month seems to go by without
e discovering another former team-mate has lost their battle
gainst it, including many from my Town days – Bobby Ross,
on Cockerill, Matt Tees. Stewart Gray, Owen Simpson and
ave Boylen all struggle now with dementia. I visit the latter in
leethorpes as often as I can, to sit with him and talk of old times.
can see the recognition in his eyes but he simply can't get the
vords out to respond.

I owed it to all of my old friends to travel back to the scene of
o many of our football adventures, to share our stories with those
hat need them most. Grimsby was the main, but not only, topic of

conversation. I also spoke of what came before and after my tir
as a Mariner, of all that I was taught and subsequently learned, t
humble experiences as a player in the Football League that th
helped me on my travels as a scout across Europe.

It was an emotional afternoon, upsetting and uplifting. As I sa
my goodbyes, I said I would return for future meetings – a promi
I kept. In the days that followed, I became ever more reflectiv
spurred once more to dig out my scrapbooks and continue t
process of piecing together my past. I can only hope that hearir
my tales does those fans some good. It certainly fills me with pric
and joy to tell them.